An Apostle of Charity

Igino Giordani

An Apostle of Charity
Father Luigi Maria Monti

New City

London   Edinburgh   Dublin

First published in Italian as
Un apostolo della carità: P. Luigi M. Monti
© Editrice Ancora, Milano, 1963

Second Italian edition
©Editrici Monti, Saronno, 1993

First published in English by
New City
57 Twyford Avenue
London W3 9PZ

Translated by Frank Johnson
© New City, London, 1998

Cover picture:
'Padre Luigi Monti riflette sul malato l'amore di Cristo per tutti gli uomini' by V. Messina, 1975

Cover design by Tomeu Mayans

British Catalogue in Publication Data:
A catalogue record for this book is available from the British Library.

ISBN 0 904287 57 2

Imprimatur in Curia Arch. Mediolani die 1-2-1963,
† J. Schiavini, Vic. Gen.

Typeset in Great Britain by
New City, London

Printed and bound in Great Britain by
The Cromwell Press, Trowbridge, Wiltshire

Contents

	Introduction	9
1.	THE COMPANY OF FRIARS	
	Birth	11
	First Job	14
	Dedication to God	16
	Montina	19
	The Death of Mamma Teresa	20
2.	THE PERSECUTION OF THE COMPANY OF FRIARS	
	The Revolution of 1848 at Bovisio	23
	The Arrest of the Friars	25
	The Prison at Desio	30
	The Sons of Mary	32
3.	THE IDEAL HOSPITALLER	
	Cyprian Pezzini	35
	The Experiment	40
	The Dark Night	44
4.	LUIGI MONTI IN ROME	
	The Santo Spirito Hospital	48
	Pezzini's Expulsion	51
	Pezzini's Death	54

5. FIRST TRIALS AT THE SANTO SPIRITO

   The Commander   57
   The New Concettini   61
   Novice Master   63
   Illness   66

6. THE INSTITUTE SPREADS BEYOND ROME

   Our Lady of Rest   70
   Fruits of Suffering   75
   A 'Sacred Visitation'   78

7. THE FOUNDATION OF ORTE AND CIVITA CASTELLANA

   Orte   81
   Starting the Work   83
   The Concettini at Orte   85
   The Death of Dossi   88
   Civita Castellana   91

8. CLOUDS IN THE SKY

   Changes in Rome   96
   Orte - Championed by People and Authorities   99
   In Defence of Monti   101
   A New Constitution   104

9. DON BOSCO INTERVENES 1876-7

   Pius IX and Don Bosco   108
   Monti Saves the Institute   111
   Don Bosco and Bro Luigi   115
   Father Angelini   118
   Monseigneur Turriccia   120

10. DISAGREEMENTS WITH TURRICCIA 1878

    Fresh Attacks on Autonomy   126
    Leo XIII   129
    Cardinal Innocenzo Ferrieri Intervenes   132

11. THE FOUNDATION AND THE FOUNDER

    The Founder   136
    The New Constitution   142
    Examination of the Texts   146
    The Approval   147
    The Character   150

12. THE REBIRTH OF THE INSTITUTE IN A CLIMATE OF SECULARISATION

    Expansion   153
    Events at the Santo Spirito   156
    The Hospital at Nepi   161
    Caring for Orphans   162

13. THE HOUSE AT SARONNO

    A Viscount's Residence   166
    First Fruits   169
    Expulsion from the Santo Spirito   172
    The Growth of the Educational Work   178

14. THE STRUGGLE FOR PRIESTHOOD IN THE CONGREGATION

    Fr Angelini's Dissent   182
    The Opposition Grows   188
    Fresh Attempts   191
    Facing Up to Failure   197

15. THE MAN AND THE INSTITUTE

The Institute	202
Man of Character	204
Virtues	207
The Formator	215
Fatherhood	220
Formation of the Young	223
Seeing Jesus in the sick	227

16. THE MAN OF GOD

Man of Prayer	230
Son of the Immaculate	236

17. THE PEACEFUL PASSAGE

An Old Man amongst Young	240
The Final Illness	246
Death	250

INTRODUCTION

The second edition of the biography of the servant of God, Fr Luigi Maria Monti, comes some thirty years after the publication of the first edition. The author of *An Apostle of Charity*, the well-known sociologist and critic Igino Giordani, died on 18 April 1980, but his lasting fame and influence is a valid recommendation for the book. As Giordani himself says in the preface, it was written 'with complete objectivity, taking care to value Monti's thoughts and works on the basis of facts, backed up by documentation.' Other factors in its favour are the critical reconsideration of the facts and the characters from both the political and ecclesiastical worlds, in the life of this servant of God.

The author's special consideration of the prevailing social climate gives a fresh appreciation of the work of the servant of God.

The sanctity of Luigi Monti emerges naturally, without being forced, 'because his personality,' says the author in the Preface, 'does not fit into the normal pattern of hagiographies which make saints into extraordinary creatures, already almost embalmed when still alive.' As well as a profound ecclesial vision, Monti's sanctity has also given the author a special spirit of discernment that has enabled him to gain a great insight into the fundamental hallmarks of the personality and the work of this servant of God.

In fact, Igino Giordani writes, in his summary of the life of Luigi Monti: 'Although I have read the biographies of many saints, rarely have I come across a story with so much disappointment and incomprehension heaped upon one man. He responds with limitless patience, irresistible strength and discernment which untangles, bleeding, from amidst the thorns, the thread of God's plan.' It must be said that the congregation he founded was and is a plan of God, because it is still growing today in the Church and in society.

Good fruits come from a good tree.

Thus, works of charity come from apostles of charity, and the servant of God, Fr Monti, was such an apostle.

Igino Giordani is one who has proclaimed this.

In this second edition of *An Apostle of Charity*, the chronological details have been removed and those pages which recounted events not of general interest have also been omitted, none of which has devalued the book. On the contrary, the facts associated with the life of the servant of God in this edition become more incisive, which makes it a truer representation of Monti's basic ideas.

Rome, 8 September 1993

Fr Giovanni Cazzaniga

1
THE COMPANY OF FRIARS

BIRTH

Bovisio is a peaceful little town, seventeen kilometres from Milan on the Lombardy plain. The houses, typical of the Brianza region, surround a courtyard which serves as a meeting place. Here, amidst hens and rabbits, the women gossip and in the evening the men sit around chatting. It is a place with a strong sense of community and, at least in the last century, it encouraged a communal life, which, inspired by charity, tittle-tattle apart, led to the sharing of sufferings and joys.

One of these houses, perhaps the poorest in the whole town, was a building in the San Cristoforo district, down by the river Seveso. The house opened out into a courtyard leading to a public passageway. On the river side there was, and still is, an apartment with two rooms on the first floor and two on the ground floor, one of which opened on to the courtyard and the other on to the street. The latter served as a workshop for carpentry and cabinet-making. These were flourishing industries in Bovisio and most families in the town earned their living through them, as indeed many still do today.

The young Luigi Monti worked for years in this tiny workshop. He was the eighth of eleven children born to Angelo and Teresa Monti, hardworking and devout Christians. Born and baptized on 24 July 1825, Luigi grew up under his mother's lov-

11

ing care, between the parish and the courtyard. The education he received was simple and homely and consisted of moral and religious instruction which, in the tradition of the ancient patriarchs, his parents gave him with his evening meal in the dim light of an oil lamp.

The whole atmosphere of the place was captured in this roadside building, where other families educated in the same ancient tradition lived. Luigi had been named after St Aloysius (his second baptismal name was Gaetano, after his godfather) so that he might be inspired by the saint's example. When his parents returned from their day's work in the fields, they would find young Luigi sitting by the fireside, reading those words of eternal life, words which took root in his ingenuous soul. From an early age, besides working and playing, Luigi started to pray and to meditate and, in this blending together of the supernatural and natural life, the truths of faith were imprinted on his soul. He had a great hunger for life, and almost a need to escape, to break free. His home environment was too small for him. The rows of mulberry trees and the cornfields on the fertile plain could hold him no longer. He soon felt the need for a wider horizon.

His father belonged to a confraternity, *la Compagnia del SS. Sacramento* (the Blessed Sacrament Society), in which his duty as head of a human family was simply lived as a participation in the family of God and as a member of the Church. Whether he was scything, or pruning or doing some other job in the fields, or whether he was conducting the church choir with great diligence and dedication, it was all done out of love for God. Taking part in the liturgy, he practised his royal priesthood in the house of God, as he did in his relationships with his neighbours.

In fact, working and thinking for love of God was already almost a kind of perpetual liturgy. He and his wife and children had God in their hearts. God was their wealth and their joy, and they were proud of it, honouring him with prayers and works, starting with their own daily work.

Although they may not have said it in so many words, both work and suffering, for them, was a work of God, the revelation of the will of the Father who is in heaven. Their house became a church.

The holy pictures on the wall, the blessed palms, the souvenirs of pilgrimages, were an invitation to those visiting the house to contemplate things divine. God was Lord of the house, where quarrelling and lies seemed like double offences, as if committed in church.

At home and in the street, and more often in the workshop when he started work, Luigi was in great demand amongst his peers. A big, lively lad, with a light-hearted nature, he attracted them with his natural talents, his deep piety and by his great love for the things of God. They were also drawn by the way in which he spoke about Jesus and Mary. He had a great love for Our Lady, like a loving son in contemplation of his Mother. He was also a natural leader.

His physical abilities were apparent when he threw himself enthusiastically into playing games, and his sharp intelligence enabled him to make astute judgements of situations and inspired his discerning actions. He was one of those people who do everything wholeheartedly, and fortunately he chose to follow the right path.

Like the simple upright folk from his part of the town, he called a spade a spade, and liked to make clear-cut, yes or no decisions. He was not a waverer.

His human upbringing, together with divine graces, set him on God's pathway, and he marched along it, like the craftsmen of his homeland, head down, and never a backward glance.

From the round, ornate church of St Pancras in the town centre, the parish priest, Fr Charles Ciceri, soon noted the gifts of the young Luigi, particularly his thirst for knowledge, and kept a keen eye on him.

In the meantime, Fr Charles admitted him to the sacraments,

as he did the children of all good Christians, finding him gentle and keen to be instructed in the catechism and in the practice of the faith.

FIRST JOB

At the age of forty-seven, Luigi's father died and the family was plunged into abject poverty.

Luigi had finished elementary school in Bovisio and was only twelve years old at the time, nevertheless he wanted to make his contribution to the family income by going out to work.

He was taken on by a cabinet maker in Cesano Maderno and every day the boy walked the one and a half kilometres to and from the workshop.

With his natural ability and good will, and motivated by the desire to bring the much-needed cash home to his mother and brothers and sisters, Luigi soon learned the skills of the trade. In fact it reminded him of the family of Nazareth and he developed a special love for and understanding of St Joseph, who had made his workshop into the temple where Jesus grew up.

Coming home each evening on foot made him feel close to Joseph Sarto and John Bosco, poor boys like himself, who, encouraged by the love of their heavenly Mother and their earthly one, never stopped working. This same love also enriched his yearning to be closer to his peers, something which was being revealed to him as his vocation. He spent hours and hours talking with them. In fact, these conversations, interposed with songs, became a kind of spiritual recreation, supported by reading the lives of the saints and the ascetics. They say that whoever sings prays twice, and in country areas hymns act both as sermons and spiritual exercises, correcting and teaching, refreshing and giving joy, as well as uniting people in the spirit.

In that atmosphere of recollection the young people exchanged experiences and impressions and it confirmed the miracle of the presence of Jesus who promised: 'Where two or three are united in my name, I am in their midst' In fact, St Vincent de Paul made this coming together of souls, this communion which opens us up to the spirit of God, the strength of his institutions.

Luigi's mother was happy as she observed all this and she thought her son would join a religious order. Surely, a boy who lived purity like St Aloysius and who gave glory to God through love for his companions was destined to be consecrated to God. And she was right, except that she could not see exactly where or how this would come about.

Work and prayer were the only things that interested Luigi. They were the components of sanctity and they brought fullness of life, joy and strength. Other things did not interest him, nor did he go looking for them. It was still some time before the troubles of 1848 and Lombardy, at least as far as the citizens of Bovisio were concerned, seemed to tolerate pacifically the military regime of the Austrian Field-Marshal Radetzky.

Luigi's spirit became enriched with many gifts and inspirations, and at the beginning of 1842 he felt a strong desire to listen to a great preacher who was preaching a mission at Varedo, a neighbouring town. Every day he went along to the mission, captivated by the profound preaching of someone who seemed, to Luigi, to be inspired. The preacher was Fr Angelo Taglioretti, of the Oblates of Rho, thirty years a Missionary, a holy man who was at the same time both cultured and austere.

The seventeen year old cabinet maker was so completely taken by what he heard that he wanted to introduce himself to the preacher and ask him in confession which way he ought to follow to become a saint. Those who are already in the seminary or in the convent have already found their way, but what about a young man who lives in the world and works as a cabinet maker?

On 27 February that year, the fourth Sunday of Lent, Luigi, along with four companions, went to the shrine at Rho to make a general confession and to receive holy communion. The huge crowd made it difficult, and therefore more worthy of merit. It

15

was not until midday that they managed to get to the confessional where Fr Taglioretti recognised that in the young man's soul there were aspirations not commonly found. After giving him many wise suggestions, he encouraged Luigi to intensify his apostolate among his peers, and to develop this communitarian piety to give glory to the Lord through works.

Luigi was impressed by this and, after communion, he returned home very happy, so much so that for the rest of his life he remained grateful to that priest, whom he held in high esteem, and through whom many young men were directed towards Monti's congregation.

As he returned to Bovisio that evening with his companions, Luigi decided to give himself totally to God as an apostle. At communion that day he had reaffirmed his decision to work only for the glory of God.

DEDICATION TO GOD

Back in Bovisio, Luigi Monti seemed transfigured. Single-minded and with a firm will, once he had decided to give himself to the Lord, he started to live like a consecrated person. He prayed a lot, did many penances - some of them very hard - frequently received the sacraments and increased his work in the apostolate.

With this deeper hunger for God, he started to cultivate his companions more systematically and with a greater sense of urgency. He would gather them together every evening in his little ground floor room, which, with one door opening on to the courtyard and the other on to the street, was easily accessible.

His fervour, his word, and the atmosphere of piety attracted forty or so boys from Bovisio and surrounding areas. They met together until about eleven o'clock and, just like St Catherine of Siena's family, they listened to readings from the lives of the saints and the ascetics, and were especially fond of St Alphonsus Liguori.

Luigi would explain the passages, adding examples and encouragement, the fruits of his reflection during his working day. His companions would listen to him, spellbound, because his words, which mirrored their own experiences, seemed to spring from their daily lives as workers and as laymen. In such a way their status as simple workmen was elevated to a spiritual plane. It was similar to the Gospel-inspired movement for social reform which had just started at that time, particularly in Belgium and France. They sang plain chant as well as popular hymns, more often than not in honour of the Virgin Mary. Son of the people and with the soul of the people, Luigi felt increasingly the need to communicate the attraction to devotion to Mary. He cultivated the purity of his soul with great diligence, following the example of his patron saint, St Aloysius, and it was through him that he drew closer and closer to Mary. Every evening after the singing and the instruction, Luigi and his companions would say the Rosary together. During the month of May they added special prayers and hymns, and every Saturday they did penances in honour of Mary, just as they did for St Joseph on Wednesdays. Theirs was a Marian devotion and that little room where they met was like an image of the house at Nazareth. There was nothing elaborate about their evening gatherings, everything was simple and clear-cut like the fields which surrounded Bovisio and the hills with the churches on top.

They also said prayers to the Sacred Heart and ended with the evening invocations. Finally, Luigi would choose a spiritual motto and an ejaculatory prayer for the next day, which he offered his companions as words of life. So, with a Christian farewell, they left in an attitude of silent recollection and made their way back home under the mysterious cover of nightfall which by now had spread over the fields. Whatever they had understood and resolved to do in the evening, they put into practice the following day at work, where they all read the nine offices of the Sacred Heart of Jesus. When the clock struck the hour, they would make the sign of the cross, honouring Our Lady by reciting a Hail Mary and an ejaculatory prayer.

With such a temperate and devout group of young men whose prayer life was so ordered and who lived such virtuous lives, it is not difficult to understand why the local people gave them the name 'the company of friars'. The young women who followed Monti's sister and lived the same spirit in the same way became known as 'the friaresses'.

The nickname was not without justification. Religious habit apart, the young men followed the three counsels of perfection, as far as their state of life allowed. They kept clear of dangerous relationships, practised physical penances and, especially during Carnival, they did not go into bars. They fasted on Saturdays in honour of Mary and on Wednesdays in honour of St Joseph. In other words, they practised a life of perfection, taking the Virgin Mary as their model. Under her virginal watch they worked and prayed, spoke and walked. As often as possible they made invocations to her, their particular favourite being the Chaplet of the Immaculate Conception.

These were the years leading up to the proclamation of the dogma of the Immaculate Conception in 1854, and it was in this atmosphere that Monti contemplated Mary above all in the essential beauty of the Immaculate Conception. His contemplation of this first moment of the insertion of the divine in the human was instinctive and all done under the light of love. Luigi saw it as the springboard for the transformation of both the spirits and the institutions of the modern age, according to the dynamics of the Incarnation.

Monti's 'friars', formed by him to be free of instincts and passions, free of pride, quarrels, vanity and lust had a notable effect on the ordinary people. Their sanctity penetrated the lowly dwellings of the country folk, was talked about in the village squares and instilled a new directness in personal relationships, both in the town and outside. But it was a sanctity made up, not only of teaching and prayers and renouncing the world, but also of works. They offered help to the sick and the needy, of whom there were many amongst such humble, uneducated people. In order to help them, the 'friars' gave their own money, time and effort and, where necessary, begged for alms.

A popular, communitarian sanctity was developing. In fact, it was a genuine precursor to those movements which were to culminate in the *consecratio mundi*, which Pope Pius XII entrusted to the laity. It was also a forerunner to that reawakening of the awareness to the royal priesthood brought about by Pope John XXIII at the Second Vatican Council.

MONTINA

The young people followed the communitarian technique of St Vincent de Paul, which was in fact none other than that of the early Church and of many religious families. Initially they found strength in coming together to share their experiences and practise mutual correction. But from this shared life there emerged a lesson for the world outside, as people began to say of them: 'See how they love one another.'

They met regularly every evening after work and every morning at dawn in the church. In springtime, on Sundays after Vespers and the other liturgical services, they would take a trip to one of the home towns or villages of their number, going up into the hills or the woods. Their favourite place, however, was Montina.

Montina was the name given to a green ridge, one of the first you come across on the Brianza plain, a humble rise which spreads out over a thousand metres and which reaches a height of about thirty metres. From the top, the young people had a panoramic view of ploughed fields and green trees, signs of human work and God's providence, almost an expression of nature and supernature.

Under Monti's watchful eye they spent the time together joyfully, talking, singing and meditating until dusk, when, still singing and full of joy, they returned home. In this way they lived many hours of peaceful joy, contemplating the air of the fields, the flora of the moorlands and the song of the rivers. It was the joy of God and of nature. The memory of those trips, which seemed to refresh the mind and purify the soul, would remain nostalgically in Monti's heart in old age.

Sometimes, they would make a pilgrimage to a well-known shrine, like the one at Rho at the Holy Mountain near Varese, to honour Our Lady and venerate relics. Purity of heart made the countryside seem more beautiful than normally. The variety of trees and flowers made the homeland of the angels and the saints feel nearer.

It was a time when working people were beginning to be deprived of the life of the spirit under atheist tyrannies or through the scepticism of new economic theories. Those young working men, through their hunger for a more meaningful life, cultivated the divine-human economy of the Incarnation, looking for the presence of God in people and in everyday events.

Their solidarity and unity of hearts, translated into a service of love by the 'friars', was very moving to witness. So much so, that more and more young people were attracted by it and came from neighbouring towns and villages to join Monti's followers. They all gathered together at Bovisio on Sunday and their example of communion lifted the whole population of the town, so effective was the apostolate of Monti's confraternity.

Now, today, we would call it the life of the Mythical Body, but Monti probably did not use this expression then. At least, he did not express it in words, he just lived it. In fact, what he was doing was reawakening in this primitive, almost feudal backwoods, the sense of the communal life with God and neighbour. And it was this that was to become the most effective reaction against the materialistic atheism of future generations.

THE DEATH OF MAMMA TERESA

Monti did not stop there. In September 1843, the year after his meeting with Fr Taglioretti at Varedo, he met another young priest, Fr Luigi Dossi at Cesano Maderno, where Monti went to work every day. Fr Dossi too had met with a group of young people in a kind of oratory, at Usamate until 1838. It was the same period in which Don Bosco, Murialdo and Canossa, who had died seven years before, had founded their congregations. Fr Dossi had been transferred to Cesano Maderno in March 1842 and, after a brief settling-in period, he once again took up his apostolate among the young. Luigi too was attracted by the luminosity of Fr Dossi's soul and by the fervour of his apostolate. Luigi confided in him joyfully, and he received wise counsel and spiritual encouragement and, above all, a brotherly relationship, which was to grow continuously. They met frequently either at one or the other's house or, more often, at Montina, to share confidences and songs to their mutual benefit.

On 11 July, 1845, Monti received some bad news while he was at work in Cesano Maderno: his mother lay dying at Bovisio.

He had loved mamma Teresa dearly, she who had been like Mary for him. She had always supported his work in the apostolate through her prayers and advice. As soon as he heard the news he ran home arriving breathless, only to discover that the poor woman, broken by illness and sheer fatigue and only fifty-seven years old, had died. She had died a holy death, having received the last Sacraments. Not only Luigi, but all those brothers and sisters he had united in the same company, mourned her loss. Now he was really head of the family.

On the advice of his Uncle Peter, Luigi assumed his responsibilities with great courage. He left his job in Cesano and started to work at home as a cabinet maker, in the tiny ground floor workshop where, every evening, whilst waiting for his companions, he had done some small job or other.

Now Luigi found himself imitating St Joseph more than ever, running the family business and working as a carpenter. In the upper room there was a gentle creature who followed him closely, his sister Maria Luigia. She reminded him of Our Lady, through

21

her piety, her purity and her apostolate, and not just because of her name. On the other hand, his younger brothers Anthony and Joseph, who worked in the family fields, reminded him of angels, because of their virtue and their faith.

This new situation also became a stimulus to grow closer to the Lord. Luigi was not yet twenty years of age, the age at which people normally start to take decisions about the direction of their lives. So, he gathered together all the enthusiasm of adolescence and youth and tied them together in a vow of consecration.

From 1843, he had renewed vows of obedience and chastity before Fr Luigi Dossi, his spiritual director, every year on the feast of the Immaculate Conception. On 8 December 1846, at the age of twenty and after eight days of spiritual exercises, he pronounced, with great joy, perpetual vows of obedience and chastity, according to the monastic rite. Now he was a friar within, he belonged totally to God and the evangelical counsels became his rule.

To complete the consecration, Monti and Dossi declared their intention to found a religious congregation, where they could recollect themselves with the best prepared of their companions. The young man returned home and began to collect funds in order to give life one day to that community which would fulfil his spirit, hungry for perfection.

In the meantime, his complete detachment from the world, whilst remaining in it, was gradually taken up by his companions, as well as by the young women who gathered round his sister. But the vows of these young people remained temporary, to be renewed every year on the feast of the Immaculate Conception.

In this way a community developed which, in a certain sense, was a prelude to what were to become known as Secular Institutes. When the company was dissolved, they continued to live the same spirit. Some joined religious congregations, others married, but each kept chastity and obedience according to their state.

2
THE PERSECUTION OF THE 'COMPANY OF FRIARS'

THE REVOLUTION OF 1848 AT BOVISIO

Luigi Monti's work was confirmed as a work of God through the persecution and calumny it suffered, something that no genuine work of the Lord can avoid.

People who do not live charity, even though they may be church-goers, do not always accept others who come together to do good, to become saints. The good they do acts like a reproof to pagans who do none and to the Pharisees who try to confine it to a set of rules. So, in their eyes, a group of young people who renounce sexual relationships and visits to inns and hostelries, and who do not take part in idle gossip, evokes a strong suspicion that they are revolutionaries, people who want to change the world. 'We have found the one who was inciting our nation,' the Sanhedrin said to Pilate about Jesus.

It was ever thus. Saints have always been disdained by Pharisees, a type which has continued to exist down the centuries. The Pharisees are the ones who produce reasons for not doing anything, for keeping the status quo, for not changing – all formulae for defending their accumulation of wealth.

The first Pharisees, in order to remove Jesus and his work from their lives, accused him of political subversion. For Caiphas,

Jesus was a revolutionary. For the Roman emperors, Christians were political activists whose words and actions threatened to overturn order in society, which itself was no more than disorder held together by social injustice.

By the end of 1847, in Lombardy as in other parts of Italy and Europe, to ruin someone all you needed to do was to accuse them of conspiracy. Plots were being hatched by secret societies and revolutionary groups and there was a general air of political and social intolerance. The whole of Europe was undergoing a crisis of uncertainty, like a premonition of a catastrophe, which for Metternich could not have been more frightening. Austria-Hungary was, at that moment in history, a model of political immobility, while the rest of Europe was feeling the shockwaves of the French Revolution. At the end of 1847 Karl Marx launched the communist manifesto, which was an early warning of a future upheaval.

'Revolution is about to break out in the Italian peninsula,' grumbled Metternich. And the Hapsburg monarchy, guardians of the status quo, began to sense that many of the peoples of Europe, the Magyars, the Italians, the Germans, the Czechs, the Romanians and others would not tolerate oppression any longer.

In fact, half of Europe was affected by revolutionary movements, from Vienna to Paris, from Madrid to Belgrade, from Berlin to Palermo.

The Austrians were expelled from Milan after a heroic five days of street fighting, and on 25 March Charles Albert came into the picture, defeating Radetzky's army at Goito, Pastrengo and Santa Lucia. In May Lombardy announced its union with Piedmont, but after defeat by the Austrians in July, Charles Albert was forced to hand back Ticino, and the following March he was decisively defeated at Novara.

Faint echoes of these events reached Bovisio. The peasants and artisans were poorly informed. When the provisional Committee decreed mass conscription, Monti's young Catholics obeyed. Despite this, however, the revolutionaries interpreted their tranquillity and their spiritual detachment as a lack of patriotism and they accused them of supporting the Austrians. Then, when the Austrians returned, Monti's followers were accused of being Piedmontese partisans. They were also accused of being a 'secret society', one of the many 'fraternities' which had been formed in the Milan area at the beginning of 1850, to prepare for the liberation of the fatherland in collaboration with Mazzini's revolutionary organisation. The Austrian imperial records describe Monti's society of friars as a conspiratory sect to be sent to the gallows.

The group of young men who are working today (1963) in Monti's carpentry workshop at Bovisio have their own ideas about the meetings that were held there both before and after 1848. They refer to them as meetings for 'partisans'. In fact, they say that they were imprisoned and maltreated by Nazi troops from Germany and Austria during the Second World War. Others, however, who were better informed, understood the real revolutionary significance - that of the Gospel revolution, of that work made up of prayer, of consecration, of daily human commitment which pre-figured the concerns expressed in the papal encyclical *Mater et Magistra*.

THE ARREST OF THE FRIARS

In 1933, during the fascist regime, Philip Meda did some research into the archives of the magistrates' court at Desio.[1] He discovered a report written by that court for the court of appeal in Milan, dated 15 September 1851. It was under the heading 'Secret Society' and spoke of an 'inquisition' carried out 'against many individuals under this jurisdiction who for some time have been meeting in a secret society under the name of 'Company of Friars'.' Fifteen of these 'many individuals' from Bovisio, Masciago, Cesano and Seveso were named, including

Luigi Monti. The 'sect leaders' were recorded as Frs Luigi Dossi and Charles Tresoldi, for they could not imagine that the head could be a modest carpenter. Referring to other sources of information, Meda writes: 'It is easy to see that this episode from the autumn of 1851 was just one of many sad examples of political aberration at the service of private prejudices and local disputes. Often, as in our case, people who were not only totally inoffensive, but deserving of much better treatment, were on the receiving end of it...'

At the end of 1848, Fr Charles Ciceri, the parish priest of Bovisio died. He had always looked kindly on a movement which involved so many young people in the life of the Church. His successor was a shy man, influenced by the suspicion and intrigue of that period of fear following the revolution. Wanting to avoid any trouble, he asked Monti to dissolve the company. When there is a choice between what is right and what is safe, sometimes the latter is preferred in order to keep to the quiet life. And anyway, what need was there for vows of obedience and chastity?

'There's something fishy in all this!' he said and he threatened to report the friars to the archbishop as heretics. Poor Monti was dumbfounded. He tried to defend himself, but such an attitude wounded his concept of ecclesiastical authority.

So, the next day he went with a companion, Ercole Albuzzi, to the shrine at Rho to seek the advice of the parish priest Fr Ramazotti. Fr Ramazotti was a man of God, who assured the two young men that both their proposals and their activities were perfectly in order and told them not to be afraid.

Monti returned consoled and reassured the whole company.

But worse was to come when a new parish priest, Fr Caldara arrived in April 1849. Either fear, or his Jansenist upbringing, caused him to dislike the young bigots who dared to introduce new ideas and upheaval into the humdrum existence of Bovisio.

'I don't want all this bigotry amongst my people and I don't want the Company of Friars. And if they don't put a stop to all their activities I'll do it for them. I'll set the town council on some of them and I'll send the others for military service.'

The priest summoned Monti and told him to close the society. When Monti said he could not see any reason for so doing, he referred the case to the commissioner at Barlassina, presenting the young carpenter as head of a subversive organisation, a secret society, something that the friars did not even know the meaning of. All the commissioner needed do to save his skin, and perhaps even gain promotion, was to denounce them, and to throw the young rebel into jail while he awaited worse punishment.

Meda relates that in the same year, 1850, Monti was requested to appear before Desio magistrates' court for questioning, without knowing why. He assumed it was to do with the Company, and it was. Before going to court, however, Monti paid a visit to his spiritual director, Fr P. Dossi, to ask his advice on how to handle the questions. Dossi told him that God would suggest to him what to say.

He went along to the court and stood before the judge who said:

'Who are you?'

' Luigi Monti di Angelo.'

'Do you know why you have been called before this court?'

'No sir, this is the first time I have been before a judge.'

'Tell me how this Company of Friars was formed.'

'I'll explain briefly. After listening to a missionary from Rho I was pleased to know that he was happy to hear my confession. He encouraged me to gather together other young people to do good deeds, so I immediately started the Company. And as a number of young people already came to my house in the evenings, we gradually began to grow.'

'I've heard that at Cesano Maderno there is a priest who also has a company like yours. Perhaps you are linked to that one?'

'No sir.'

'You don't know that priest?'
'Yes, I know him, but the companies are separate and each runs its own affairs.'
'Have you never been to confession to that priest?'
'Yes sir.'
'What did he say to you?'
'You shouldn't inquire about the secrets of the confessional...'
'You're right. We won't talk about it.'
The judge continued the questioning and Monti spoke openly about the Company.

In the end, the judge turned to the Chancellor and said, 'It's the first time I have examined a case like this,' and he left the court laughing and saying, 'Secret society, anything but!' He then released Monti.

No matter how much the Commissioner schemed, he was not able to carry out his plan to imprison Monti and his hopes of abolishing the Company came to nothing.

The following year, 1851, while Monti was with two companions, Custode Radice and Peter Caronni, at Fr Luigi Dossi's house at Quinto Romano, the police went with a warrant to search his house at Bovisio. There they found the damning evidence: manuscripts of sacred music and plain chant, readings from St Alphonsus Liguori and other saints. All this highly dangerous material was confiscated and held under lock and key. General Giulay, symbol of imperial might and power and noted for his zeal for inquisition and repression, was notified straightaway. It was also just at the time when the people's sense of fear had been heightened by the news of the impending visit of the Emperor Franz Josef. A few weeks later, on the evening of 7 September, the judicial authorities arrested thirteen young men. They put eleven of them in handcuffs, but two of them were without, because the police did not have enough of them. Joseph Monti, Luigi's brother and the director of the Company was one of those arrested.

The local people, surprised and confused, organised a demonstration against the parish priest whom they blamed for the arrests. The mayor intervened to protect him from a possible violent attack and to have the young men released.

Fortunately, they had arrested thirteen of them. The order issued by General Giulay to the Commissioner at Barlassina was drastic: 'I grant you, Honorable Commissioner, permission to arrest and imprison all the members of the said company, and if you arrest no more than four, shoot them on the spot, without trial. If there are more of them, you must follow the penal code.'

It is not clear why four could be shot there and then, but not five. Was it due to a shortage of ammunition? Or was it fear of a negative reaction by the local people? In fact, this is the kind of logic employed by all despotic regimes and by the pathetic characters who work for them.

The thirteen became sixteen a few days later, with the arrest of Luigi Monti, Radice and Caronni, besides Fr Dossi's houseboy from Quinto Romano, where the round-up was completed on the afternoon of 11 September.

Monti pleaded successfully for the release of Sante Pennati, the houseboy.

The newly-arrested men were also sent to Desio. On the way there they spent the night joyfully in the jail at Bettola. They behaved as if they were on their honeymoon. They kissed the walls and declared how lucky they were to be able to imitate in a small way their Divine Master. As they had been arrested after midday, they were given no supper. Some of the young men lifted Luigi up to a tiny window from which, he threw some money down to a group of children below, asking them to go to Fr Dossi's and buy some food. Two hours later it arrived.

The prison commander provided a woollen blanket for Fr Dossi to pull over himself on the wooden bed. The next morning they were sent to Bollate, where they had breakfast in the prison there. After stopping at other prisons on the way so that the guards could change, they arrived, still handcuffed, at Bovisio, where almost everyone had turned out to welcome them. Monti asked them not to say anything to his relatives, as they were already upset by the arrest of his brother.

At Cesano Maderno, the hometown of Radice, Seveso and Caronni, there were protests and scenes of great sadness. Finally, at nine in the evening, after stopping in the jail at Barlassina, the prisoners reached Desio, tired and hungry. They had marched 40 kilometres on foot, their only meal being a little soup for breakfast.

THE PRISON AT DESIO

'When Monti entered the prison with his companions he was shocked by the appearance of the other thirteen young men already there. Their faces were pale and wan, but he very soon realised that this was due to the lack of air in the cell, which caused such a deathly, suffocating atmosphere. The cell was about seven paces square and the only way for air to enter was through a tiny grille. There was also a toilet in the room, with a wooden seat which barely covered it.'

Desio is a small town, still dominated by its beautiful basilica with its Lombard tower. Right up until 1975, it had kept the prison cells in the same conditions as its Austrian overlords: low ceilings, narrow stairways, primordial toilet facilities which produced a terrible stench.

After two weeks cramped up in a tiny warren on the ground floor, Monti and his companions were transferred to a dingy first floor cell where there was the danger of suffocating in the foul smelling air.

They had been in prison about 20 days when the warder told them that they were about to receive a visit from the judge and that they should all line up before him as a mark of respect. When the judge arrived with his entourage he said in a very severe tone of voice, 'At last, here you are!... You're all well here.' Monti took his courage in both hands and said: 'My Lord, we ask the grace to be examined.' But the judge cut him off in midsentence saying: 'Now you're asking for a grace, eh! You belong to secret societies; you listen to a false priest [Fr Dossi]; you read evil books [the lives of the saints, the works of St Alphonsus Liguori!] and you have started a church in your house.' Monti replied, 'My Lord, these really are lies.' Then, grudgingly, the judge offered his hand to Monti and said: 'I'll be seeing you!...' and he left.

Nevertheless, despite the discomfort and the filth, these young men did not lose heart, because they did not lose their union with God. In fact, it was stronger than before. They formed a kind of ad hoc community with, naturally, Monti as its head. He kept them going, encouraging them, teaching them hymns and warming them with his wit.

People gathered outside under the windows to listen to their pure and harmonious singing in honour of Mary. It was as if the songs had come down from heaven.

The prison authorities could not make head or tail of it.

After Monti and his companions had spent a month or so in prison, numerous individuals and families wrote to the powers-that-were, asking for their release. The mayor, Fr Dossi, the Brambilla, Cornaggia and Carretto families and Archbishop Romilli all pleaded for the release of the young innocents put under suspicion by 'a priest who cannot see beyond the end of his own nose,' as Meda said. In fact, the archbishop actually made an appeal directly to the Emperor Franz Josef who happened to be in Milan, but, being a rigid bureaucrat he simply passed it on to the official enquiry.

For all its diligence, the enquiry failed to establish the connection between plain chant and a treacherous conspiracy. So, after consultations with magistrates courts, regional courts and various other offices, conducted through rigorous correspondence and punctilious interrogation, they concluded that the 'friars' were innocent, and after 72 days in detention they were released.

In April 1933, that suffocating cell, number 16, where they are said to have been held, was converted into a chapel and blessed by the saintly Cardinal Schuster of Milan. The sixteen 'friars' processed from the prison in pairs down the road which led to the nearest church, where they gave thanks to God. In prison they had hungered for the sacraments and now they were able to satisfy their hunger.

God was their strength: 'If God is with us, who is against us?'

Then Luigi, on behalf of his companions, went to thank one of those who had done most to secure their release. She confessed that she had felt envious of those young men who had been worthy enough to suffer for Christ

The episode clarified many aspects of Monti's work. It certainly showed that he and his companions were completely given to serving God and had no political agenda whatsoever. Victims of a cowardly lie and its associated arrogance, they showed themselves to be men of rare virtue. Having suffered badly at the hands of repulsive enemies, they were ready to forgive them.

The newness of their apostolate, living as consecrated people in the world, like in a monastery, was such that it completely astounded even a priest.

The action of those lay friars, who brought monasticism into the workshop caused a split. The idle, the cowardly, the guardians of the establishment saw in it the seeds of subversion, even though all this was happening in a tiny community, in a remote village.

THE SONS OF MARY (1852)

Luigi stayed at home for three days with his sister, Maria Luigia. She too had given her life to God and Luigi felt strengthened

Bovisio:
The baptismal font where the little Luigi was baptised on the day he was born, 24 July 1825. He always had fond memories of this holy place.

The house where Luigi Monti was born.

The workshop where Monti worked as a carpenter for eight years and where he gathered together other young men in the evenings for prayer, catechism and singing.

by her love for him. However, he soon went back to Quinto Romano to take up his carpenter's tools again. It became more and more clear to him that this job was an instrument of the apostolate in Fr Dossi's community. A few days later Caronni and Radice joined him there.

They began again with greater vigour. There was a burning desire all over Italy, but particularly in the North, to raise the religious awareness of the people, who in their turn wanted to raise themselves socially and politically. A general overview of the needs of the times led them to build up nuclei of young men to be trained as apostles to tomorrow's society.

Fr Dossi had gone to the Carthusian monastery of Pavia for a few days. In the setting of the magnificent traditional liturgical celebrations, he spoke to the superior of the Carthusians asking him for suggestions for drawing up statutes and structures for his nascent community. The abbot assured him that such a community would provide a backbone for an institution that was already in existence, but decadent.

And so it was. When Fr Dossi returned home, he heard that there was a community at Brescia founded on similar lines to his, by the venerable Ludovic Pavoni. Under the direction of priests and lay assistants they had gathered together children of the area, especially orphans and abandoned ones, under the name of the Sons of Mary Immaculate. Fr Pavoni, a saintly priest, died suddenly in 1849 and his congregation went through a crisis which was reflected in a lack of vocations.

Fr Dossi went to investigate and introduced himself to the Superior-General of the Sons of Mary Immaculate, Fr Joseph Baldini. Moved by the desire to serve God's cause, they agreed that they should unite their efforts rather than found new institutions.

It was agreed that the Brescia congregation would make available its leaders, statutes and its approval by the church authorities. For his part, Fr Dossi offered a host of ardent youth, like a stream of young blood in an organism that was already tried and tested, but reduced to three priests and four assistants. Monti accepted, quietly following the judgement of his spiritual director. On 7 August 1852, Dossi and five young men moved to Brescia and became part of the congregation of the Sons of Mary. It was a beautiful congregation and much loved for its name, which put love for Our Lady in a completely new light. Monti followed him on 28 November that year. He saw it as a leap ahead in the divine adventure and he set himself to work with great alacrity.

Note:

1. *La 'Compagnia dei fratti' in Brianza perseguita come Società segreta*, (in: 'La Lombardia nel Risorgimento Italiano', Milan, 1933 anno XVIII, 24 July, 1933, pp 43-69)

3
THE HOSPITALLER IDEAL

CYPRIAN PEZZINI

The talents of Monti the worker were immediately appreciated by Dossi and Baldini amongst the Sons of Mary. While five of his companions were teaching their particular trade to the orphans, he was charged with the supervision and the instruction of the sick, as well as setting up the surgery, the pharmacy and the infirmary. His main training was in nursing and it was while caring for the sick that he saw the value of this work of mercy in a new light. Throughout the centuries great saints had been formed beside the sick bed, including the young Aloysius, whom Monti had always looked on as a model.

The development of the apostolate in the field of the care of the sick was born of the universally acknowledged need to resurrect the hospital service as a work of mercy, at a time when it had become simply a job, often badly paid and poorly organised.

In fact, it was Fr Dossi himself, always sensitive to the needs of the apostolate, who cultivated in Monti an interest in, and a love for, the care of the sick. On his visits to the hospital at Brescia he saw the brutality and the uncaring attitude of the secular 'professional' nurses. He thus conceived the idea of religious nurses, dedicated to service of the sick, and not just there to earn a wage. They would have the conviction that they were serving Christ, and would do it out of love for God.

Fr Dossi's aspirations were supported by Sister Maria Crocifissa Di Rosa, the holy founder of the Handmaids of Charity, whose vocation was to care for sick women in the hospitals. The saintly Sister Di Rosa wanted to set up a similar service run by a male congregation for those in hospital and she urged Fr Dossi to start one in Brescia. With great admiration for their spirit and for the 'prodigious progress' as he called it in a letter written in 1855[1], Fr Dossi intended to 'implant and copy in the male branch' the Handmaids of Di Rosa. He wanted to involve Monti and his friends from Bovisio, but how could he do it? Like Monti, he was a religious and dependent on a superior. At that point Divine Providence came to his aid.

Something similar had already been tried at Cremona in 1846. Mgr Ferdinand Manini, chaplain to the Handmaids of Charity, had gathered together a group of young people to serve the sick, with charity, in the public hospital. Because of the political turmoil they had to withdraw in 1849 and the bishop entrusted the work to the religious congregation of St Camillus de Lellis, to which was added Manini's group of young people.

One of the most lively of these was Cyprian Pezzini, born in Cremona in 1817. He wanted to keep the spirit of Manini's group intact and he left the hospital with the idea of starting somewhere else the thing that had failed at Cremona.

Not much is known about the events of which Pezzini was both author and victim. What is certain is that he offered his service of charity at Astrio, near Brena sull'Oglio, from where Sister Di Rosa invited him to go to Brescia to meet Fr Dossi. She had spoken to the latter about Pezzini in glowing terms. It was 'a happy moment' for Fr Dossi, who at last saw the possibility of his dream of having a team of religious hospitallers coming true. Pezzini was free, motivated by a holy ideal and experienced in hospital work. Fr Dossi could 'make available the sacrifice of thirty young men' from Monti's 'Company of Friars' at Brianza.

The whole thing was agreed between Dossi and Monti and was wholeheartedly adopted by Monti. Above all he offered himself for the intimate vocation which the Lord was cultivating in his soul, longing to serve God in his neighbour and to help wherever the needs were more immediate or graver.

There was undoubtedly an urgent need to educate the young, to counter the damage caused by widespread secularism and to produce well-informed citizens for the rapidly evolving society. But now Monti saw as equally urgent, the service of the sick, threatened both by physical illnesses and by moral degradation which often led to desperation.He saw how productive it would be to uplift the human person, the child of God, through works of mercy carried out by a host of young nurses in a religious order, able to give, at one and the same time, the benefits of physical and spiritual health.

For this reason he was undergoing training as a nurse, a pharmacist and a surgeon and at the same time he was deepening his knowledge of the religious life. There was a particular difficulty, however: both Dossi and Monti were dependent on the superior of the Sons of Mary.

But Pezzini's offer, made through the saintly Sister Di Rosa, plus the availability of Monti's young men, all of whom were independent, meant that an autonomous institution could be started. The realisation of this fact gave Dossi 'a feeling of happiness'. But, as he was to confess in his letter, it was 'passing'. Immediately there were trials caused by misunderstanding and various kinds of difficulties.

First of all, they could not get things going at Brescia, so they went to Bergamo, where, in 1853, Dossi sent a nucleus of young men led by Pezzini. Under the guidance of the industrious Pezzini things started to improve, until the beginning of 1855. The hospital chaplain, a Capuchin Franciscan, struck by the integrity of the lives of these young men and by the spirit of dedication in their work as nurses, had the idea of incorporating them into his own Order, as a special section of the Third Order. He set about the task and managed to obtain the approval of the Bishop of Bergamo, the authorities of his own order and of the Roman Curia. On 22 February, 1856 everything was finalised; obviously, both the style and the aims of the organisation changed.

This was a suffering for Fr Dossi, because he had wanted to set up the male section of Sister Di Rosa's community and not a Third Order. He wanted it to live independently of an order. If anything, it should have been linked to the Sons of Mary. The Provincial of the Capuchins did not want this hybrid formula either. He felt that admitting young men who were not trained in the Franciscan way and who were destined for other tasks than those normally performed by the Order was likely to produce more problems than benefits.

The first damaging result was that Dossi withdrew Pezzini and his young men. He was developing a different ideal which he wanted to translate into a new institution suited to contemporary circumstances.

With great humility, Pezzini withdrew to Brescia with Dossi and Monti, blaming himself for problems at Bergamo. As Dossi's representative and as head of the community he held himself responsible. Pezzini's action in Bergamo and Monti's, later on, in Rome, show how the shape of the new community, born in Sister Di Rosa's heart and embraced by Fr Dossi, was stamped precisely and clearly in the spirits of the two apostles of charity.

One can understand just how bitterly disappointed Dossi was after the failure in Bergamo. Monti went through this trial as if it were his own and he learned another lesson from it about the difficulties that can arise even when good people acting with good intentions intervene to do good. He was living the 'prelude' to the suffering he was to undergo later in Rome, in similar circumstances.

Gathered round their common master and spiritual father, Monti and Pezzini grew to know one another more intimately, sharing projects, hopes and experiences and strengthening their own vocations.

Monti knew he should wait before proceeding prudently and obediently, but Pezzini, impatient to realise his ideal, decided to go to Rome. He went with a letter of introduction from the Bishop of Bergamo to Mgr Angelo Mai. Fr Dossi, in fact, had already guessed that Pezzini would come across difficulties at least as great as those in Bergamo.

However, Dossi could not do much to save the situation. In the summer of 1855 he was struck down with cholera as an epidemic spread throughout the Italian peninsula.

When he recovered he gathered together the various threads, including Pezzini, who was happy to work under such an expert, safe and well-loved master. Now Pezzini did everything with the approval of Dossi, who became the prime mover in the next stages.

On 8 December 1855, the feast of the Immaculate Conception, Dossi and Radice moved from Brescia to Bussolengo, near Verona. Dossi became director of an institute for wayward children, thus giving birth to the second branch of the Sons of Mary. The transfer came about after certain difficulties with Fr Baldini, the superior at Brescia.

It seemed as if there were two heads of the community at Brescia, with two men who were so different from one another. This led to the formation of two factions with the two priests at their head.

In those conditions, Monti felt a strong desire to be reunited with Fr Dossi, his spiritual father and his inspiration. He visited Bussolengo frequently, for at Brescia he felt as if he were in exile.

THE EXPERIMENT

Pezzini arrived in Rome on 19 March 1856. He was received on various occasions by Archbishop Salvatore Nobili Vitelleschi of Seleucia, Commander of the Santo Spirito, the highest authority in the main Vatican hospital. Not wanting to waste an opportunity, in October of that year the Commander entrusted to the Capuchin Fathers Pezzini's plan for a Christian inspired service run by nurses consecrated to God. The offer was gratefully accepted and Vitelleschi started to get things moving straightaway. He hurried the process along because he was due to give up the post.

He asked for references on Pezzini from the Archbishop of Milan, the Bishops of Cremona, Verona and Bergamo, as well as from Fr Dossi, with whose backing he had introduced himself. The references must have been excellent, for Vitelleschi proposed the idea to the Holy Father at an audience on 29 January 1857. The Pope gave his approval with great joy and invited them to start immediately.

At the behest of Archbishop Vitelleschi, Pezzini left there and then for Lombardy to gather together the young men and start the job.

He went to Bussolengo, near Verona, where Fr Dossi was running his institute for wayward children, and where he also met Monti, who had come over from Brescia.

At Fr Dossi's request, Monti was asked to go to Rome to take charge of the operation and to be a companion for Pezzini. It seemed as if the two young men were made to understand one another and complement one another. Pezzini was ardent, enthusiastic but prone to depression; Monti was solid, prudent with a sound knowledge of people and things. Both of them were spiritually linked to Dossi and both subject to him. By 26 February Pezzini was able to send the names and personal details of the young men to the Commander. Pezzini himself gathered other young men from the Bergamo, Como and Sondrio districts.

On 23 March he wrote to the Jesuit Fr John Blosi saying he 'had gathered the number needed to make a start' and that he had notified the Commander.

There were twenty young men to begin with and there were others on the waiting list should they be needed.[2]

They met at Bussolengo, at Dossi's institute, having been trained by Monti as professional nurses with a religious formation.

When they came to choose a name for the society on 25 March 1857, Monti, at Pezzini's request, proposed that of Sons of Mary.

For six years he said he had been a Son of Mary and he always wanted to be a Son of Mary.

Pezzini objected because there was already another congregation of the same name. He would have preferred the name Servants of Mary. However, this title too had been chosen by someone else, and Monti joked that he would rather be a child than a servant. He remarked that if a servant does something wrong he is kicked out, but if a child is guilty of some fault he is not.

So, Sons it was, but to distinguish themselves from others they agreed to add 'of the Immaculate Conception', to commemorate the dogma proclaimed by the Pope three years previously.

On hearing that Pezzini had 'eighteen young men recommended for their moral qualities'[3], the Commander submitted a 'report' to the Holy Father. It was based on his opinion of Fr Dossi, formed through his contact with Pezzini. He asked for authorisation to start an experiment with the new institution at the Santo Spirito. In this way everything would be ready when Pezzini arrived in Rome with the young men. In order to get things moving quickly, Pezzini had urged Fr John Blosi S.J. to write, which he did on the 23 March: 'I would like Archbishop

Vitelleschi to let me know when he can leave. If it is to be soon, may I beg Your Grace to move things along quickly, so that there will be no major delay.'

The Commander presented the following report to the Holy Father on 28 April, 1857:

'Most Blessed Father,

'Those filled with the spirit of charity are the ones best suited to provide for the many needs of the sick, to whom they have dedicated themselves. People who are motivated only by money cannot do the job properly.

'In order to provide the poor sick people of the Santo Spirito hospital with the best possible care, the undersigned has in mind to bring together, with co-operation of the Capuchin Order, the chaplains of that pious establishment, a selection of charitable individuals who, having produced an abundant harvest, would work like zealous labourers to gather it.

'At this moment, Most Blessed Father, eighteen persons, noted for their moral qualities, are ready to lend their hands to this holy undertaking, just as soon as the blessing of Your Holiness comes down upon them to make it come to fruition. There are many requests for other workers for the necessary tests and experiments.

'The new institution at present has no external and legal form as a religious community, but it has all its own internal rules and discipline. It is called the Friars Hospitaller of Mary Most Immaculate.[4]

'A priest from the religious family of the Capuchins would take on their spiritual direction.

'The immediate direction would be left in the hands of the 'pro tempore' Commanders.

'After a successful experimental period, a permanent rule would be proposed to Your Holiness with the idea of validating, on Your Apostolic Authority, a new order, which would be distinguished by all the prerogatives of a Regular Institute.

'Meanwhile, the Undersigned beseeches Your Blessedness to

grant his approval to introduce this new institution to the Santo Spirito and to experiment with it in the ways and methods explained above.'

In the audience granted to the Commander, the Holy Father kindly deigned to authorise the experiment. In his 'report', Archbishop Vitelleschi refers to 'eighteen persons, noted for their moral qualities'. These were the young men nominated by Pezzini to the Commander and gathered together at Bussolengo.

Pezzini and Monti, intent on preparing the young men for the new mission, could not leave straightaway for Rome because of the length of time it took to issue the two of them with passports. In the meantime, an anonymous letter from Rome informed them that new developments were taking place there. The news alarmed Pezzini, always easily upset, and it took all Monti's persuasive powers to convince him to return to Rome to see what was going on.

In Rome, Pezzini discovered that the Capuchin chaplains were already recruiting individuals with whom they intended to start the experiment authorised by the Pope.

Their sub-prior, Fr John Baptist from Genoa, dilly-dallied with Pezzini, before eventually gathering together 12 young men, the number established in the negotiations between the Commander and Pezzini. So it was that on 3 July 1857, the experiment with the institution proposed by Pezzini got under way.

Pezzini did not find anyone to help him maintain his rights, and discouraged and humiliated he implored the Friars Hospitaller to accept him. On condition that he did not claim any rights, he was clothed in the blue habit with the name of Bro Cyprian of Cremona.

In the meantime, knowing nothing of events in Rome, Monti was waiting with the young men. When Fr Dossi asked Pezzini what had happened, he replied: 'With all the calamities and mishaps, all that was missing was Bro Luigi's nail, to be nailed to the cross.'

THE DARK NIGHT

And the cross had been there – for some time. Monti was not able to leave. They needed transport which was difficult to come by. They needed passports to pass through three states and, with all the red tape, these were not easy to obtain. There were no railways and to travel to Rome on foot or by horse and carriage was no small effort. Then, to cap it all, Monti fell ill. And as if all this were not enough, Dossi, the superior, had gone off to preach in the Verona region, to raise money for the house. Dossi's deputy added insult to injury by making offensive comments such as: 'What are you doing here? You're always ill... You cannot stay here, you're not going to Rome, what on earth are you going to do?'

The malice of these questions added to the fact that he could not work because of his illness, provoked a spiritual crisis within Monti. He saw himself as useless, as a failure who, seven years after leaving Bovisio and his family to join the Sons of Mary, was still without a base, a misfit scorned and derided. He wanted to live as a religious, but he still did not have an institute to which he could be consecrated. He wanted to nurse the sick, but there was no hospital where he could start work.

His spirit was enveloped in a kind of mist which could be regarded as a kind of dark night in miniature. This gathering of shadows included his physical sickness and the human uncertainty manifested in the disintegration of his youthful ideals and the separation from friends and family. It was as if heaven and earth had obliterated him. He prayed for hours before the Blessed Sacrament but his heart remained 'arid, cold and insensitive' as he was to confide in a friend. He felt abandoned by God and by human beings, with no moral or physical strength...

In that desolation, which all the saints have suffered in one way or another, the Lord came to him. One day in September 1857 when the others were making the Novena for Our Lady's Birthday and he was suffering alone in his room, a voice spoke to him, quite clearly, in his soul: Luigi, go into the chapel and tell your trials once more to Jesus in the Blessed Sacrament.

Shaken, Luigi ran straight to the chapel, knelt down by the grille which opened on to the altar and, once more recounted his trials to Jesus, who himself was closed in and alone in the tabernacle out of love. Suddenly the chapel was illuminated with a radiant apparition, an apparition of Jesus and Mary.

Here were two loves, two ideals made persons. It was the Immaculate Conception, on the left, who spoke to him: 'Luigi, why are you so sad and downhearted? Take courage and don't be disheartened. Could I abandon you after all you have done for me? After winning over those young men in order to preserve their innocence and to help them live in chastity? Take courage, I will never abandon you'.

After the Immaculate Mother it was the son, Jesus, who confirmed her words: 'And I, how could I abandon you after you have done so much for my poor sick ones? Courage Luigi, don't be sad. In every mishap, in any turmoil that you might go through, I will help you…'

All Monti's human experience, interwoven with mishaps and turmoil, was sealed by that divine promise.

That vision was like the sun breaking through the clouds again and it brought new life to the heart of the young man. He was now thirty-two years old and it gave him a kind of second youth. He started on his path again with all the vigour of one of the Lord's labourers who has been tempered by trials.

The young man, with his humility and with his head firmly on his shoulders, did not mention the apparition to anyone, except to Fr Dossi in confession. Dossi, his spiritual director, just back from the mission in Bussolengo, explained, taking him gently through this period of downheartednes, that it was a divine action to make him a saint: 'These are the signs with which Jesus lets you know he wants you to become a saint, and human beings are the instruments…'

So with renewed strength he started again - to suffer. Months passed, a whole year passed and no solution emerged. However, during this period his aspirations grew and his vocation became clearer: he was to dedicate himself to the Christian service of the sick, for which work he was to gather together other young men. The winter of 1858 arrived. The roofs and trees were covered in white snow and everything shrouded in grey mist. One night, perhaps triggered by the vague and scarce news of Pezzini's tribulations in Rome, Luigi had a dream. He dreamt that he was falling down a slope towards a precipice. Just as he was about to drop into the chasm, the Heavenly Mother appeared and stopped him with her arm, saying: 'Luigi, where are you running to?... Can you not see the precipice? If I had not come to your rescue, wherever would you have ended up?...'

After the chastisement came the tender caress.

'Well, I want to let you know that, just as I helped you and saved you on this occasion, so will I help and save you in any moment of danger or need. And even if sometimes it may seem a hopeless case, take courage all the same and don't be afraid of anything, for I will always be with you.'

Luigi woke up to a completely new perspective: earthly dangers and heavenly assistance. And, with even greater determination, he set about doing the will of God. And this was expressed by Pezzini's gesture. For he, by submitting himself and joining the new institution, was able to bring his friends from Bussolengo too. So, Monti, with Dossi's assent and blessing, was able to apply himself to the new mission in Rome. But he was alone. A simple tradesman from the country, he was making such a long journey for the first time, to set up something which was so uncertain. With great trepidation, he left his spiritual director Dossi, and his natural brother Anthony who lived in Bussolengo, and travelled by rail to Rome. On 22 April 1858, he arrived in the capital of Catholicism, the city of the Pope.

NOTES

1. The phrases in quotation marks are from Dossi's letter, stored in the Conceptionist archives.
2. Pezzini's letter to Fr John Blosi on 23 March, 1857. (Conceptionist General Archives, Prot. no 5) It says: .'.. as well as having completed the required number, as in the two notes sent to Archbishop Vitelleschi, I am also keeping others in reserve so that whenever the need arises I know where I can lay hands on them.' The names of six of these young men are known. The Commander is asking for information regarding the moral qualities of three of them, Pancras Cattaneo of Bovisio, Andrew Camnaglio of Desio and Vincent Corno of Lesmo, from the Bishop of Bergamo and the Archbishop of Milan. Pezzini speaks of the other three in the letter already referred to. They are: Bernadine Abati, Alexander Venturi and Martin Tartaglia. Writing to Fr Blosi, he says: 'I would be grateful if you could assure me that their documents have been sent to Archbishop Vitelleschi, as I was given to understand before my departure. If they are still in your possession, may I request that you kindly send them as soon as possible to his Grace.'
3. The Bishop of Bergamo and the Archbishop of Milan affirmed the moral qualities of the first three. Another three were guaranteed by Fr Blosi and of the twelve gathered together at Bussolengo, Pezzini, Monti and Fr Dossi were guaranteed.
4. Friars Hospitaller was the name given by Pezzini and Dossi to the institution right from the beginning. (Pezzini: Regole; Dossi: letters quoted 3-7, 1855).

4
LUIGI MONTI IN ROME

THE SANTO SPIRITO HOSPITAL

It cannot be mere coincidence that Luigi Monti set up his work of service to the sick, run by consecrated lay people, in a hospital such as the Santo Spirito in Sassia. It was the principal pontifical hospital, which, in the eyes of Christendom, was a symbol and model of all European hospitals inspired by Christian charity and built by the Church.

For generations it had been the first, the largest and the most venerated. It was the hospital *de Urbe*, a monument of piety, built in the Vatican, on the Tiber, by that great builder of modern Europe, Innocent III, the greatest Pope of the Middle Ages. The Romanesque bell tower is all that remains of the original building, but it was re-built by Sixtus IV and carefully maintained by his successors down the centuries. It developed into a kind of citadel of charity and of art and its centre opened out into the high, spacious Sistine ward, interrupted by the chapel erected by Palladio. The chapel stood in the midst of the rows of beds, like Jesus in the midst of the multitude. The nurses walked down the aisle of the church and the first thing they did was to go to confession, thereby disinfecting their spirit. Following the wish of the founder, the poor and the sick were welcomed as *quasi domini*, like lords, by the General Master and Preceptor.

In each of these great buildings, often under high and grandiose arches, great saints like Philip Neri and Camillus de Lellis had brought their healing, giving charity to the sick. It was in these very same places that great artists like Palestrina and Animuccia had produced soothing melodies on the organ. The name Sassia recalls the Saxons, whose *Schola Saxonum* (later *Schola Anglorum*) had flourished in that quarter, made sacred by the martyrdom of St Peter and the Christians put to death by Nero. Since its foundation, no less than 1,000 poor people, out of a total population of 35,000 inhabitants, had been given permanent assistance.

Innocent III had the original idea and provided the funding for the building of the Santo Spirito, King John Senzaterra had given the land and Guy de Montpellier had brought his Friars Hospitaller, the order of the Santo Spirito. They were originally laymen, but, in time, they became priests, Canons Regular of the Holy Spirit. Gradually, however, they detached themselves from nursing and, with the accumulation of material goods, also from poverty.

By the end of the sixteenth century there were around 1,200 hospitals affiliated to the Santo Spirito, which thus acquired the title of 'Arch-hospital', It was a very important centre and the power it wielded was a source of temptation.

Leo X had made the hospital a commandory and its director became a Commander, installed in his own palace, adjoining the hospital. It was a sumptuous palace built beside the church of the Santo Spirito with a courtyard surrounded by two rows of arches supported by columns, twenty above and twenty below.

The hospital suffered the consequences of the sacking of Rome in 1527 when the Landsknechts attacked it, throwing the patients into the river and killing friars, monks and children.

In 1715, Lancisi, an illustrious doctor, gave his valuable library to the hospital, for the medical training of the doctors.

The hospital was ruined financially by the French Revolution, but it was put back on its feet by Pius VII and particularly by Pius IX who, in 1847, suppressed the Order of the Holy Spirit, which was defunct, and replaced it with St Camillus' Ministers of the Sick. They stayed there until 1856 when the Capuchins were introduced as chaplains.

The Conservatorio delle Esposte[1] was also part of the Santo Spirito hospital. With the decline of the Order of Hospitallers, Pope Gregory XVI had to entrust the work to the Sisters of Charity in 1844. They put some order back into that environment where more than 400 patients had been suffering continuous disorder and upheaval. Gradually the sisters widened their scope and began to look after the sick on the wards.

In that spring of 1858 numerous institutes for good works were flourishing. It was perhaps the city most blessed with institutes dedicated to the works of mercy. There were hospitals, orphanages, homes for waifs and strays, hospices and confraternities. And they were needed, because, out of a population of 200,000 inhabitants, at least 70,000 were unemployed and living off their wits or begging. Pope Pius IX, generous and warm-hearted as he was, was doing all he could to help the poor in the heavy atmosphere of the political revolution which was fighting against temporal power, and the ideological revolution whose aim was to dismantle the papacy. In 1848 he was forced to flee to Gaeta and in that flight he suffered Christ's passion as the passion of the Church.

When he returned to Rome he started to make unannounced and informal visits to hospitals and hospices as well as to churches and convents. He also went with architects such as De Rossi and Visconti to explore the catacombs and underground passages. He would often pass through the city at night, down dark streets, or ones dimly lit, from 1853 onwards, by gas lamps.

In 1854 he proclaimed the dogma of the Immaculate Conception which was to release a new wave of Marian devotion in the world, bringing with it a new spring in the Church.

Monti's letter from Rome to Fr Dossi reflects the atmosphere of the new dogma. In it, after telling him how, when he left Bussolengo, he had felt like having a good weep, Monti adds:

'The only consolation is the thought that I have never ceased to be a Son of Mary and now I am a Child of the Immaculate Conception. So, I think that I have gained something with the title, being a child of the Immaculate Conception, for I can say that I am always a child of the Virgin Queen of Heaven and earth. I repeat: this is a great consolation to me.'

PEZZINI'S EXPULSION

So it was that Monti went to work in the hospital which was so dear to the Pope of the Immaculate Conception. He went there with his ideal in his heart and a little bundle under his arm. He knew virtually nothing about the Company of Friars Hospitaller. As he waited for Pezzini who was working on the wards that afternoon of 22 April, 1858, he was taken aback at the sight of nurses dressed in the religious habit, but proud that he himself was not a religious. When Pezzini finally arrived, Monti wanted to know why they dressed like that and why he had not been told beforehand.

'I did not tell you,' replied Pezzini, 'because I was afraid you would not have come if I had.'

He went on to recount all his troubles to Monti, who was both shocked and saddened. Luigi lowered his head and expressed doubt that the Capuchins would be able to establish a stable congregation with the kind of young man he had seen passing by. 'However,' added Luigi, 'with regard to our duties, we will try to be as precise as possible.'

Luigi's judgment of the situation was seasoned with humility and realism. He knew full well, particularly from his own experience, that the success of a religious undertaking such as this one depended not so much on the religious habit or the brethren, or the superiors as on their personal virtues and deeds. He expressed the golden rule of the ascetic life that has held down through the centuries.

'We will try to be precise in our duties, and not to give any reason for complaint, to serve the sick in a true spirit of sacrifice, respecting everyone, especially the superior. You will see that, if we do this, things will change and, in time, the work will come back into our hands.'

This was foresightedness, and wisdom. With such prospects he donned the blue habit and, following Capuchin tradition, he was called Bro Luigi of Milan. His arrival at the hospital acted as a brake on the impulsive Pezzini and, by giving a living witness to the rest of the staff, it helped project an image of the kind of person they had both contemplated.

What Luigi Monti had predicted soon came to pass, that nurses like the ones he had seen that first day who had no religious or moral training, could not form a congregation. Pezzini was not always able to contain himself when he saw certain types of behaviour. On one occasion, unbeknown to Monti, he wrote down all his criticisms, accusing the sub-prior Fr John Baptist, a Capuchin, of incompetence. He sent the letter to the Commander. However, out of a sense of loyalty, he told Fr John Baptist what he had done.

The latter reported him to the Commander, who at that time was Bishop Camillus of the Narducci-Boccaccio family. Permission was given to remove the habit from Pezzini and send him away as soon as possible.

Bro Cyprian of Cremona was not the sort to give in easily. He was stubborn by nature and he said that Our Lady had given him the habit and that he would rather be 'martyred' than remove it. Monti quickly read the situation and tried to calm Pezzini down by persuading him to remove the habit in the knowledge that things would eventually sort themselves out. But Pezzini insisted that the Immaculate Conception had clothed him in the habit and not Fr John Baptist: 'Let them lock me up in prison,' he said 'but I will not remove the habit.'

'If you don't do it,' insisted Monti patiently and affectionately, 'then they will.' And he motioned to four companions who were in the room with them. And so it was. The four young men ripped the habit off Pezzini, gave him some ordinary clothes, and put him in a room on his own.

Pezzini eventually calmed down and, with a great sense of resignation, sat down and ate something. Humiliated, he left the room under the weight of a third failure: Cremona, Bergamo and now Rome. He felt as if he had lost everything, beginning with his honour. Monti's heart had been wounded just as much as Pezzini's. This was not what he had dreamed of at Bussolengo as he waited to come to Rome and for a moment he felt homesick for the serenity of Fr Dossi's house, but it was only a passing temptation.

In the meantime, his superiors also kept an eye on him. And when, a few days later, Pezzini, who had gone to live in a tiny garret room, came to visit Monti, he too was nearly expelled, for being Pezzini's accomplice. Monti warned his companion not to come back until there was a new superior.

In fact, Fr John Baptist was removed prematurely from his post in August, by the Pope himself. Pezzini saw this as a confirmation of his criticisms and wrote to the Commander and the superior of the Capuchins asking to be readmitted, but they did not want him in that, or any other, hospital.

So, with a small amount of money given him by some good folk, he opened a tiny hospice for the chronically sick at Longara and in February 1859 he invited Monti to join him there. Pezzini wanted to set up a free institution which depended only on the bishops, like the one they had both dreamed of from the beginning. Monti saw, with a clear head, the problems: lack of funds, houses, personnel and approval... Monti tried to dissuade his friend from going ahead with the project and promised that he would do everything possible, when the time was right, to have him readmitted to the Santo Spirito hospital.

Monti's prudence, humility and rigour in entering the new community so unexpectedly, showed his religious maturity and the quality of his religious formation, especially when compared to that of his colleagues.

He had come to found a particular work and thought he had an ideal companion in Pezzini. Instead he found himself in the midst of a group of young men who did not understand the dialects of Rome or Lazio and whose temperaments were so varied.

The intention of the Capuchins was to expand the work of these nurses to all the wards in the hospital. To this end they recruited as many as possible, as quickly as possible until they had gathered seventy young men, none of whom was adequately prepared, either professionally or religiously. It was, for Luigi, the first station on his way to Calvary. He passed it with great strength, ready to sacrifice himself following the example of his Divine Master, supported always by the virginal love of the Mother Most Pure.

PEZZINI'S DEATH

He was struck with another suffering when Pezzini, contrary to Monti's advice, had undertaken a pilgrimage, on foot, to the Holy House at Loreto. He arrived at the Santo Spirito hospital physically destroyed with tuberculosis and asking to be admitted.

When Pezzini returned, ill, Monti was away in Lombardy. Pezzini had not been able to live a religious life, but he died a holy death on 7 June 1861 at the age of forty-two. He too had sacrificed himself to give birth to the congregation of the Sons of the Immaculate Conception.

In a sense, Pezzini was a companion of Monti and a pioneer of his work. He could have been an invaluable collaborator if he had not been broken by the painful events which thwarted his apostolic ideals.

His good faith, his spirited enthusiasm, his purity of soul had been recognised by a saintly soul, Maria Crocifissa Di Rosa, the gifted mistress of the apostolate of service to the sick.

But these qualities did not serve him well. The whole of his life, from Brescia to Bergamo to Rome, was like a rising mound of difficulties blocking the fulfilment of his dream. In a way, Pezzini prefigured the kind of superhuman strength of Monti himself in the face of the opposition to his great ideal.

In Rome, Pezzini was a kind of precursor of Monti at the Santo Spirito hospital. It was typical of many Christian hospitals where heroic virtue, medical practice and a whole baggage of tradition encrusted with arrogance and diffidence, were mingled together. Bro Cyprian tried to introduce the youthful enthusiasm of the Sons of Mary Immaculate, almost like an injection of that Marian virtue with which the Holy Spirit was beginning to renew, not just the Santo Spirito hospital, but the whole of the laity.

Pezzini's programme was the same as Monti's, born in similar circumstances from a similar love for the Virgin Mother, and it was inspired and illuminated by the same master and spiritual director, Fr Dossi. The union of those two young men should have enabled the building of a firm foundation on which to build the work. On the one hand there was Pezzini's zeal and enthusiasm, along with his rebellious spirit and tendency to depression. On the other hand there was Monti, straightforward, patient, steadfast in the face of trials, never allowing his attention to wander from his goal, a man who knew just how much work there was to do and how much effort it would require to complete it.

In the complicated Roman society where diplomacy and tradition were the order of the day, Pezzini dreamed of setting up a nursing congregation under direct episcopal control. He had neither the time nor an appropriate method for acquiring the qualities necessary to achieve his aims patiently, over a long period. He simply could not wait and in his hurry he broke the web of work which Monti had been weaving. Monti's greatness lies above all in the determination with which, trusting in Our Lady, he stuck to his guns and, head down, broke down a succession of barriers erected by man and by events. Pezzini's problem was that he wanted to jump the gun and in doing so he came up against the system which, at least temporarily, was against him. Monti picked himself up again after his failures, Pezzini was crushed by them. He was a young man with little experience of life who, whilst a strong idealist, appeared to be weak on realism.

Pezzini was pure spirit who gave himself in a heroic way and who, if he had survived the setback at the Santo Spirito from where he was violently ejected, would probably have become Monti's right hand man and possibly even co-founder. But his spiritual life was very basic, almost instinctive, and he had not learned to die, like the seed which, if it is not buried underground, does not decompose and does not produce fruit. In fact, his dying to himself happened during the final phase of his life, away from the hospital environment. It ended with a holy death in the very hospital where they did not want him alive. It was like a sacrifice which gave life to the institute, the seed of which his faithful companion carried in his heart.

As he lay dying at forty-two years of age, the Immaculate Conception smiled at Pezzini and he went to meet her, taking with him the greetings of his friend who had set off, head down, on his own Via Crucis.

It could be said that Pezzini had contributed ideals, but above all he contributed bitterness and this became the material for the foundation of Monti's work. Thus the Conceptionists should regard him as a gifted pioneer whose life was both an encouragement and a warning.

A hundred years after his death he can look upon the work of the Sons of the Immaculate Conception with that radiant, joyful smile, which was rarely seen on a face so lined with sorrow while he was on earth.

Notes

1. A place where abandoned infants were looked after.

5
FIRST TRIALS AT THE SANTO SPIRITO

THE COMMANDER

The condition of the Santo Spirito hospital was much the same as at many other institutions balanced on a knife edge between past and future. They were balancing between venerated traditions and modern techniques, between their religious/ecclesiastical status and the influences of the secular world. Opposing forces were trying to take over the management, the doctors were often in conflict with the clerics, the lay nurses bickered with the religious ones and the nuns were blackmailed by the auxiliary staff. The Commander was afraid of the reputation of the friars.

Misinformed and instigated by the lay nurses, the people who came to the hospital started to call the friars *Concettini*. This was a way of making fun of their consecration to the Immaculate Virgin. The nickname caught on and spread. Strangely enough, it eventually lost its negative connotations and was the name commonly used until 1923 when it was officially replaced by the title Conceptionists (*Concezionisti*).

Due to the conditions in the hospital the *Concettini* were subject to all kinds of difficulties, so much so that many suffered from poor health. They were formed in the Franciscan spirit of poverty and humility and for this reason the Capuchins tried to find a way of founding an institute, or at least a way of linking them to one of their third orders.

Archbishop Narducci, who succeeded Vitelleschi, issued a decree on 26 June, 1858, taking on the responsibility for expanding the community of hospitallers, although this was confined to the San Carlo ward.

It was he who wrote a report to the Holy Father which resulted in the sub-prior, Fr John Baptist of Genoa, being moved to Trieste, the most distant point of the Italian peninsula. It was he too who suggested to the new sub-prior, Fr Ubaldo, to call all the available friars together for a meeting in his palace. Monti, now Bro Luigi of Milan, charged with gathering the largest number, led seventeen into the Commander's apartments. On seeing the inquiring look in Monti's eye on the occasion of this unexpected and unusual meeting, Fr Ubaldo reassured him: 'Don't be afraid. And anyway, the Franciscan habit will protect you,' laying his hand on the habit as he did so.

The hospital governing body, with the Commander, was already waiting for them. The Commander started to read a new rule which, he said, had already been approved by the Holy Father.

The new rule went back to the original set up, whereby the Friars Hospitaller came under the direct and sole control of the Commander, who had full authority to admit or dismiss them and to regulate their life and growth. Their spiritual life and only their spiritual life, on the other hand, remained entrusted to the Capuchins. In effect, it was a return to the original constitution. However, the news stunned the Capuchins, who felt they had been deprived of a work which they had jealously guarded. It also stunned the Hospitallers who feared the constant changes and interventions that could affect their institute.

Asked to express their thoughts, the young Hospitallers protested that they wanted to remain under the jurisdiction of the Superior General of the Capuchins, as they were already professed as members of the Third Order of St Francis. The Commander said: 'What do you mean? You are in my house, I keep you out of my own pocket, and you don't want me as your superior?'

The Friars' sub-prior, Bro Camillus (Cesari) of Bologna, asked permission to speak. 'It's not that we don't want to recognise Your Grace as our superior, on the contrary it would be a great honour for us. It's just that we would like the protection of a religious order such as the Capuchins who are widespread, so that we can have spiritual guidance wherever we become established.'

At that point Fr Ubaldo intervened and declined, or at least in front of the Commander he appeared to decline, the protection of his order to the Concettini. Obviously, he did not want to become involved in an argument.

The young hospitallers were taken aback and embittered, so much so that Bro Camillus had to intervene to keep their spirits up. 'It doesn't matter if the Capuchins don't want us,' he said, 'There are plenty of other religious orders here in Rome, we can ask one of them.'

Then Monti asked to speak. 'My Lord Commander,' he said, quietly but firmly, 'I agree with Bro Camillus. It's not that we don't want to be under Your Grace's jurisdiction. In fact, in the hospital please command us and we will always be most obedient to Your Grace's commands. What we mean is that we want to be under a religious order so that we can have spiritual guidance wherever we go. Your Grace cannot oblige us to stay under his jurisdiction as was the case when you arrived. Your predecessor, Archbishop Vitelleschi, never had any intention of having us under his jurisdiction, and I was sent for that very reason, by the superior of the Sons of Mary, to set up this institute and afterwards to take it to Lombardy and to other places.

Half of what he said was simply a reiteration of what Bro Camillus had said, but the other half was an explosive expression of his own thoughts, as a free working man, full of common sense and dignity. The Commander replied: 'I see, you don't want to be subject to me, so I am sending you away, all of you,' and he dismissed them. In the meantime, the prior of the hospital, Fr Francis Maria of Porto Maurizio, was ordered to reduce the number of friars to no more than ten, and ten meek ones at that. With great difficulty, the prior was able to maintain a community of eighteen Friars, the minimum requirement for the San Carlo ward. Nevertheless, it was clear that things were leading to dispersion.

So, the prior of the Friars, Bro Crispin of Rome, and Bro Luigi of Milan, the most authoritative amongst them, decided to go to Cardinal Della Genga, Prefect of the Congregation of Bishops and Religious, to save their order.

The Cardinal realised what was going on and promised to do something. If the Pope had the formation of a nursing institute at heart, the Cardinal had to give them a stable structure, if not, it was better to send the young men home before they ruined their health.

At Cardinal Della Genga's side was Cardinal Giusti. A few days later, when Crispin and Luigi went to the Commander for the second weekly visit, he welcomed them kindly and, embracing Luigi, he asked: 'I have been to see the Holy Father and do you know what he said to me?'

Luigi had heard about the audience, but he said simply: 'What did he say to you, Your Grace?'

'He said that I was an anti-Concettino...'

He smiled wryly and continued: 'It's absolutely true that I persecuted you quite a lot in the past, but I did it to test your vocation.'

Monti was a simple craftsman, used to straight talking. The Commander's change of heart did not put him off the track and he replied calmly: 'Your Grace, look how many vocations we have lost. And the young men who have left us have gone to other congregations.'

'Yes, but those of you with a real vocation have stayed.'
'But your Grace,' replied Monti frankly, 'not all asses can carry the same burden.'

THE NEW CONCETTINI

In effect, there was a move to start again. Firstly, the Friars Hospitaller were allowed to open a novitiate in a rented house of their own, a short distance from the hospital, near the Holy Office, behind the colonnade of St Peters. In their own, albeit modest, house they would be able to offer a religious formation to future nurses. Until now, their education had, in contact with the lay nursing staff and the relatives of the patients, been influenced too much by the world.

Before opening the novitiate, Monti had asked the Pope for permission to acquire a house in the country where the Friars could rest for a few days after having worked day and night and having endured all kinds of hardships in the attic room where they lived.

When the Pope passed on the request to the Sacred Congregation for Bishops and Religious, he had written a note: *Non novi hominem.* He did not know who Monti or his confrères were, but knowing, as he did, about the various goings-on at the hospital, he must have known about the nascent community. When Monti called on the secretary of the Sacred Congregation to find out the Pope's reply, the secretary, on the basis of the note, chastised them for having rented a house outside the Santo Spirito, by the colonnade.

'Who gave you permission?'
'The Commander of the Santo Spirito,' replied Luigi.
'And this rag,' said the secretary, pointing to the blue tunic, 'who told you to wear it?'
'Archbishop Vitelleschi!' they replied together.

'And what did you all do before taking this habit?'

'I was a blacksmith,' said one, 'I was a student,' said another. 'I had been a religious for six years, in the Sons of Mary,' declared Monti, 'and my superior sent me from Brescia with the specific aim of setting up this institute.' And he added that just a few days previously he had received a letter from Fr Dossi inviting him to return to his 'convent' if things went wrong in Rome.

It is obvious that Monti was aware of his responsibilities and, despite the setbacks, (or 'continual battles' as he referred to them in that conversation), he carefully safeguarded the ideal of the Sons of Mary for whom he considered himself the herald. He must have spoken firmly and with great emotion, because the prelate changed his tune. He expressed his admiration for 'the religion of the Sons of Mary,' whom he knew well and he encouraged them not to lose heart in the face of the inevitable trials. The Church walks with leaden feet.

Non novi hominem! - so said Pius IX. However, a few days later, the Holy Father had occasion to meet the young nurses during his visit to the Santo Spirito. They were there, all lined up at the entrance to the San Carlo ward, with the doctors, chaplains, clergy and nosey-parkers. The Pope went over to them and exclaimed: 'There they are, my Concettini!' and with fatherly, light-hearted words he beckoned them to come to him and kiss his foot.

That welcome was a great surprise for the whole staff of the Santo Spirito and for all present, for the Company of Friars hospitaller lay under a heavy cloud of suspicion.

There were various reasons why there was such an aversion to the Concettini: their newness, their humble origins (most of them were working men), the extreme poverty in which they lived (their only reward was board and lodgings and a cheap tunic), their lack of influential backers (and in those days this was a sign of weakness). Added to all this was the fact that theirs was a new community still without an official rule and with no approved structures, whilst their relationship with Capuchins and the Commander had still not been defined and was plagued with disagreements and uncertainties.

It is easy to see why, even without being expelled, many young men left in search of a better regulated, more tranquil, religious community. But above all it is easy to understand how Monti, in the midst of all these problems managed to survive, just because he was well aware of the goal he wanted to arrive at, supported by a religious faith and life which were way beyond the ordinary.

As well as the internal difficulties, there were the external pressures from the people who came to the hospital. They brought with them, not just the normal gossip and tittle-tattle, but also all the ideological and political undercurrents spread by liberals and anticlericals. Small wonder that Luigi had to have a character as strong as the stone foundations which support the pillars of Rome's churches from Castel Sant'Angelo to Gianicolo along the muddy banks of the Tiber.

NOVICE MASTER

In January 1859, the Capuchin chaplains wanted to give the Friars Hospitaller a superior, to be elected, with a rule and a chapter. Fr Angelo dal Tufo, sub-prior and spiritual director of the Friars, wanted Bro Bonaventure Bernardi of Modena as superior. He was an educated man, but his religious formation was still incomplete. The Friars, on the other hand, wanted Bro Luigi Monti, who in most people's eyes seemed blessed with rare talents, personal virtues and the ability to lead others.

'What shall we do?' Fr Angelo asked Bro Luigi. 'I would like Bro Bonaventure to be elected, but the family would prefer you.'

'What shall we do? It's simple,' replied Bro Luigi. 'Let's do everything in our power to have Bro Bonaventure elected.' And he proposed an electoral system to that end. Fr Angelo, whom he considered his superior, would have two votes and the proxy of the working nurses. Bro Luigi would vote for Bro Bonaventure and would encourage others to vote the same way, so that there would be a clear majority.

When it came to the election, however, despite all the legal arrangements, Bro Luigi was elected. He then set about persuading the Friars that Bro Bonaventure was the better choice. He tried to make them see that Bro Bonaventure had all the necessary qualities and that if the latter were to become proud of his position, he (Luigi) would help correct him. Reassured by Luigi's words, there was another ballot and this time Bro Bonaventure was elected, though only by a single vote majority. The former superior, Bro Crispin of Rome, was nominated as his deputy and Bro Luigi was nominated novice master. In fact, the position of novice master was the most urgent and the most delicate, for on him depended the future of the religious family.

He had wanted to strengthen the family now under construction and he had sacrificed himself for it. In fact it was he who incarnated the ideal to be followed, the kind of congregation required and the goal to be reached. His work in the formation of the novices made a decisive contribution to the institute of the future.

The novitiate was inaugurated in February 1860 with the admission of the first postulant. The following month another three arrived. Obviously that kind of religious life, which glorified work and allowed young men who did not know any Latin and who were beyond adolescence, to dedicate themselves to the Lord, attracted souls to it. There would probably have been a flowering of vocations if it had not been for a fault in the statute which had not yet been eliminated and which led to violent trials the following April.

One of the Friars, Vincent, who was Spanish and had joined them at the end of 1859, became very cynical and had begun to criticise everything and everybody, including Luigi. Luigi

Bussolengo (10 miles from Verona): The house for abandoned children (1856).

This was the town where Fr Luigi Dossi of the Sons of Mary founded his first community; the house is shown in the photograph overleaf.

Luigi Monti joined him in 1857, while he was waiting to go to Rome. It was in the chapel of this house, in a moment of great difficulty, that Monti had an apparition of Jesus and Our Lady. They promised him special protection for his mission for the rest of his life.

A prison cell at Desio.

The prison at Desio where Luigi Monti was incarcerated was demolished in 1974. It was rebuilt on another site on the outskirts of the town, but some photographs remain. The chapel, blessed by Cardinal Ildefonso Schuster, was sited in the cell where Monti and his young companions lived as in a monastery. There they prayed and sang together in an atmosphere of great peace, for they knew they were innocent - a fact fully recognised by the law at a later stage.

The photograph shown overleaf is of a prison cell. It gives some idea of how hard life was for prisoners at that time.

tried to make him understand that a religious cannot be idle or constantly complaining. As Vincent had no intention of changing his ways, he had to be dismissed. As he was about to leave he threatened to cause trouble. The following day he returned to collect a bag which he had left deliberately in the hospital.

He walked into the refectory while the Friars who were not on duty were eating their modest meal, went right up to the superior and bawled out: 'Pay me, Judas!'

The Friars went across to him and forced him out of the refectory, whereupon he started to shout out like a madman: 'Murderers, you're killing me. They've knifed me.'

And he threw himself to the ground as if fatally wounded. Doctors, nurses and students came running from all quarters.

While all this was happening, Bro Luigi was working in San Carlo ward. When he heard what had happened he realised immediately that it was a trick. Four or five days later, as if under an inspiration, he went, with the deputy, to see the new prior of the hospital, Bishop Joannin, and said: 'The wound must be an artificial one, because I assure you that the Friars are innocent.'

The Bishop was not convinced and shook his head in denial, but Monti insisted: 'I am certain that the Friars did not even touch him.'

Bishop Joannin was struck by the sincerity of Monti's words and, dismissing him, he went to the wounded man's bedside. There and then he accused him of being a trickster and of wounding himself in order to ruin the Concettini. He threatened to have him arrested.

The culprit showed no reaction, and while they waited for the doctors to arrive, the bishop demonstrated how the holes in his tunic did not correspond to the wounds which, in any case, were all superficial.

'Triumph!' exclaimed the delighted bishop, turning to the Friars. 'The trick has been discovered and your innocence proved.'

The dying man got up straight away from his bed and quickly disappeared. Not only did the Friars not have him arrested, they gave him some money to help him make ends meet and wrote off the debt he had contracted.

THE ILLNESS

The family of the Friars Hospitaller of the Immaculate Conception was in continual crisis, however, because they did not turn to the person who knew and lived its spirit most intimately. Its story, for the first nineteen years, is a succession of interminable external and internal problems. The problems which at times were petty, at times tortuous and violent, can give us some idea of the strength of spirit and of the patience and humility of Bro Luigi Monti. Many of his confrères became discouraged and, overcome by the inhuman conditions and the physical and spiritual difficulties they had to endure, asked to leave, and returned to the world in search of the peace that was so lacking within them.

It was true that a nurse's job was a difficult one, requiring an iron constitution. What they really needed was solidarity around them, not the incomprehension and misunderstanding which were the norm in the dull, daily routine of the job.

Monti knew where he wanted to arrive, and his ideas did not always coincide with those of the chaplains who, understandably, wanted to produce a Franciscan creature. His ideas did not always coincide either with those of the Commanders, who took other needs and practices into consideration.

The crisis lasted for the best part of twenty years.

Bro Luigi gritted his teeth in the face of the storms which from time to time seemed about to blow the roof off and scatter ideals and projects to the four winds. With the tenacity of a founder, or of a pioneer or, more precisely, of a saint, he passed through the tempests without crumbling. To this end he made himself everything to everyone. He covered the gaps left by others, spent hours and hours labouring in the wards, in the pharmacy and in the dispensary. And for the same end, he proved himself to be the most obedient to the chaplains and to the Commander, whilst in his heart he kept the ideal of a new, independent community.

After much suffering, in 1860 he witnessed the closure of the novitiate which had come to life as a result of sacrifices proportionate to the hopes of the Friars. Then, one after the other, he saw twenty of the thirty Friars leave the community. They could not put up with the reprimands of the doctors, many of whom had never taking a liking to the religious community. Neither could they tolerate the scorn of the lay nurses who saw them as competition.

That summer, one of the best Friars, Jerome Biassoni of Milan, was struck down with typhoid fever and died at the age of thirty. Bro Benvenuto Tasca of Bergamo and our Bro Luigi took to their beds with the fever and were comforted by a blessing sent specially for them by the Pope at an audience with the remaining Friars held on 21 August.

At the end of October, Luigi and his sick companion were advised to go back home to Lombardy to convalesce. A collection was taken to pay for their journey home. This resulted in a grand total of sixty lire, which they took with them to the port of Ripagrande on the Tiber, in Rome. They told their story to the captain of the small merchant steamer and he offered to take them free of charge to Genoa, from where they would go to Milan.

At that time there was no railway from Rome. All they had for the journey were a few sandwiches and a bottle of broth.

However, when they reached Civitavecchia the vessel stopped. They found another ship bound for Genoa and paid seventeen lire each for a third class ticket. This left them with twenty lire to pay for their food for the train journey from Genoa to Milan.

Fortunately, the captain was a good man and when Monti became seasick, he offered both of them coffee, soup and other items of food.

After two days at sea they docked in Genoa. They spent the night with the Capuchin fathers and next morning took the train to Milan, from where they walked to Bovisio. They were nearly dying with hunger, but they still had one lira left.

At home, Monti had to listen to all the arguments and apprehension of the poor folk regarding the campaign for the unity of Italy.

A month later he was back at Bussolengo among the Sons of Mary, looking for his Fr Dossi. He was in dire need of both physical and moral refreshment. He had reached the half-way stage in his life in the midst of trials of every sort.

When Dossi saw him, he was shocked at how thin and emaciated he looked. Dossi welcomed him with fatherly affection. He had never stopped thinking about his long-distant son in the hope that he would return to join his own community. The Sons of Mary were delighted to have him with them. In their communion, Monti relaxed in the serenity of the plains of Lombardy/Veneto, and above all in the peace of a more serene union with God.

For a year they put him on a special regime of complete rest and his natural vigour began to return almost to normal. When they tried to recall him to Rome, Dossi refused to let him go, on grounds of ill health, and he was right to do so.

When he felt a bit better, Luigi started to perform various tasks including nursing and looking after juvenile offenders, first at Bussolengo, then at Vicenza.

It should not come as a surprise that Monti undertook these simple tasks. They represented all Monti's apostolic ideals, for they involved the education of the young, leading to the formation of the society of the future and, in essence, of the Church of tomorrow. They were also obeying the will of God as he had understood it over the previous few years, namely the care of the sick. But always, whenever the opportunity arose, the nurse in him gave way to the teacher. He had a growing desire in his heart to give himself to young people, to form them according to the model of Mary Immaculate, so that they would all be, in a general sense, Sons of Mary.

He stayed with the specific Sons of Mary for four years altogether, helping them in all sorts of ways and receiving in return the benefits of Christian solidarity and a deeper moral formation. Fr Dossi did everything possible to ensure that he would stay with them for the rest of his life.

But Monti belonged to the congregation of the Friars Hospitaller, Sons of the Immaculate Conception, and it was they whom he held in his heart constantly, longing to spread them throughout the world. He felt they were his family, germinated from his own heart, and he felt responsible for them. So, whenever Dossi tried to persuade him to stay, Monti humbly and respectfully expressed his wish to return to his own 'family', until the worthy priest was convinced that it was the will of God. At the end of the summer of 1864 Dossi let him go, giving him his blessing.

Monti's departure was difficult for both men. It signified a distinction of vocations and of foundations. When Bro Luigi arrived in Rome at the beginning of October 1864, he was given a joyful welcome by the community of the Santo Spirito.

6
THE INSTITUTE SPREADS BEYOND ROME

OUR LADY OF REST

That day, 8 December 1864, was the day on which the Church promulgated the encyclical *Quanta Cura*, which accompanied *Sillabo*. They both revealed the concerns of the papacy in the face of theories and movements which seemed to undermine the Church.

In this situation Monti was the faithful subject of the Pope.

And his faithfulness was put into practice immediately, for on that very day he was appointed vicar, counsellor, reviser and novice master. To these he added the job of carpenter, something he had never completely given up and which he did in his spare time.

This was a period of relative calm.

Two years later, on 4 October, the institute received the decree of praise from the Holy See, which was the first step on the road to full canonical recognition. This was conferred on 10 May 1865 with a decree of approval as a congregation with simple vows, renewable annually under the instruction and direction of the superior general of the Capuchins. The benevolence of these religious and of the Friars Hospitallers' superior, Bro Bonaventure of Modena, an exceedingly severe and almost despotic character, permitted them to rent St Pius X's Casaletto. They paid a rent of 2,000 lire a year, an enormous sum in those days, for the house, which was situated beyond the Vatican, on the outskirts of Rome in the midst of green fields. In the new house, which was spacious and well-ventilated, the Friars could have a good rest, especially during the summer period, and look after the old and chronically ill. They also transferred the novitiate there.

All this increased the institute's debts and Prince Doria Pamphili, who had already given them money as well as personal guarantees for the foundation of the Hospice of Our Lady of Rest, came to their aid again. But the debts continued to rise until they owed 3,000 lire. The creditors' impatience led Bro Bonaventure to make a direct appeal for help to the Pope, whose love for such a modern and worthy congregation was growing. The superior went with Bro Luigi Monti to an audience at Castel Gandolfo and was given authorisation to draw up a contract for a loan of 15,000 lire underwritten by the real estate of the Santo Spirito hospital.

Success went to the head of the superior of the Friars Hospitaller who began to behave like a member of the nobility. He bought a carriage and two horses, had a new and very grandiose kitchen fitted and acquired all kinds of expensive furnishings. He also admitted a large number of young men to the institute, without scrutinising them, so that, in just over a year, the number of Friars increased from fifteen to sixty or so. This involved, above all, a huge financial commitment.

Out of his love of poverty and his duties as a counsellor, Bro Luigi suggested to Bro Bonaventure that they should be more careful in their use of money. Bro Bonaventure, who wanted 'yes-men' as his counsellors, took it badly.

So began another *Via Crucis*. Monti took on the daunting task of running the Casaletto. He should have been teaching a severe ascetical life and an ordered workday to those raw recruits, most of whom had come with no real vocation. He set about the task with great zeal, patience and determination. Inevitably however, the badly prepared ones and the incurably lazy ones interfered with the formation of the good ones, who then, under the bad influence of the former, lost any vocation they might have had.

It was in this atmosphere of chaos, which Bro Bonaventure managed to keep hidden through his authoritarianism, that the chapter was held on 13 January 1866. The twelve Friars who composed the chapter, under pressure from the sub-prior of the Santo Spirito and the Friars' chaplain, Fr Angelo dal Tufo, and his confrère Fr Alphonsus of Rimini, re-elected Bro Bonaventure as superior. Bro Luigi and his travelling companion, Bro Benvenuto, were unanimously elected as local superiors.

Bro Bonaventure emerged from chapter with his authority increased. Bro Luigi had had his responsibilities doubled, for besides running the hospice at Casaletto he was also given the administration of the community. Bro Bonaventure became even less tolerant than before of observations and suggestions and he had built around him a sort of personal party. Bro Luigi, with his simple and direct way of behaving and his naivety, seemed to be an obstacle. He realised this and resigned as a counsellor. What was the point of him carrying that title if advice was not accepted, much less, required?

Bro Luigi's action was adjudged insubordination by Fr Angelo dal Tufo, an insubordination that he described as 'a pestiferous seed of discord amongst the Concettini Friars.'

In fact, it was dal Tufo himself who was the 'pestiferous seed of discord.' With the support of Bro Bonaventure, he stood against his own superior, the most worthy Fr Francis of Porto Maurizio. In May 1867 dal Tufo asked for Fr Francis to be removed and denounced him in front of the General Minister of the Capuchins. Fr Francis was a man of great virtue who supported Bro Luigi and Bro Benvenuto.

At the most critical moments, the two Friars scrupulously followed Fr Francis's advice. Bro Luigi realised that this situation could ruin the institute and he tried to defend its structure and spirit up to the point of appearing obstinate in front of the superior, something which he was to do on other occasions. Undoubtedly, his tenacity was impressive at a time and in circumstances when many would have compromised, just to save themselves.

One thing is certain, Monti had no feelings of resentment towards his 'older brother', It was clear that Bonaventure, seeing the failure of his leadership, had no further desire to work for the community, and isolated himself. Bro Luigi, who had seemed so proud, presented himself to Bro Bonaventure in complete humility, even to the point of kneeling at his feet and asking him to continue to run the congregation.

It was charity, acting on humility, which was at work in Luigi.

However, the disagreements at the Santo Spirito continued, causing grave damage to the discipline of the order. Bro Bonaventure tried to cover up the relaxation of the religious spirit by imposing severe external measures such as excessive fasting, going barefoot and wearing skull-caps. The Friars became increasingly agitated, to the point where an argument broke out which one could call the battle of the skull-caps. Monti was recalled from Casaletto by Pius V to restore some sense of order, but the difficulties were more serious than he had imagined.

Monti felt that to restore peace Fr Alphonsus should be asked to leave, but this so upset Fr Angelo dal Tufo that he resigned as chaplain to the Concettini. For three days the Friars went without Mass and communion, until Francis of Porto Maurizio suggested that Bro Luigi should make an act of submission to Fr Angelo. Without delay, Bro Luigi made this act of humility, but Fr Angelo was not satisfied and demanded a full submission, *perinde ac cadaver*, not only to Fr Alphonsus but also to Bro Bonaventure.

However, this went against Bro Luigi's conscience. Of the five counsellors, Luigi was one of four who, together, opposed Bro Bonaventure's behaviour. They felt that it was a waste of time appointing counsellors if their advice was not taken. So there was a kind of paralysis in the institute. At the top there were Bro Bonaventure, the Capuchin Fathers, Angelo and Alphonsus and a few Friars. On the bottom were almost all the Friars Hospitaller, with Fr Francis and Bro Luigi. There were in fact two factions.

Fr Angelo referred the situation to the Superior General of the Capuchins, describing Bro Luigi of Milan as an 'ungrateful and ambitious assailant', and the cause of schism. He called Fr Francis a 'spineless poor old man' and asked for the healing intervention of the 'loving father, an expert and skillful doctor', capable of 'cutting out the cancer of all this evil at a single stroke and of applying an immediate, health-giving and effective remedy'.

According to Fr Angelo, the remedy would consist in removing Monti and Fr Francis. This would be facilitated by the resignation of Bro Luigi in order to simplify the argument.

The Superior General believed he could resolve the situation by naming Bro Bonaventure as the only superior, assisted by two deputies, one for the Santo Spirito and one for Casaletto. The idea was to put Monti with the chronically sick at Casaletto and forbid him from communicating with his confrères. Out of respect for the wishes of his superior, the deputy at Casaletto forbade Monti from administering medicines and from keeping a lamp for use in pharmaceutical work, even though he was working in the pharmacy. This was in September 1866.

The nature of the man of God was revealed in these circumstances. Removed from the council and from every position of leadership, he enclosed himself in obedience, hiding himself away and dedicating his free time to teaching a group of more than twenty boys from the surrounding vineyards.

Nevertheless, he continued to nurture in his heart the hope that the religious community that he dreamed of for years would one day flourish. He accepted this 'burial' as being like the seed, which if it does not die, does not produce fruit. He hoped that this would be a contribution to the work.

Whenever he could, Luigi spent time with the boys. He was looking for innocence and he tried to protect it, by forming Christian souls. This was his ultimate aim. If he was dressing wounds he did it for this reason: to look after souls and build in them the empire of the spirit.

Though all these problems existed and have been described for the sake of the historical record, they did in fact contribute to the development of the new community. It was a community which, providentially, the Capuchins protected with the authority of their order and to which they gave great gifts of Franciscan charity which the new era called for.

FRUITS OF SUFFERING

Monti was comforted in his isolation by his correspondence with Fr Luigi Dossi, who wrote to him on 21 March 1867 from Ala:

'My dearest Luigi,

I would like to write you a very long letter, but my visiting and packing to leave for Isera, near Rovereto, where I am substituting for the parish priest, forbid me from doing so. How much consolation your letter brought me! Well done Luigi, a true son of Fr Luigi Dossi. I have suffered and still suffer, but thank God, always with resignation. Jesus offered me the most bitter of chalices, but he gave me the strength to drink it and I thank him for it, just as I thank you Luigi, for the efforts you have made to lighten my load. Yes, you read my thoughts. If it proves impossible to come together here, my intention, having acquired houses in Rome, is to implore the Holy Father to let us set up a congregation in the Papal States and in the Tyrol. But for the moment we will have to postpone it. Who knows, perhaps you are destined to play the part of Joseph in all of this, going ahead of the Friars, for their salvation, into Egypt!

'That's all for now, but my heart pours out greetings and blessings on you and on your brothers in religion.'

The correspondence with Dossi shows how he had never stopped hoping that his own community would reclaim such a precious element as Monti. For his part, Monti would have grabbed the opportunity, as had other Friars, to leave an association where he was being crushed, if he had not been so totally convinced about his mission of suffering and humiliation. He did not even leave when, in June 1867, an old confrère from the 'society of friars' saw the state he was in and invited him to return to Lombardy. In the same way, he declined politely but decisively, an invitation to join the Fatebenefratelli, who would have welcomed him joyfully, so admiring of his gifts were they.

He remained faithful to his vocation, held firm by a deep, interior trust even in the midst of desolation. The Lord had given him the task of suffering, suffering for his community, and he accepted it without complaint. They stopped him from doing anything and he let God do everything. Where he could not act, he prayed.

In the autumn there were revolutionary moves in Rome which were soon put down. In November Garibaldi tried to take the city with his volunteers, but he suffered a bloody rout at the hands of the Pontifical and French troops. Some 200 wounded soldiers were treated at the Santo Spirito which was used as a military hospital.

The year 1867 was dismal from every point of view. It was an even darker night.

On one occasion, Monti bumped into Fr Angelo and said, 'Remember Father, the war that you are waging against me is not, as you believe, against me, it is against you and your advisers.'

THE INSTITUTE SPREADS BEYOND ROME

Monti's words proved true, for, having got rid of Bro Luigi to impose the despotism of Bro Bonaventure, Fr Angelo realised that Bonaventure was working to destroy the authority of the Capuchins over the Friars Hospitaller, to put himself in their place, the exact opposite of what Fr Angelo wanted.

The Capuchins wanted to perfect the constitution of the Hospitallers according to the Franciscan spirit and rule and Fr Angelo had, in fact, obtained the approval of the Holy See for some modifications he had devised. But Bro Bonaventure did not accept them and he wanted to transfer jurisdiction from the Capuchins to the Vicariate of Rome, in order to establish the autonomy of the institute. The disagreement exploded during a meeting at the Santo Spirito. Bro Bonaventure declared that all the disorder of the last few years was the result of their being under the jurisdiction of the Order of the Capuchin Friars and therefore the fault of the spiritual directors who had interfered in things about which they had no knowledge. He even blamed their administration for the financial mess, which others had said, quite rightly, was due to his megalomania. He repeated his accusations against the spiritual directors at a sitting of the council on 7 January 1868. He also accused them of failing in their duty as catechists and formators and in protecting Bro Luigi and others, whom Fr Angelo had wanted to expel in the past, but whom he now wanted to reinstate in leadership roles.

Bonaventure had got the message. However, not only had Fr Angelo contemplated reinstating Bro Luigi, but, having heard of Bonaventure's intention to turn to the Vicariate again to throw off the Capuchins, he went, as a last resort, to see Bro Luigi at Casaletto. He tried to appeal to Luigi's feelings, knowing how much this Friar loved the institute. He explained how Bro Bonaventure had presented a petition to the Pope in order to modify the structures of the institute, which, because of its enormous debts, His Holiness could have dissolved. Only he, Bro Luigi, could save the institute by writing a letter to the

General of the Capuchins, signed by all the Friars and inviting him to put things in order. The Friars, if invited by Bro Luigi, would certainly sign such a petition and the General would be in a strong position to go to the Holy Father and obtain a favourable intervention.

Bro Luigi wrote the letter, out of love for the institute.

He wrote the letter and with it the General went to speak to the Pope. The Pope ordered an inquiry (a sacred visitation) and entrusted it to a Capuchin, Fr Eusebius of Monte Santo, assisted by a venerable old Olivetan, Abbot Sante Urbani.

A 'SACRED VISITATION'

Forty-six Friars were interrogated. Almost all of them gave an excellent impression of goodness and gentleness.

Thirty-two of the forty-six explicitly expressed the desire to remain under the Capuchins, five were indifferent and nine against. The nine against were the ones who belonged to Bro Bonaventure's council. 'They', said the report presented to the Holy Father by the two Apostolic representatives, 'represent all that is ignorant and bad in the Concettini...' So the report proposed sending them away, either temporarily or permanently, and electing Bro Luigi of Milan and Bro Felix of Jesi as superiors.

The proposals were accepted by the Pope and carried out.

However, Fr Angelo, who held on to his ideas and his fears, worked things so that Bro Felix was elected instead of Bro Luigi, and not as superior of the 'older brother', but as procurator. In this way power effectively remained in the hands of a Capuchin specially appointed by the Minister General.

So that it did not look as if it was going against the wishes of the Pope, who had expressly wanted Bro Luigi as superior, Fr Angelo made Luigi secretary to the procurator as well as bursar to the two houses. Under the affectionate pressure of Fr Francis of Porto Maurizio, Bro Luigi accepted this position of responsibility, which left him open to all sorts of humiliation, but all on the condition that he would resign as soon as Bro Felix took on the full exercise of his office.

This was the position in which Luigi found himself. He was the only one capable of running the institute and yet he was not allowed to. All he could do was to restore some order wherever there was a mess, as for example, in the finances, where innumerable creditors were pressing for repayment of money lent to Bro Bonaventure, who had left debts amounting to more than 40,000 lire.

Monti absorbed all this until Fr Angelo's animosity reached the point where the former was forced to resign and withdraw to Casaletto. When Luigi left the Santo Spirito things went from bad to worse. Bro Felix, who struck one of the Friars in front of a patient, was removed from the position of procurator and replaced by Bro Clement Gamberini, who immediately started to run things in Fr Angelo's way, the idea being to wear down Bro Luigi and expel him. Fr Angelo, in fact, was convinced that the source of all the problems in the community was Bro Luigi whom he defined as 'the professor of laxity, disobedience and insubordination.' From this it can be seen that the accuser did not fully understand the words he was using, if he was accusing of laxity someone who seemed to be guilty of the exact opposite.

Because he wanted to serve his neighbour through the works of mercy, because he wanted to become a saint with his companions in his ideal, for years Monti had battled and risked being expelled. If his feelings had been solely human he would have rebelled and left some time before. But he knew that he had to suffer, and suffer he did, even though he knew the true nature of this ill-treatment. He never lost his temper and, despite his frankness, he was always respectful of those in authority.

Because he loved his religious family so much, at the critical moment when he realised that he was undergoing a very difficult trial, he turned for help and advice to a very high-profile person, Cardinal Edward Borromeo, who was universally recognised for his integrity. He told the cardinal what had happened in his community and how war had been declared on him at the Santo Spirito, while at the same time the General of the Fatebenefratelli had invited him to join his order. The cardinal understood the worth of the man and how vitally important his presence was amongst the Friars Hospitaller, if they were to be safeguarded from the terrible trial they were undergoing. He advised him to stay, and stay Luigi did.

7

THE FOUNDATION OF ORTE AND CIVITA CASTELLANA

ORTE

Monti's isolation and maltreatment increased. His superiors wanted to wear him down by stopping him from doing anything. He had always longed to give himself heroically in the service of suffering humanity and now he was prevented from doing so.

At forty-three and in his prime, he was forced into inactivity. This weighed on him until he became convinced that the only way he could serve the Lord was to go on the missions, something he had dreamed of doing when he was a young man. Perhaps the Lord had allowed this detachment from action and condemned him to inaction so that he would leave for distant lands where hard-working apostles were needed more than ever.

Then, out of the blue, the General of the Capuchins asked to see him. Bro Luigi was fully expecting that he would be expelled from the institute. In fact, he was offered a lifeline for it, having been asked to install the Friars Hospitaller of the Immaculate Conception in the lay hospital at Orte in Lazio.

The director of the hospital at Orte, Count Nuzzi, had previously expressed the desire to have a nucleus of Friars Hospitaller to revive the hospital which was in decline, if not actually dying. There was a lack of nursing care, of charity and of hygiene. It was dominated by the undertaker who regarded it as the ante-room of the cemetery.

This undertaker was greatly assisted by his wife who, like him, made sure that the poor patients who happened to be there did not have even the most rudimentary care.

Obviously, knowing the conditions of neglect, no sick person wanted to go there and the thirty beds in the male and female wards were as dirty as they were empty.

Various authorities from the Orte hospital had turned to the Santo Spirito and to Monti himself, asking for a nucleus of Friars. Monti went, with his trusty Fr Francis of Porto Maurizio, as a guest of the Capuchins at Orte, to assess the situation. On his return he made a proposal to his superiors to accept the work at Orte, which would allow the young family of hospitallers to expand at a good rate. However, the proposal did not go down well with those, like Fr Angelo, who feared that expansion beyond the Santo Spirito would mean an escape from their authority. The Father General, following Fr Angelo's suggestions, took over the negotiations with the authorities at Orte, but he conducted them in such a way that they were heading for failure.

He called for Bro Luigi and confessed that things were going badly 'So I thought to send you to the place, knowing that you are practised and skilled in these things. Talk to the governing body of the hospital and see if you can come up with a solution. Remember', he concluded, 'if it goes well, then it will be to your advantage, but, if it goes badly, you will suffer the consequences.'

It was both a demonstration of trust and a threat. Bro Luigi, who knew the people and the situation, saw the dilemma and, for a moment, he was perplexed. Then his constant love for his longed-for community won the day and he accepted the challenge. However, just like the simple peasant who moves only on

stable ground, Monti was prudent and asked for a formal written proposal. The Father General wrote in his own hand:
'Venerable Bro,
'To smooth out every difficulty and organise the installation of the Friars Hospitaller of the Immaculate Conception at Orte, we send you, on behalf of His Reverence, to finalise an agreement with the Directors of that pious establishment and to preside over the setting up of the operation and anything else which may need organising, trusting in your experience and in the spirit of discretion with which you are gifted.
May all be to the merit of Holy Obedience and with the blessing of the Lord who will also pray for us.'
Your Reverence I remain, Bro Nicholas, Minister General.
The letter of obedience was dated 20 November 1868 and the following day it was carried out. The following day was the feast of the Presentation of Mary and also that of Fr Francis of Porto Maurizio, his venerable spiritual director who, on that very day, died a holy death.

STARTING THE WORK

Luigi left Rome, alone and without the prayers and advice of Fr Francis who, for ten years, had guided and defended him. He had none but God on his side - and thus he lacked nothing.
So, with God at his side, he began the negotiations with the Vicar General at Orte, who introduced him to the hospital board of governors. Monti explained his ideas so clearly and with such vigour that they were all satisfied and expressed the desire to draw up a written contract to be submitted to the Congregation of Charity under whose jurisdiction the hospital came.
The contract was drawn up by Bro Luigi himself, with his usual discretion. He took into account the poor financial situation of the place and offered initially two Friars, rising if necessary to four, at a monthly salary of 40 lire each.

The agreement was drawn up in two days and on 23 November the Congregation of Charity accepted unanimously the very modest conditions proposed by Monti. That same evening, Count Nuzzi, the director, gave him the keys of the hospital. It was one of the purest of joys for the intrepid religious who, up to that point, had had to climb up his own Calvary, almost alone in the face of opposition and envy. At last a lamp was lighting up.

He gave notice straight away to the General of the Capuchins, to whom he suggested waiting patiently until the contract made with the hospital chaplain expired, and for him to be replaced by a Capuchin at the same level of remuneration. Monti also asked for the release of a second Friar, as agreed in the Orte contract, suggesting three names, one of which the General could select by 1 December, the day the new contract came into force.

This was the beginning of an exchange of letters with the Father General which revealed to him all Monti's gifts which, until now, had been hidden under a cloud of gossip and hostility. In the same way, Monti was able to appreciate the prudence and goodness of the General, in whom he found the qualities of Fr Francis.

While he was waiting for the other Friar to arrive, he set about cleaning the hospital. Using all his energy and experience, he cleaned and reordered wards and toilets and every other room in the place so that, in just a few days, what had been a hive of neglect became a shining hospital with a completely new face. The hospital, poor as it was, had survived on modest loans from the director, but Monti's untiring hard work attracted the benevolence of Zi' Barbara. Barbara Primanni was an old lady, full of goodness, who was happy to offer him food and whatever else was needed and she remained a generous benefactor for the Friars.

The Friars Hospitaller of the Immaculate Conception started their work officially at Orte on 8 December 1868, the feast of the Immaculate Conception. The whole town celebrated the feast, having seen the vital problem of the public health service so magnificently resolved.

THE CONCETTINI AT ORTE

Situated on a typical Etruscan plateau, split by gorges with walls of reddish rock, Orte seemed to be barricaded around its cathedral, dressed in undergrowth and topped by ruins. The narrow winding streets made, and still make, the buildings seem like fortresses designed to keep out brigands. The majority of the population of around 3,000, most of whom were farm workers, walked down every morning to work in the fields alongside the Tiber and its tributary. Every evening they walked back up again as bells rang, reminding them of the faithfulness of generations who had worshiped in that church.

The hospital of which the Concettini took possession was buried amongst the apartment blocks piled one above the other, and was accessible through a square with two entrances, one which led to the hospital and the other into the church.

Having cleaned the hospital, Monti started to repair the church, following his double-edged commitment to cure both the physical and the moral, those sick in body and those sick in the spirit.

His experience as a nurse was really providential for those poor country folk, with his ability to perform simple surgery and extract teeth. Every so often a lacerating cry would rise up above the roof tops and another poor soul left the hospital delighted to be relieved of his agony.

Monti spent his day between the church and the hospital, prayer and work, although for him work was also prayer.

He served the poor whenever he could.

He loved to teach catechism and hymns to the children. He took them on walks and enchanted them with his stories. He also formed in them the concept of serving others, a concept which they then put into practice by working in the church and in the hospital.

At Orte too he soon became aware of the moral shortcomings of his own community. The first two Friars sent to work with him were very mediocre in their religious lives and their behaviour was correspondingly mediocre. Bro Luigi's patience and charity helped them lead a life which was more in tune with their ideal. The two Friars, drawn by the example of their superior, gradually came to understand the sacred value of their ministry and began to carry it out in an ever-increasing spirit of self-giving. In fact, the people of Orte began to hold the Friars in high esteem, as the General of the Capuchins reported to the Sacred Congregation of Bishops and Religious: 'The hospital has changed its face and the Friars are loved by everyone. And whereas before the poor did everything to avoid going to hospital, even when gravely ill, even healthy people want to be cared for by a Hospitaller Friar.'

But at Orte, as before, difficulties emerged in the relationship between the Concettini and Capuchins.

For example, on 20 December, the chaplain to the local convent commanded Bro Luigi to set aside two rooms for him in the hospital, so that he could move in when he retired from his post and become the spiritual director of the three Friars Hospitaller. This was completely contrary to the agreement drawn up between Monti and the General of the Capuchins. The whole thing reminded Monti of Fr Angelo's way of behaving, in other words, it was a command issued by a superior to a subordinate.

Money was needed to provide these two rooms. The Friars did not have any and they did not feel they could ask the hospital governors for it, as the latter had already made a heavy financial commitment to the reordering of the hospital itself. Monti wrote to the Capuchin Father General to explain the situation. Ten days later the Father General replied, fully agreeing with Monti: 'It is certainly neither necessary nor opportune to have a full-time spiritual director and it would be even less prudent and economic for him to live on site. Please inform the Reverend Chaplain or anyone else that I have not given my permission and if they want something they should consult me.'

During his stay at Orte, people came to Monti requesting all kinds of assistance, from pulling teeth to blood-letting and emergency surgery. Because of this he started a course in basic surgery at the University of Rome on 5 February 1870, and he compiled a 'recipe book' himself which contained instructions for mixing fifty or so different medications. The 'recipe book' began with an introduction or, as he called it, a 'recipe for health' which revealed the primary aim of all his studies and pharmaceutical preparations. It said:

'To enjoy good health of mind and body, take root of faith, green branch of hope, rose of charity, violet of humility, lily of purity, wormwood of contrition, wood of the Cross. Bind it all together with a thread of resignation. Boil it on the fire of love in the vessel of prayer, with wine of cheerfulness and mineral water of temperance and cover it well with the lid of silence. Leave it all morning in the serenity of meditation. Take a cup of it every morning and evening and you will enjoy good health which, with a true heart, I desire for you.

From the much accredited pharmacy of the most loving Heart of Jesus our Saviour.'

The Concettini left Orte in 1923, but the memory of their generous service there lives on. Just ask the older citizens and they will recall the tears of the people at the death of Bro Amadeus Gregori and for that limitless generosity which was not tainted by bureaucracy or mercenary interests.

THE DEATH OF DOSSI

The success of Orte encouraged other towns to ask for the Friars Hospitaller to come and work in their hospitals. In January 1869 Montalto di Castro put in a request, followed in April of the same year by Canepina.

Montalto asked through the Capuchins, but Canepina went directly to Monti. The Curia of the Capuchins examined the request carefully and turned it down on the grounds that there were not enough suitable candidates. Monti, on the other hand, went to Canepina on 25 April and, as the vicar forane was not there, he went on, '*pedibus calcantibus*', as he jokingly wrote, to Caprarola, where he met him. He was given a very courteous welcome, but nothing came of the visit because they would have had to put up a new building, and in the existing political climate it was a much more daunting task than the good vicar had foreseen. Nevertheless, Monti did not hesitate to assure the Father General: 'It won't be long before we take over more hospitals.'

At that time it took a lot of courage and an unusual degree of foresight to advocate an expansion of the hospital work. But Bro Luigi was a hard worker with a strong ideal and he stuck to it with all the tenacity of a founder of a new work in the Church. At Orte, as already mentioned, he did everything himself, as nurse, administrator, pharmacist, porter, catechist, teacher... If he had to go to Rome - and the means of transport of the time were not very fast - he would go and come back in a day, so as not to leave the pharmacy and the sick bay.

He was struck by a great suffering when, in September of that year, he received news of the death of his first spiritual director, teacher and friend, Fr Luigi Dossi. He had died desolate, as his community had been suppressed and its members dispersed. It was the spirit of the age which was ill at ease with everyone, to the point of opposing the common good. This kind of reaction became common in the period after the French Revolution. Consecrating oneself to the apostolate was regarded as a danger to one's enemies and a reproof to one's friends. Such an attitude paralysed the forces of good.

Bro Luigi analysed these events, he saw them and he wept over them. He prayed more fervently to the heavenly Mother for the soul of his unforgettable master and father, from whom he had received the most profound inspirations for his apostolate and who had set him off on the hard, but beautiful road to God. He never forgot that great soul who was both a protector and preceptor. He applied Dossi's teaching instinctively, reacting to harshness with the resources of the spirit. So, he was faithful to the commitments he had undertaken. He showed unconditional fidelity to the Church, had a constant union with God and imitated Mary. With all these heavenly resources he was able to give untiring service to his brothers and sisters on earth. His was not simply a service to the sick, it was also charity, understood as dedication of the soul, with the aim of looking after both the physical members and the spiritual fibres: health and holiness. So, having materially restored the church next to the hospital, he re-awakened the sense of worship and made it first the heart of the institute and then of the whole town. The church became the meeting place where many people came to pray every day around the sacrifice of the altar under the watch of Mary. He became the teacher and friend of swarms of boys who gathered round him every day to learn how to sing, how to serve in church and how to live in the world.

The Vatican Council, which had been announced in 1864, opened on 18 December 1869 in Rome. It was taking place in the context of political turmoil and also theological challenges, which were coming particularly from Germany and France, and from England, still smouldering after the dogma on papal infallibility. Also, criticisms of the Encyclical *Sillabo* were still being spread furiously everywhere.

Like all good Catholics Bro Luigi was concerned when he saw members of his Church in open disagreement, something which gave advantage to the Church's enemies. As he prayed, humbly, in silent recollection in his hospital, with the Virgin Mary as his guide and model, he became more and more convinced of the urgent need of bringing about harmony among Christians. He could see the disorder of the outside world bringing pressure to bear on the ecclesiastical authorities, even within religious communities themselves. The discord and the vivisection into different factions erected even greater obstacles to the formation of a religious spirit of humility and obedience in fraternal charity.

A young knife-grinder from Trent, Angelo Sauda, arrived in Orte one day, with his boss, to practise his trade. While he was there he fell ill and he experienced the love of the Friars Hospitaller. In fact, he was completely taken by their ideal and wanted to live it, consecrating himself, like them, to God to serve him in the sick. Monti was convinced that Angelo had a real vocation and welcomed him into the family of the Sons of the Immaculate Conception, changing his name to Bro Stanislaus.

And Bro Stanislaus grew in virtue and merit and became more and more closely bound to Monti, to whom he owed a debt of gratitude. From 1871 till 1872 he was called to do military service in his native region. He was imprisoned for draft dodging and Bro Luigi wrote to him on 12 June 1871: 'We are all very sorry that you have been put in prison, but we are consoled by the fact that you have offered all your sufferings to the Lord. No servant is greater than his master!'

The following year when he heard that Stanislaus had been exempted from military service Monti wrote to him again: 'I can see that the Most Holy Mary wants you as her child. Yes, come and join us, I am waiting for you, the Friars are waiting for you, but most importantly, Mary, our most beloved Mother is waiting for you.'

CIVITA CASTELLANA

In September 1870 the temporal power of the papacy came to an end and a month later saw the closure of the Vatican Council. In December disastrous floods offered an opportunity to the anticlericals to admire the heroism of the Friars Hospitaller, who were assisting the victims of the Tiber. The Santo Spirito hospital, built on the river's edge, was itself badly flooded. On 28 December the flood waters burst into the Baglivi and Benedettina wards while the doctors were seeing the patients. In the chaos, amidst all the shouting and wailing, the Friars Hospitaller hoisted the sick on to their shoulders and carried them all to safety. It was during the emergency that Bro Stanislaus Sauda contracted phthisis, which, in just a few years would destroy him. He launched himself, with the other Friars, waist deep in water, until he was completely exhausted. As if all this emergency work, which lasted for twenty days, were not enough, the Concettini also had to endure insults resulting from the political changes.

The blow inflicted on the papacy, in the name of liberty, was provoking anticlerical rumblings even in sleepy provincial towns, even in Orte. A man by the name of Pantaleone had been put in charge of the Santo Spirito in Rome, and his immediate intention was to get rid of the Concettini.

At Orte, these rumblings did not manage to distract Bro Luigi from his care of the sick. In fact, his talents and the sacrifice of his confrères as they constructed more and better facilities demonstrated the benefits of an enterprise which was as spiritual as it was material. The hospital church was becoming increasingly the centre of worship for the whole town, and the reputation of the Friars had spread so far that not only nearby towns, such as Civita Castellana, invited them to set up hospitals, but places far away, like Tradate in Lombardy.

At Civita Castellana Monti was invited to take over from the

Fatebenefratelli, who had had to leave the well-appointed modern hospital there because of a shortage of personnel. A formal invitation from the governing body was received on 26 December 1871. Monti accepted it enthusiastically. He was no longer afraid of being blocked by Bro Clement, as, a few days before Luigi and the Friars had invited Clement to Orte, where Monti had convinced the procurator to let him open new houses and to take on more young men. On New Year's Day 1872 Monti took possession of the hospital at Civita, taking over the running of it with one of the Friars from Orte.

This was a great joy for him, as it was the first beautiful fruit of his labours. The hospital at Civita was very well resourced and even had facilities suitable for those Friars who needed a rest.

Civita Castellana was easily reached from Rome by the Via Flaminia. It is situated on a green plateau, split by gorges with rocky sides topped by undergrowth. At the entrance to the town a fine three-storey building, the St John Decollato hospital, rose high into the sky. It shared its name with the church next door. The building is still there today, but for some time it has been used as a school.

Whenever the Friars Hospitaller of the Immaculate Conception are mentioned to the senior citizens of Civita, their faces light up as they recall their good works. They too remember Bro Amadeus Gregori and they blame sectarianism for the departure of the Concettini who, to their dismay, were forced to leave in 1923.

Monti brought Bro Joseph Maria Petrolli, also from Trent, who had been sent to Orte from Rome, to work in the pharmacy. Monti's intention was to help Bro Joseph recover his physical strength, for he had overworked himself at Orte. The work in the pharmacy required great care and precision. Pharmacists had to prepare medications based on doctors' prescriptions, and any errors could prove fatal. However, Bro Clement Gamberini, the superior, cantankerous and moody as he was, recalled Petrolli to the Santo Spirito. Monti was greatly disappointed by this for he was afraid that Petrolli's health was not strong enough to cope with the work and the stressful atmosphere at the Santo Spirito. At the same time, Bro Clement ordered Monti to return to Orte and he obeyed.

However, the governors of the hospital at Civita pointed out that in their contract it was stipulated that Bro Luigi should be the director, a contract that had been sanctioned by the Sacred Congregation of Bishops and Religious. In order to sort out the problem, Bro Clement went to Civita on 6 February 1872. But no matter how much he tried to depict Bro Luigi as 'insubordinate to his superiors', to the three hospital governors, he had to give way to their request either to leave Luigi there or to send back Bro Joseph.

This accusation of insubordination was born from Bro Clement's fear for his own position in the light of the successes at Orte and Civita. Bro Clement, who did not share Monti's deep aspirations for a life of perfection through sacrifice in hospital service, would have preferred Monti's way of life to be less severe, more worldly.

Despite the pleas from the governors of Civita and the authorisation of the Sacred Congregation in Rome, Monti tried to obey his superior. So he travelled from Orte to Civita just to give a hand to the Friars in the pharmacy, and to try to educate them in the style of the Sons of Mary Immaculate. When it seemed to him that they were capable of carrying on by themselves he returned to Orte.

In the meantime, the relationships between Bro Luigi, his superiors and the community in Rome were, if not entirely peaceful, at least based on mutual toleration. In effect, Rome turned a blind eye to Orte. Bro Luigi maintained a humble, constant contact with the General of the Capuchins and respectfully carried out his duties to Bro Clement. But in the eyes of many of those at the Santo Spirito, Monti was mistaken in not aligning himself either with Fr Angelo's group or Bro Clement's, or in not wanting to organise a third faction to attack the endemic laxity.

Monti was as straight as a die. He set his sights on God and let himself be guided by Our Lady. Besides, his humble country upbringing did not allow him to become involved in intrigue and with people whose intentions were bad. What made things worse for someone who, like him, had to deal with the curia, was the fact that he was so plain speaking. For him, yes meant yes and no meant no. He did not clothe his opinions in diplomatic verbosity or in clever ambiguity. Had he been cunning or ambitious, he would have buttered up the men at the top, sending them presents and paying them compliments, as many others did. But he never did this and so he was not liked by those who were involved in the daily practice of compromise which oscillated between formal deference to religion and actual approval of vice. He kept a straight back, like a mountaineer on a rock face, never bending, with no bowing and scraping or giving presents. This was interpreted as a reproof, an offence almost. It seemed like pride, as if someone wanted to do things in their own way instead of falling in with the majority.

There were no serious disagreements because of the distances, but on the other hand, the distances meant that accusations accumulated against the distant 'Friar', who tried increasingly to keep his distance, while he was blamed because he always remained in unity, in obedience.

If no rupture occurred, it was due to Monti's discipline and spirit of toleration, which simply made him swallow bitter pills in silence. Bro Clement made his life as difficult as he could. If Luigi was coming from Orte to Rome, Clement made his reception by the Friars degrading and hostile. He was not given a bed to sleep on, forcing him to lie on a mattress in a ward, among the sick at Santo Spirito or with friends outside the hospital.

THE FOUNDATION OF ORTE AND CIVITA CASTELLANA

The moral and economic chaos which ruled at Orte was there for all to see. Bro Clement spent crazy amounts of money. For example, every so often, to buy some popularity, he would throw lavish banquets, inviting doctors, students and important people. He even brought the former Bro Bonaventure, now married, to live at Casaletto, and allowed his wife to use the community's cupboards, linen, crockery and cutlery.

These and other factors combined to produce a row between Fr Angelo, who had been relegated to Casaletto, and Bro Clement. First of all, Fr Angelo tried to have him removed as director and when this failed, he abandoned Casaletto, leaving it without a spiritual director.

8
CLOUDS IN THE SKY

CHANGES IN ROME

In Rome, there was a new regime after the taking of Porta Pia. The Santo Spirito hospital lost the financial support of the Vatican and most of the legacies, which were the fruit of Christian piety but which the wave of anticlericalism had dried up. In fact the hospital was up to its ears in debt. This meant that they had to bring to an end the age-old tradition of free care and treatment for all. The director of the hospital was an MP. who was a member of a twelve-person hospital commission for the city of Rome.

Pius IX, who had always shown a great personal interest in the institute, had to retreat behind the walls of the Vatican where he was forced to remain. He could only watch as religious ideals were dissipated here, as in almost all the institutes founded on and nurtured by papal charity.

The Capuchin General, Fr Nicholas of San Giovanni Marignano, under whom Monti had suffered misunderstanding, was replaced and the Commander of the Santo Spirito, Bishop Ricci, was replaced by Bishop Luigi Fiorani.

Bishop Fiorani did not know Monti, but he had heard about him through malicious talk and gossip, so that he was convinced that, in Monti, he was dealing with a proud and ambitious man.

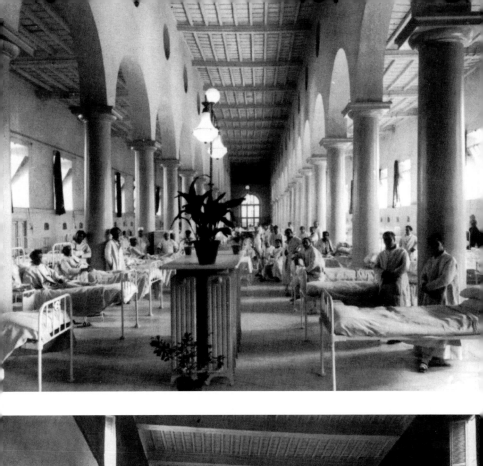

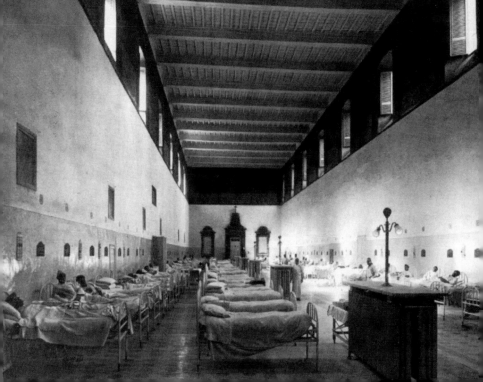

The sick person is the suffering Christ. This is why hospitals were built with the same sacredness with which churches were built.

During Monti's time at the Santo Spirito the best doctors and pharmacists were employed and the religious offered good care of the sick.

The problems were mainly with the auxiliary workers. The Sisters of Charity and the Friars Hospitaller, Sons of Mary Immaculate, were brought in to remedy the situation.

Luigi Monti worked as a nurse and a phlebotomist and helped in the pharmacy in two periods: 1858-60 and 1864-6. From 1877 to 1891, as superior general, his main task was to animate the whole of his religious community.

At the end of 1872, a dispute broke out between the spiritual director, Fr Francis of Lanciano, and Bro Clement Gamberini, who accused the former of insolence. The end result was that the Supreme Pontiff intervened, dismissing Fr Francis and expelling Bro Clement from the institute.

Bishop Commander Fiorani and the faction which supported the former superior pleaded for mitigation and consequently Bro Clement was punished by being transferred as subordinate to Civita Castellana.

Because of this, a new chapter was held on 28 November at which a particularly inept Friar, Crispin Fredduzzi, was chosen as superior. Bro Salvatore Bronelli was to go to Orte.

Monti did not take part in this chapter. His letter of invitation was delayed in the post and arrived six days late. The envelope had been addressed to 'Bro Luigi Monti of Milan - Orte' and had been delivered to Milan, from where it was sent to Orte. His absence from the chapter was interpreted as an act of pride and as a challenge, which brought rebukes from those present, and especially from the Commander.

Bro Luigi knew nothing of all this. He only found out when a letter from the prior, Bro Ambrose of Milan, arrived. It said:

'Dear Bro Luigi,

'On seeing Bro Benvenuto's way of working when he came to Rome for the general chapter, the Commander, Bishop Fiorani, was very annoyed. So he has ordered me to come to Orte to warn you. His threats were such that I broke into a sweat just listening to them. In order to remove any suspicion of your guilt, I would advise you to go to or to write to the superior general elect and show him that you are a true subject, and not what you appear to be. I hope you have already done it, but if you have not, for the love of God, do it.

'Always your friend in Jesus and Mary
Bro Ambrose.'

Monti took this letter, which spoke of warnings and threats, to Mgr Mengacci, the Capitular Vicar, who was running the diocese after the death of the bishop.

Mengacci realised there was a danger that Monti could be removed from Orte and so he sent a commission of three priests, including one who was a representative of the municipal hospital in Rome, to speak to the Commander of the Santo Spirito.

He wrote a memo in which he explained the task entrusted to the three priests. It went as follows:

'1) They will tell Your Grace of the great good which the Concettini Friars do in this town, under the leadership of the above-mentioned Bro Luigi; of the high esteem in which they are held for their most exemplary conduct; and for the self-denial and activity they display in carrying out their duties. They will also tell of the gratitude felt by citizens of all classes for the services given, especially to the poor sick and the needy.

2) They will tell Your Grace of the great activity carried out by the above-praised Bro Luigi in the expansion of his institute.

3) They will tell Your Grace how Bishop Mangacci clearly recalls having taken these two houses in our diocese under his protection, and how well pleased he is with the way they are going.'

The Vicar goes on to express his sorrow at the way in which Bro Luigi was treated on the occasion of the general chapter, and concludes by asking the Commander to leave things as they are at Orte, adding that the departure of the Friar would have led to the closure of the hospital. This meant that the hospital was a success because of the wisdom and heroism of Bro Luigi and his confrères, who gave themselves in daily sacrifice, which had a salutary effect on the people.

Bishop Fiorani read the letter and listened to the commission, who verified every assertion with statements expressing the highest esteem for Monti. But, as Fiorani was full of prejudice, the greatest concession he made was to agree to meet Monti in person and listen to him.

Monti introduced himself to the *redde rationem*. Being prudent, he armed himself with statements from the hospital rector, the surgeon and other important people. Fiorani arrived accompanied by a superior of the institute, Salvatore Bronelli of Petrella, the very person who had just been elected prior of Orte. As soon as Monti came into the room, Fiorani launched a hail of insults, calling him proud, ambitious, capable of directing the institute, yes, but not before submitting himself to the prior there present.

Bro Luigi remained humble under that trial, until he heard the following:

'Go back to Orte and await further instructions!' Then he replied calmly: 'I will return, because I am responsible for the pharmacy there. So I will do my spiritual exercises and then I will do no more and no less than that which God wants.'

He went back to Orte, to work, and to wait for the new prior whom he would obey.

ORTE - CHAMPIONED BY PEOPLE AND AUTHORITIES

Nine days later, on 28 November, the new prior arrived, but he did not introduce himself to Bro Luigi.

Accompanied by the superior, he arrived bringing an array of gifts and introduced himself first to the Capitular Vicar and then to the mayor. He told them both about the decision taken in Rome to remove Monti, who was working in the hospital totally unaware of what had been decided for him.

But neither the Vicar nor the mayor accepted the decision. In fact, they were most indignant and strongly deplored the way in which Monti had been persecuted. They said that the local people could only speak well of him and explained that the people might well rebel against such an incomprehensible decision. Then the mayor, who was also the hospital administrator, raised his voice in a threatening manner and declared that he wanted no superior other than Bro Luigi. Faced with such explicit declarations, the two superiors from Rome made a quick turn-around and joined with the mayor and the Vicar in praising Bro Luigi. They said they agreed that he was irreplaceable and promised to report all they had heard to Rome in order to prevent any changes.

When they arrived back in Rome they changed their tune again and started to heap accusations on Monti, both to the Commander and to the new bishop, Dominic Mignanti, who happened to be in Rome. In fact, they spoke to the latter with such venom that he was shocked that two religious should show such a lack of objectivity. They showed the bishop a letter requiring Monti to return to Rome under obedience and he promised to deliver it personally (which he never did). He asked them to suspend any decisions until he returned to his diocese. They promised to do this, but had no intention of keeping their promise. They spread plenty of malicious gossip, in and outside the Santo Spirito, against Bro Luigi of Milan. His only fault was that of developing the institute and serving the sick people of Orte, rather than supporting the ambitions of the guardians of a moribund institution. The latter seemed to be totally unaware of the anticlerical storm which was sweeping through Rome, Italy and the whole of the Church.

They had no understanding of either people or events and they thought they could solve their problems by getting rid of Bro Luigi. Luigi, however, understood very well the real intentions of the two superiors, even though they had actually promised the bishop that they would not make any changes. Luigi wrote to Fr Adeodata Orlandi, parish priest of Orte, 'These men aren't capable of behaving prudently and they think they can resolve things by destroying them and warning people of their intentions.' In fact, despite the promises made, they did not wait for him to return and on 20 January 1873 they sent Bro

Gregory Coriddi to Orte with a mandate to remove Monti and send him back to Rome. Once again the Vicar and the mayor strongly opposed the move. In fact, the mayor threatened to send the police to remove Bro Gregory if he did not go of his own accord, and quickly.

There was sharp contrast between the mayor, who as representative of the people wanted to save the hospital, and some of the Friars who, representing their own wretched interests, wanted to move the institute. In the meantime, the new prior designate of the hospital, Bro Gregory, went back home without telling anyone, which shed some light on the internal structures of the Santo Spirito, where the hospitallers lived.

Bro Stanislaus Sauda, a simple soul hungry for God, suffered a lot in that atmosphere of jealousy and disunity and he wrote to Monti, his 'father' and friend at Orte, describing it as 'a continuous martyrdom.' In fact, the best of the Friars were leaving the community to join other religious institutes. From the moment he was recalled to Rome, Bro Stanislaus no longer felt at peace and he prayed, for himself and for the others, to be reunited with Monti, even at the cost of starting another institute... just to be with him. He summed up the situation at the Santo Spirito with an observation which typifies his simplicity: 'there is nothing new, only continuous discord and gloom.'

The choice was clear: either form a body with Monti and so save their vocation, or leave an institute which was infused with the evil spirit of discord. The same spirit of discord had also taken root in the hospital at Civita Castellana, after Monti, as an act of obedience, had withdrawn from it.

IN DEFENCE OF MONTI

To stop Monti being removed from Orte, all the clergy of the town gathered together and sent a document to the new bishop. The document was a carefully logged record of each stage of what they called the 'persecution' of the good Friars being carried out by ambitious hypocrites and giving 'most grave scandal, particularly in the present climate.' They were referring to the satisfied sneers of the liberals who had come to power after 1870, and who could hardly believe their eyes at the public display of perversion given by certain religious orders. Such behaviour complemented the anticlerical theatrical productions and newspaper articles much in vogue at the time. It all helped inflame the increasingly violent argument between papists and liberals.

The clergy also mentioned in the document the 'shameful state of the finances' of the Friars' house in Rome. They contrasted it with the success of Monti's Concettini at Orte, where they had re-built the hospital and the church and spread an 'immense good... in every class of the population', largely because of Bro Luigi.

They went on to talk about the various manoevres, initiated by the recent 'general chapter' in Rome, to remove Monti from Orte. They said that he was described as 'insubordinate' simply because 'in promoting the spirit of the institute, he had to remove the mask of hypocrisy from those who were trying to destroy it.'

The document was exhaustive, vibrant and relevant to the political climate of the day, which did not tolerate displays of disunity. But it did not have any noticeable effect at the time. In fact, on 15 June 1873, Monti received a letter from the faithful Stanislaus, telling him of a diabolical plan aimed at expelling Friars Benvenuto Tasca, Placid Crescentini and Bro Luigi himself, from Orte. In the face of such fury, Monti could no longer stay calm, and every day he became more embittered until he became convinced that the only alternative was to leave the institute before being kicked out of it. He went to see the bishop to tell him of his decision.

'Don't destroy these people and this house which cost you

so much sacrifice', said the bishop, alarmed at Monti's request, 'I give the orders here. I will defend you and if there are any problems I will speak to Bishop Fiorani. You just obey me.' The bishop, whom Monti described as rather 'cold and shy', did not normally react so violently and usually tried to avoid trouble.

That was all Monti needed, for their rule insisted on obedience to the local bishop. Bishop Mignanti was, by now, well aware of the 'real persecution' of which Monti had been victim and he decided to go and see the Pope personally to let him know the truth of the situation. He went to Rome and spoke to Bishop Fiorani and, on the advice of Monti, he also spoke to the Commander, Bishop Borgnana.[1] The intervention of the two prelates may not have modified Fiorani's views, but it was enough to prevent Monti's removal from Orte.

More than a century later, it is difficult to comprehend the blindness of people like some of the superiors at the Spirito Santo. Even more incomprehensible is the fact that all this took place within the context of the violent anticlericalism which broke out after the ending of the temporal power of the papacy. The whole of Lazio was affected and there was a general tendency to remove clergy and religious from all public institutions.

In such a highly-charged atmosphere there was a reason for such small-mindedness: even the most intelligent of people could not easily see beyond their political passions. To develop the ideal of an apostolate of service to the sick, as conceived by Monti, meant rooting oneself in God with exceptional determination. In fact, he was already completely in the arms of his protectors, Jesus, Mary and Joseph. They were the only bulwarks solid enough to weather that storm.

Humanly speaking, nothing remained, or so it seemed, but in the end the truth came out. Despite the deterioration of much of the institute, those Friars least involved in the various factions saw that the pride, the personal rivalry, the vanity and all the other negative circumstances, could be overcome if there was someone who kept faith and remained in charity. That person was Bro Luigi, who incarnated such qualities. His energy, faith and dignity, together with his Christian humility, administrative wisdom and heroic service, were such that the more mediocre the surrounding circumstances, the more he grew in stature in the eyes of the people.

In the end, the majority of Friars saw that there was no one else but him. Sent away, isolated, despised and defeated, he was saved only by his personal qualities, and so, for their own salvation, they turned to him.

A NEW CONSTITUTION

In October 1874, Rocco Tonnoni, one of the most respected Friars in Rome, wrote to Monti telling him of the next general chapter: 'Our Friars,' he said, 'are all ready for you. Now there is nothing to fear, because Commander Fiorani is now in charge of us and it is as if the Pope himself were our superior... I hope to see you soon as my superior general.'

The letter contained many other things. For example, it said that Fiorani had overcome his aversion to Monti and had admitted that the latter was the only person capable of taking on the job. Fiorani also admitted that the Capuchins had had their share of troubles after Fr John Baptist, at the Pope's command, had been removed.

Clearly something new was being born amongst the Friars Hospitaller of the Immaculate Conception. Above all there was an air of expectation that they were about to emerge from the depression in which they had been languishing for some time.

At their request a sacred visitation was arranged with Pius IX, who sent Bishop Scipione Perilli to represent him. It began on 26 November 1874 and four days later Monti, who had come specially from Orte, appeared before it. Ten days after that, a report was produced.

Three proposals were made to restore order to the institute: a rule approved by the ecclesiastical authorities, a regular novitiate and an 'enlightened government.'

The Pope accepted the proposals and asked the Commander who would be capable of setting up an 'enlightened government.' Despite the fact that the Commander had shed most of his prejudices against Monti and was convinced that only he could do the job, he chose another, Bro Gregory Coriddi.

Bro Gregory was nominated at the beginning of 1875 and Monti was confirmed as superior at Orte.

The constitution, drawn up by the Capuchins and the Commander, reflected the conflicting interests of the two, for each of them wanted to keep the institute under its wing. Pius IX made a sharp comment: 'The General of the Capuchins is the superior of the Concettini and so is the Commander. So, the superior of the Concettini is not worth a bean.'

He drew a line through the paragraphs regarding these points and added a note saying: 'The superior should be just like the superior of all other religious orders.'

They obeyed him. The General of the Capuchins was to be simply a spiritual supervisor. The Commander of the Santo Spirito had the simple title of protector, but without any powers of jurisdiction. The superior of the Concettini was invested with full, independent authority, with the Santo Spirito as its mother-house.

The new constitution was approved on a five-year trial basis by Pius IX on 30 April 1875, to the joy of the vast majority of the Friars who were received in a special audience. Bro Luigi was present at the audience and saw the dawning of a new development, which he later wrote about: 'The great Pontiff of the Immaculate Conception entered the room where the Concettini were kneeling. He addressed them, 'Oh! Here are my Concettini' and, turning to his own clerics he continued: 'Being unable to sleep last night, I started to think about my Concetti-

105

ni. I've noticed that in Piazza Mastai there is a little garden where a small house could be built, big enough for twenty-five or thirty people. This could become a novitiate, where instruction and spiritual formation could be done, but not practical work.' He added, turning towards the Friars, 'as you have done up to now, when as soon as someone joins the family he is immediately clothed in a habit and sent on to the battlefield. The king first of all gathers the recruits, he clothes them, then he puts a gun in their hands and with this he sends them on manoevres. It was amazing and I don't know how you managed to survive up to now! But no more, from now on you will have a place for your spiritual exercises.'

Thus Bishop Perilli's second proposal, that of a novitiate, was assured.

The problem was, however, that many things had been affected by the polluted atmosphere of gossip and arrogance. The Concettini were so badly affected by it that some threatened to resign and others not to submit to the new regime. Another apostolic visitation followed and, of the thirty-nine Friars interviewed, all but four expressed a desire for autonomy, as laid down in the constitution. After further inquiries and disagreements a new election was held. On the Pope's instructions, this was prepared by the first apostolic visitor, Bishop Perilli who, in agreement with the Servite Friar Alex Biffoli, also appointed to look into the situation, reported his concern regarding aspects of the religious life. He proposed that the Holy Father 'should nominate as superior Bro Luigi of Milan, the present superior at Orte, the current superior being only a temporary appointment. Monti, who has been a Concettino for many years, is the only one who has the capacity, the intelligence and the disposition to govern. He was also favoured by the majority of his confrères when they were interviewed. This would put a stop to any dispute which would render the trial constitution desired by Your Holiness impracticable. The dispute, if it were to continue, could, some time in the future, lead to the end of this new and holy institute, which has great ideals, is sublime in the practice of charity and gives glory to Your Holiness, who instituted it.'

Before Perilli presented his report to the Pope, recommending Monti as superior, Bro Gregory pronounced these words in the council: 'If we do not ensure that Bro Luigi is brought back from Orte to bring to an end, or at least, minimise the enemies who are conducting the relentless war against the institute, very soon we will see an irreparable catastrophe. The family cannot endure these trials much longer. The institute is running a great risk and without Bro Luigi it will be difficult to save it.' He concludes: 'Certainly, I confess that I find myself incapable of tackling the enemy who is growing stronger by the day. It is God who wants the institute in the hands of Bro Luigi, for it is all too clear that without him, it will perish. In fact, I have already told him that this institute was born of his inspiration and it is through his work the Lord wants it to flourish.'

Notes

1. Member of the Hospitals Commission for Rome.

9
DON BOSCO INTERVENES
1876-1877

PIUS IX AND DON BOSCO

On 10 November 1876 the Friars made a plea for help to the Pope, explaining how it was not possible to profess holy vows under the current rule and regime. They asked that the decree of the Sacred Congregation of Bishops and Religious be brought into force, saying that, as long as they remained subject to the opponents of that decree, the institute would never be able 'to prove itself'.

But already, before he received their request, Pius IX had thought of a way out of the quagmire. Through Cardinal Aloysius Bilio, the Pope turned to Don John Bosco, the great and saintly organiser of works of mercy for the Church. 'The Capuchins', wrote the cardinal to Don Bosco on 29 October, 'do not seem suited for such guidance and the institute needs a better system. So the Holy Father thought that the right man would be Don Bosco.' He added that the Pope was very keen that either he himself or another Salesian should accept the honour and that he had said, with a smile: 'If Don Bosco comes, tell him that I will pay his travelling expenses.'

Don Bosco obeyed, and the Pope told the Commander of the Santo Spirito that the guidance of the Friars Hospitaller had been taken away from the Capuchins and given to someone else. The Commander could not wait to break the news to the Concettini and he brought Bro Luigi, post haste, to Rome, saying he had 'something which concerns you and with which you will be very happy.'

Bishop Fiorani asked Monti to prepare the Friars to receive the new arrangements, which Monti did, as can be seen from this letter to the Commander, dated 22 November:

'Your Most Reverend Grace,

'I believe it my duty to update you on the mission you gave me on my last visit to Rome. My brothers at Orte and Civita Castellana were greatly consoled by what His Holiness has done for the much-tried institute of the Immaculate Conception. They proclaimed unanimously: 'It is a miracle of Divine Providence that our Holy Father has found such a holy solution, from which will come the renewal and the life of our institute.

'We cannot find the words to express our gratitude and our love to His Holiness. Your Grace, however, will, out of his goodness, compensate for our inadequacy and thank His Holiness for not having abandoned us, and for putting up with the dishonour of so many problems suffered on our behalf. We hope, in the future and through grace, to become your consolation.

'And for all the patience you have shown us through all the trouble we caused you, the Lord will reward you with many good things.'

Don Bosco intervened, and with his intelligence and experience, he understood the nature of the crisis, which was due mainly to the lack of a spiritual dimension and which affected both religious and lay nursing staff. Of the latter, some had still not made their first communion and others had not received the sacraments for many years. Many of them had been brought in off the streets, from amongst the ranks of the unemployed, in order to make up the numbers, and were in fact, religious in name only.[1] Running parallel with the spiritual chaos was the financial mess. When Count Borghese heard about the task given to Don Bosco he exclaimed: 'They say that Don Bosco works miracles, but if he manages to sort out the affairs of the Concettini, it will be the greatest of miracles.'

In fact, everything needed to be sorted out. The institute of the Friars Hospitaller of the Immaculate Conception in the Santo Spirito was a real mixed bag of people which lacked a religious spirit and which lacked above all a uniting discipline. Their mission, as Pius IX defined it was 'sublime,' but their organisation was a disaster. 'You should not reform or correct yourselves', commented the Pope, 'but create, or better, model the constitution of the Concettini on that of the Salesians.'

The appropriate term was 'create,' on the foundations of a solid religious life. For this they needed, above all, a new religious novitiate. It could be said that by turning to Don Bosco the Pope had realised that what was needed was a holy founder.

The industrious Don Bosco studied the situation keenly, for he too wanted to establish his own community in Rome. In practical terms, he formulated a reform of the Friars Hospitaller in eight articles. He proposed abolishing their status as Capuchin Tertiaries and making them instead Salesian co-operators, keeping the same name and habit as before, but thereby forming a stable link with his own congregation. However, from the first contacts with the Friars, and particularly with Bro Gregory Coriddi who had gone to Turin to meet him, Don Bosco understood how much they valued their independence. As he himself explained to the superior chapter of his own congregation at the end of November 1876: 'The thing they fear most is that we will go there and make them into Salesians.'

Don Bosco tried to cater for their express wish for autonomy, but he did not see how their community could be reformed without being brought into his own family. In fact, it seemed that the Pope too agreed that this was what should be done.

On behalf of his community, Bro Gregory wrote to the Pope

asking him to maintain the integrity of their congregation which 'first rose up in Rome just after the proclamation of the dogma of the Immaculate Conception of Mary.' and while he thanked the Supreme Pontiff for having entrusted the leadership of their community to so worthy a priest, he also expressed his belief that they should 'always fully conserve their autonomy with the aim of always doing good for the honour of the Immaculate Virgin, the only patron of the institute.'

MONTI SAVES THE INSTITUTE

Bishop Fiorani was opposed to the aspirations of the Concettini, because he saw that their 'identification' with the Salesians would bring an end to his authority, in maintaining which he had invested a lot of time and effort. He asked the Pope for an interpretation of the proposal and spoke to Don Bosco, who understood that the bishop wanted a 'dual government,' whereby the Salesians looked after the spiritual part (*in spiritualibus*) and the Commander the material part (*in temporalibus*).

As a result of exhausting negotiations, the two men agreed on the names of the local superiors of the various houses run by the institute. In his generosity, Don Bosco tried to reconcile people and circumstances, but he realised that bonding together so many different influences would mean that the institute would break up, before even getting started...

For the mother house, the one on which the others depended, Bishop Fiorani wanted Monti. In fact he could see no alternative.

The letter written from Orte on 22 November had sealed a peace between the two men and this signified a complete change of judgements and relationships. In this new spirit of reconciliation, the Commander sent for Monti to come from Orte on 4 March 1877. He said to him: 'As you know, the Capuchins are no longer there and I am there instead, as visitor *in temporalibus* with Don Bosco *in spiritualibus*.'

As such the Commander was empowered to appoint a superior for the Friars Hospitaller at the Santo Spirito. Then after a long period in silent thought, he confessed that he had made the choice of superior some time ago.

'Who is it?' asked Monti.

'You', he replied.

Monti, however, thinking of the mess to sort out and the huge amount of work required to rebuild the house, declined the honour. In his refusal there was a sense of humility and of realism, and Fiorani understood it. He promised his support to tackle Monti's enemies and insisted that Monti accept. Eventually, Monti 'surrendered' and accepted.

Prince Paul Borghese was the first to congratulate him: 'Now I can see the institute going ahead', he said to Bro Luigi. 'Another couple of months and it would have been destroyed.'

Monti left hurriedly for Orte to put things in order there and on 5 March he returned to Santo Spirito as superior general. At that moment, he was probably thinking about his friend Pezzini, to whom he had predicted, on entering Santo Spirito for the first time, that it would come back into their hands. It had, however, taken twenty years of suffering.

The new superior general set to work and, just as he had done at Bovisio, Bussolengo and Orte, he found himself having to make furniture from a few rough boards, a garden out of scrubland or a church out of a rats' nest

He arrived to find a family of forty-two Friars and thirty lay workers, the latter having been taken on to cope with the increasing workload. Most of them, both the Friars and the lay workers, had been recruited by a certain Bro Charles, a local superior who had left the community at the end of 1876. So, the community was, in part, made up of unemployed people who had joined to earn enough to keep the wolf from the door. Thus, the essential elements of a religious community, vocation and formation, were missing.

To start with, Monti engaged in a sorting process. He watched how each one behaved, at work, at rest, in the refectory and outside the house. In three months, after a warning which proved fruitless, he dismissed no less than forty Friars and lay workers. On 17 April he took possession of the novitiate.

Thus he was ready to start what might have appeared to be a reform, but what in reality was a new construction. In effect, he was trying to form a religious family from that group of workers, which up to now had been living just like any secular community. First and foremost Monti taught through the daily example of his own life.

His rule then, was to give himself without reserve. He started from the beginning. He revived the practices of piety and established a timetable which enabled them to care for the sick, to pray, to meditate, to be silent, as well as to take some physical rest and nourishment. Previously their lives had been completely disordered, the life of the body having been just as neglected as that of the spirit. More than teaching them by giving sermons on all these things, he taught by example. A nun who worked in the hospital observed: 'He was a marvellous superior, because he was always the first to do everything, especially the most lowly jobs. He carried heavy loads, walking solemnly and always in silence.'

Through his example and his charity, he set about uniting souls, the prime task of a community, if it is to be such. So that everything was done in the presence of God, he watched day and night, without rest, ready to give his life, offering help where needed, advising, warning and, when necessary, punishing. He wanted the hospitallers to be Friars and at the same time he wanted them to be real religious. He was not interested in increasing the numbers. Those who were not called to that way had to leave, which of course meant he met with opposition and maltreatment. In the most difficult cases he consulted Fr Joseph Scappini, the Salesian put there by Don Bosco as spiritual director. Bro Luigi made good use of the wisdom and virtue of this priest and he told Don Bosco, in a letter to him, how much he appreciated Fr Scappini's presence.

For example, he wrote to him on 22 May of that year: 'Very Reverend Father, please forgive me if I take the liberty of confiding my mishaps in Your Fatherhood and at the same time make you aware of the needs of the Friars Hospitaller. And that loving father has helped us as much as possible so that this much-tried institute of Mary Most Immaculate can be renewed and reflourish.

You can well imagine the turmoil and difficulties that I have to endure in carrying out my responsibility as superior. The job of weeding out the trouble-makers is exhausting. In two months we have had to dismiss eight Friars and about twenty lay workers.

The disorder was intolerable and the scandals had become public knowledge.

'Now, however, with God's help we are enjoying a bit of peace and are beginning to see some order. In the midst of many problems my conscience has never been troubled for I have not acted on my own whims, not moving a finger without the advice and knowledge of our marvellous director Fr Joseph and of the visitor Bishop Fiorani.

'Yes Most Reverend Father, now I can thank God that we have been freed from the infected members who were preventing the renewal of the institute.

'With the help of God I am ready to give my life to sustain the institute, but every time I do not see the fruits for the glory of God, I prefer to enjoy my own peace and to think of the good of my own soul.

'Meanwhile I owe a debt of gratitude to Your Fatherhood for all the good I receive from you, and that my confrères receive in the person of Fr Joseph, our wonderful director and true reflection of the Father.'

There were some who took exception to Monti's title as founder of the Institute. If he had not done anything other than what he did during those six months at the Santo Spirito, he would have to be recognised as the saviour, the rebuilder of the institute. In reality, it was he who brought a consistency, a unity, a soul to that community, where previously no-one had ever seen any evidence of real community life. He created a family out of a mixed bunch of people and infused the care of the sick with the spirit of charity.

Don Bosco was happy with all this, and Pius IX was so pleased that, not only did he write off debts of 35,000 lire which had accumulated during previous administrations, but he set up a fund of half a million lire for his Concettini, which meant they could build a novitiate and instruct the novices.

The novitiate was built in Piazza Mastai which Pius IX loved and had named himself. On the order of the Pope, building started in 1875 and was completed in April 1877. It consisted of a chapel, a refectory, a study room and four upper floors. On the inside there was a tree-lined courtyard.

With the novitiate, Monti could now form the new Concettini according to the model he had always envisaged, that is, one inspired by the life of the Mother of God.

DON BOSCO AND BRO LUIGI

The reconstruction of the institute spread the good name of the Friars far and wide in Rome, and the governors of the Fornari Hospital at Foro Traiano presented a request to Bro Luigi on 15 June for his nurses to take over the running of their hospital. A contract was drawn up and the superior sent the first Friars.

The same month, Don Bosco wanted two of his priests, Fr Joseph Lazzero and Fr Julian Barberis, who were in Rome for the episcopal jubilee of Pius IX, to give a course of spiritual exercises to the Concettini in the novitiate house. The course was a great success and established a family relationship with the Salesians. As a result, Fr Lazzero became convinced that the Concettini should eventually have their independence as a congregation even though they were happy to have the Salesians as their spiritual directors. But the old conflict reared its head again as Don Bosco, more than ever, wanted to incorporate the Concettini into his own family as co-workers and Bishop Fiorani had designs on becoming their superior himself. The third element in the story was Bro Luigi himself, whose leadership was a shining demonstration to all that the Concettini were capable of governing themselves. In fact, the Capuchins were already standing back and giving a confirmation of their detachment and loyalty.

Don Bosco thought of resolving the problem in a way that showed his charity and detachment. One day, at a lunch at the novitiate house at Piazza Mastai, he said to Monti: 'From now on, you should start to do some studies and I will arrange for you to be ordained. Then I will send you on the missions.'

The priesthood was an ideal which ought to have attracted a consecrated soul like Monti, who had dreamed about it since he was a boy. But even such a high ideal could not distract him from the intimate, unchanging ideal which he had followed through thick and thin - the formation of a religious community with a Marian apostolate. So he replied to Don Bosco, defending himself humbly by quipping, 'Most Reverend Father, I have been twenty years at the Santo Spirito and I have never had time to study.' Two canons from Orte, who were also at the lunch, backed Monti's declaration, recalling the fact that their bishop had also asked him to become a priest, but that he had declined in order to remain with his community.

However, three days later, Don Bosco sent for Monti again and, in the presence of the spiritual director Fr Scappini, he openly proposed that he and his companions should unite with the Salesian congregation.

Two great men of God were facing one another, each with a

different vision. It has happened many times over the centuries and only goes to show that saints are human beings with their own way of seeing things. Sanctity lies in the rectitude of one's intentions. In that open confrontation between the two, there can be no doubt that each of them wanted to give glory to God, something which was in fact confirmed by the events that followed.

Don Bosco promised to speak to the Holy Father about organising Monti's ordination and the latter wrote to him saying: 'Most Reverend Father, I am writing to you, not as superior general, but as a neutral. If you try to take on this institute which the Immaculate Conception wants for herself, you will lose all the esteem which the Vatican has for you, because Our Lady wants the institute to be free and all hers. Woe to anyone who touches it.'

Monti stuck to his guns, but so did Don Bosco. Two strong wills were in opposition, divided by their own convictions.

A row eventually developed, not between Monti and Don Bosco, but between Fiorani and Don Bosco. The latter was prevented from obtaining an audience with the Pope by the Commander, who did not want any rivals to his control over the institute.

Monti, however, did have an audience with the pope. He knew how much Pius IX loved the Concettini, and he was received by him on 15 July 1877.

In the presence of the Pope, Monti, who was both moved and full of joy, read an address in which he thanked him for his generous protection in the midst of 'a thousand storms,' out of which the institute had emerged victorious. He also reminded the Holy Father how the novitiate and the two 'pillars' of the institute, Bishop Fiorani for the administration and the 'most zealous Don Bosco' for the spiritual life, were also his gifts.

Pius IX replied to Monti's address and, as well as expressing his love, he sent a beautiful picture of the Immaculate Conception, painted by Silverio Capparoni. The picture was a confirmation of the Marian character of the institute over which Mary reigns.

Bishop Fiorani was present at the audience, but neither Fr Scappini nor any other Salesian was there. Fr Scappini, in fact, was ill and had gone back to Piedmont, leaving the Concettini without daily mass and with no spiritual director, for several weeks.

In his address to the Pope, Monti had mentioned the two mansions, temporal and spiritual, assigned to Fiorani and Don Bosco. Don Bosco did not like this arrangement at all, and he foresaw all sorts of problems as a result. When Don Bosco spoke to the Pope's representative, Cardinal Randi, he repeated his 'way of seeing it' which was to incorporate the Concettini into his well-established institute, while letting them keep the habit, the name, the aims and the rule. It seemed to Don Bosco that this was the real meaning of the letter of 17 November. However, if incorporation into the Salesians was not acceptable, he suggested entrusting both the spiritual and material direction of the Concettini to one person. That person should be appointed by the Pope and the Salesians should be left to carry out the task of chaplains.

FATHER ANGELINI

In the meantime, there was still no priest either at the Santo Spirito or at the novitiate. Monti, who knew nothing of the correspondence between Cardinal Randi and Don Bosco, was growing concerned over the fact that the Friars could not have a daily mass at home and had no spiritual director. On the morning of Sunday 19 August, he gathered the Friars together and said: 'Go to mass at Traspontina or St Peter's or any other convenient church and I will go on my own to Our Lady of St Augustine 'to brew up a storm'.'

This was a typically Roman expression, sometimes used by

Pius XII, and it showed the familiarity of the children with the mother, from whom they insistently ask some favour.

Our Lady of St Augustine is a statue in a church of the same name. It was extremely popular with the ordinary folk who came from all over Rome and Lazio to plead with Mary. Monti had remained an ordinary working lad who firmly believed that he was carrying out a mission close to Mary's heart and he felt he was both her child and the executor of that mission.

He stood there in the midst of the crowd before the huge marble statue of Our Lady and the child Jesus and said: 'Mother, you can see the need your institute has for a priest to celebrate Holy Mass and confession. I don't know whom else I can turn to.'

He recounted the story of his conversation with the heavenly mother in the third person. 'And, looking up at the statue of Our Lady he said, from the depths of his heart: "Mother, the institute cannot go ahead like this. You are our patron and Our Mother, you must provide for us, otherwise I will leave everything and your work will be destroyed. So, on my way back, or when I arrive home, find me a priest who will ask if he can celebrate mass for us. Or, inspire me, O Mother, as to what I must do for the good of the institute".'

A 'clear voice' spoke in his heart: 'If you don't find a priest on your way home, or at home, go to Fr Angelini of the Society of Jesus, and he will provide all you need.' Fr Anthony Angelini Rota was a popular and gifted priest in Rome who had great devotion to Our Lady.

On his way home, Bro luigi came across a number of priests, but they were unapproachable. Each one seemed closed in his own world. No priests had come to the hospital either, so he said to his deputy, Bro Jerome: 'Take off your apron and come with me.'

Bro Jerome did as Luigi had asked and on the way he realised that they were going to the place where Our Lady was sending them. They eventually arrived at Fr Angelini's house in Piazza Farnese. They were ushered in and Bro Luigi explained what had happened at Our Lady of St Augustine.

After the initial surprise, Fr Angelini reflected on what he had heard and, as it involved Our Lady, he said yes.

'From this moment', concluded Monti, 'a whole series of graces came and with them, the renewal of the life of the institute.'

In fact, Fr Angelini became the spiritual director, with the approval first of Bishop Fiorani and, later, the Pope, as well as that of the superiors of their own order.

When Don Bosco saw what had happened and saw that it was with the Holy Father's approval, without any fuss, he slipped discreetly away.

Whilst he wanted so much to pass on a spirituality to the institute, he did not want to block its independence. He could see that it was already virtually independent and was resolving any outstanding difficulties.

MONSEIGNEUR TURRICCIA

Fr Angelini was the spiritual director and Monti was superior general, but how was the Holy See to exercise its own authority? With Don Bosco gone, the clergy of Rome felt that one of them should represent the Holy See to the Friars Hospitaller. Cardinal Randi, who was looking after the affairs of the Concettini, suggested Mgr Ambrose Turriccia, a typical Roman, who had been chaplain to the papal troops.

Turriccia accepted, but he was authoritarian by nature and, because of his upbringing, he wanted, as ecclesiastical superior, to be 'the sole and independent authority', so that he could restore order to the Concettini who, he maintained, were still victim to various factions. For these reasons he sent a memo to the Pope. The Pope, who by now was physically weak and close to death, had him nominated by the Sacred Congregation as apostolic visitor for a three-year term, with sole control over both internal discipline and financial matters. He would report directly to the Holy See.

'Poor Commander', the Pope said to Fiorani, 'I dealt you a blow there, eh! Never mind. Be patient. I thought that two heads on one body would clash, so I left one on its own.'

The new visitor, having listened to badly informed sources, did not have a particularly positive image of Monti and, before even meeting him, he had decided to remove him. When Turriccia met him, he gained a very favourable impression and decided to keep Monti as superior general.

Being superior general under an authoritarian ecclesiastic like Turriccia was not easy, however. Turriccia wanted to be everything and to do everything. Nevertheless, through his humility, Monti managed to establish a cordial working relationship with the Monseigneur, through which he was able oversee the growth of the institute.

One sign of this growth was the profession of the vows on 8 December that year, the feast of the Immaculate Conception, something which had not been possible for three years.

Another sign was a marked increase in the number of new recruits, after, as already explained, the huge drop in numbers due to expulsions either for insubordination or lack of a vocation. On 25 August of that year, Bro Joseph Maria Petrolli, who had preceded Monti as superior, died, completely worn out, at the age of only thirty-two. He died a holy, but painful death, victim of his devotion to duty, 'a martyr of obedience' as Bro Luigi had described him six years previously.

While the number of Friars had diminished, the amount of work in the hospitals had increased, especially at the Santo Spirito, where the governing body became more and more demanding as the pressure from the secular world grew. Monti turned to his friends at Brianza where there were many young men who wanted to give themselves to the apostolate. His brother Anthony, a member of the now suppressed Sons of Mary, his friend Fr Giglio Albuzzi, Fr Rovella of the Rho missionaries and others stirred up a lively interest in Monti's work and helped prepare the ground for his arrival. Monti eventually arrived on 11 December and stayed for ten days. He went from Milan to Bovisio and then on to Desio and Rho, all favourite haunts of his youth. He went back to Rome with seven young men who had been recommended by parish priests and religious. He joyfully introduced his new recruits to Mgr Turriccia on 22 December at the Santo Spirito.

The following January (1878) he returned to Lombardy for a second recruitment campaign, a 'catch' or 'harvest' as he jokingly called it. He was supported by the prayers and offerings of the Friars and of Mgr Turriccia. As Bro Jerome Pezzini wrote in a letter to Monti dated 27 January: 'Mgr Turriccia asked me to let you know that he hopes you take a good catch. We pray the Rosary for you and offer our visit to the Blessed Sacrament every evening, and now we are making a novena for you. In fact, Monseigneur says to tell you that two more young men are on their way here and he hopes that you bring back at least another dozen. He expects to hear good news from you.'

The good news was not long in coming, and on 2 February Mgr Turriccia wrote the following to Monti:

'Bro Luigi in the most beloved Jesus,

'I feel consoled by the good news you sent and hope that, with God's help, things work out successfully.

'If you think you can increase the size of the catch by staying longer in Lombardy, stay there, and send comforting news. We are in dire need here. There is a lot of suffering. I have a lot of sick religious here (at least six), and all at the same time. You know what that means! Then there are other little crosses inside and outside... Let it be so! Let's place our trust in the patronage of Our Lady.'

The 'catch' this time was ten young men, but by the time Monti came to leave it was reduced to seven. The seed had been sown however, and news had spread throughout Brianza and other areas. Many more young men made the journey to Rome in response to the call of the ideal incarnated by Monti. By mid-1878 the number of Concettini had doubled.

Luigi Monti returned to Rome on 13 February. He arrived too late to see the face of the Pontiff or to venerate his body. Monti had turned to him as father and protector many times, and had always received both spiritual and pecuniary benefits. He had died on 7 February, bringing to an end a life marked by greatness, but also by political turmoil.

The Concettini felt the loss more than most. Special masses were said for Pius IX at Santo Spirito, Fornari, Orte and Civita Castellana and on 16 February they celebrated a solemn memorial mass in the church of the Annunciation near the Santo Spirito. In memory of this occasion, Fr Angelini, well-known for his epigraphs, wrote a beautiful inscription in Latin.

With the same fatherly love as he recruited the Concettini, Monti also cared for them, looking after both their spiritual and physical welfare. They needed someone to defend them, for in the eyes of the secular world, their work was seen as a commodity to be bought as cheaply as possible. The hospital governors were usually incompetent and, in the strongly anticlerical atmosphere of the time, all they did was to load more burdens on to the Friars' backs.

Many of the Friars became ill and several simply collapsed under the weight of continual sacrifice, in surroundings which were totally unhygienic. As Mgr Turriccia noted in a report on the Santo Spirito in May 1878: 'The dormitories are attic rooms, the refectory and the chapel have windows which open on to the place where the bodies are deposited and dissected, the infirmary is like a tomb without either light or air.'

This was why, since 1864, they had rented a house at Our Lady of Rest, why the year after they had built a house at Pius V's Casaletto and why, in 1875 they had acquired a small vineyard. But they were all temporary and inadequate solutions to the problem. They really needed a place of their own, somewhere where the air was clean and the atmosphere calm and which could be equipped to cater for the specific requirements of the Friars.

All this would take a lot of money, and Bro Luigi did not have that sort of money. Mgr Turriccia, however, who was equally convinced of the need for a rest house, contacted Cardinal Randi and Cardinal Nina, the Secretary of State, and obtained a loan of 14,000 lire from the Holy See. With this money and another small sum which he already had, Monti was able to buy a house and a vineyard in the country, not far from Our Lady of Rest. He called the new house St Joseph's.

Having acquired the land, Monti and his Friars set about tilling it and sowing seeds, while at the same time repairing the building. They worked themselves to the bone. Monti contracted rheumatic fever which he accepted as a trial sent by the Lord, for the good of his soul and that of the institute.

Finally everything was ready and the new house and garden were opened to the sick Friars. There they could recover in the silence and in the fresh air, as well as enjoy innocent recreation. To cap it all, Monti was given permission to reserve the Blessed Sacrament in the chapel. Everyone liked the place and the cardinal himself came to visit it in 1879, to join in the festivities with thirty-six Friars.

After thirteen years the debt was repaid and the house and vineyard were just as they wanted them.

The true spirit of the community, remodelled by Monti, could be seen during an epidemic when huge numbers of people were admitted to the Santo Spirito.

Monti himself recounts one such occasion in a letter to Fr Giglio[2], written in August 1879:

'There are 1,214 patients at the moment. Yesterday 228 were admitted. We had to bring in more beds, setting them out in three rows per ward. For us it is harvest time. The head nurse called me and told me that we had run out of mattresses. He wanted to know what to do to avoid laying patients on the floor. I replied that he could have my mattress, but that I could not ask my Friars to do the same, because they needed a bit of rest after their prodigious efforts. However, I told him to see who was willing to make a little sacrifice for the love of God. In fact, I gathered the whole community together (there are sixty beds, plus seven in our infirmary) and told them that the poor patients had to sleep on the floor. I said that if anyone wanted to make a little sacrifice to let me know, and I would give his bed to a patient. They all shouted out together: 'Take mine, I'm happy to give it to someone. Give it to a patient straightaway.' I also asked in the infirmary if they were ready to give up their mattresses and they all said, 'By all means, please take it'. However, I told them that a generous heart was all I wanted and that I would make do with the mattresses of the healthy Friars. So, in a wink, fifty-three mattresses were taken on to the wards.'

No wonder Bro Luigi ended his letter by saying: 'Truly they are great and they are a great consolation to me and to the Most Reverend Fr Angelini, our spiritual director. Prince Paul Borghese, who represents the governors of the hospital, also rightly praised them all for their acts of generosity in a letter of thanks.'

Notes

1. These are Don Bosco's words.
2. Fr Luigi Albuzzi, a Milanese priest.

10
DISAGREEMENTS WITH TURRICCIA 1878

FRESH ATTACKS ON AUTONOMY

By now the Institute of the Sons of the Immaculate Conception, under the firm guidance of Bro Luigi, was flourishing, and its success also strengthened the personal standing of the superior. However, the success also provoked envy and other such feelings which did not build the family. Some of the Friars started to have ambitions. The smooth running of the institute, the life of humble service and prayer, did not fit in with their plans. They wanted to return to the old regime, where the most cunning ones helped themselves to double rations. They were only a few, but they were sly and ambitious and incapable of living the virtue of obedience. Two such men were Bro Gregory Coriddi and Bro Clement Gamberini, both former superiors, who saw the fading of their own careers in the light of the high esteem in which Bro Luigi was now held. Bro Joseph Ceccherelli and others, who had been forgiven and helped in numerous ways by Monti, were also stirring up trouble. They began to deceive Mgr Turriccia.

A witness recalls how 'to climb the ladder of ambition, they loved to fish in murky waters. Full of suspicion and jealousy, they whispered in Turriccia's ear warnings about *the great influence* which Bro Luigi, as superior general, exercised over the whole religious family.'

Unfortunately, Mgr Turriccia did not see through their intrigue and he began to look at things with their eyes.

So began a series of humiliations and troubles for Monti, which were all the more painful because they came from someone in authority. Adopting an attitude of humility towards his ecclesiastical superior, Monti accepted all the restrictions put on his authority over the religious family. He was forbidden from spending any money, from clothing the postulants in their habits and from giving them their name. He was ready to become nothing, to become nothing for the good of the institute.

The five-year, *ad quinquennium*, experiment of the institute's Constitution was about to expire, and Monti wrote to the Pope humbly requesting full autonomy:

'Most Blessed Father,

'As the five-year Constitution is drawing to an end, the humble Bro Luigi Maria Monti, superior of the Friars Hospitaller Concettini, submits to your goodness and wisdom, our wish to be allowed to govern ourselves. This is all the more appropriate now that we have excellent spiritual nourishment through the loving and diligent care of the fathers of the Society of Jesus. We can now say that by the grace of God and with the help of our Immaculate Mother, the family is healthy and is flourishing, with a good number of novices, all of which augurs well for the institute. The eternal memorial of our Holy Father Pius IX has left us well provided for. It was also his will to see the institute of the Immaculate Conception free and in charge of its own affairs, like other secular institutes such as the Brothers of Mercy, the Ignorantelli, and others.'

Did Turriccia know about this letter?

We do not know, but what we do know is that ten days later, on 19 June, he called Luigi to the council room and, in the presence of three other Friars, gave him a severe reprimand.

Luigi Monti humbly did not reply.

The same scene was repeated five days later in Bro Clement's room where Mgr Turriccia accused Monti of a lack of charity and of spreading dissent. As a punishment, he was forbidden to speak to his Friars and they were forbidden to speak to him.

Humble as ever, Bro Luigi bowed his head, fell on his knees and begged forgiveness for all his failures. He had only one thing in his heart: that the family, as he wrote to Fr Angelini, should not be discouraged by the 'turmoil' and thereby lose its direction.

He was thinking about the new recruits who had just arrived from Lombardy and who would have been disillusioned if they had heard what was going on. He also felt a responsibility towards their priests and bishops. 'I am responsible for these young men, because I brought them here and they placed their trust in me as a father. Now I am a laughing stock who needs help himself.'

One possible solution was to hand in his resignation. Should he do that? But Fr Angelini insisted that he stay put. He realised that Bro Luigi's departure would have been a disaster.

So a row then broke out between Fr Angelini and Turriccia.

The hospital governors, who were pleased with the Friars' behaviour, asked them to take on the running of the wards for the chronically sick. The Visitor found the suggestion an excellent one, especially from the financial point of view, but Monti found it unacceptable. The Friars lacked the necessary training and the new job would put an intolerable burden on the youngest Friars. Monti knew how demanding the work would be.

This resistance provoked other rebukes for Monti, who put an end to it all by going down on his knees and asking them all to pray to the Lord for him.

How the saints react to things! Mgr Turriccia was completely disarmed and asked that none of what had been said in that room be repeated outside by anyone, including Bro Luigi.

Luigi wanted to make his confession, so he went up to Giani-

The general chapter of 1883.
Luigi Monti, whom everyone called Father, as superior general, seated in the centre, in the new habit without a hood or girdle. He is holding the 1881 Constitution, the first one he drew up. After twenty years of suffering, the Congregation of the Sons of the Immaculate Conception were given the juridical autonomy to become a self-governing congregation in the Church. So the founder announced a new code of life, in which he laid down the principles of religious consecration in the name of the Immaculate, with a second apostolate to the orphans and the introduction of the priesthood in a congregation composed entirely of lay people.
All these aims were eventually fulfilled, but at different times and after much suffering and many difficulties.

Orte: the church adjoining the hospital.
Luigi worked at Orte from 1868 to 1877. Almost a decade of activity in almost every area of hospital work, founded on the twin pillars of science and charity.
He was an apostle amongst the youth of Orte and animator of the hospital church, which he restored so that songs of praise to Our Lady could be sung once again.
He may not have been a priest, but he was a deacon of charity, an ardent announcer of the word of God and a zealous champion of devotion to the eucharist.

colo where Fr Angelini took his daily walk. As soon as he saw him, the Jesuit greeted him enthusiastically, waving his breviary at him. Surprised at this reaction, Luigi went over to him.

'Well, Bro Luigi', he said, 'what's new? Do you know that this morning I sat down at my desk to write when I heard a clear voice in my heart. It said, 'Pray, pray for Bro Luigi'. I rose straightaway and knelt down to pray. I returned to my desk again, when, lo and behold, I heard the voice again, 'Pray, pray for Bro Luigi'. I knelt down again and prayed. Once more I returned to the desk, when, just as clearly as ever, I heard the voice a third time, asking me to pray for you. So, without thinking too much about it, I knelt down once more and prayed even more fervently to God and to Our Lady to save you from any possible danger. Now, tell me, what happened to you?'

Bro Luigi listened to all this, amazed and happy.

'You did well Father', he said, 'to pray for me, because if God and Our Lady had not helped me, it would have been the end for me. However, I pray, please don't ask me to tell me what happened, because I am under obedience not to tell anybody.'

'What?' interrupted the priest, 'no one can make you do that. Speak, I will dispense you of any obligation.'

Fr Angelini made him tell everything, and sent him on his way in peace and calm. On 26 July Angelini went to St John Lateran to see the Pope's confessor, Fr Daniel da Bassano. Angelini told him everything and asked for help. That very evening, da Bassano told it all to Pope Leo XIII.

LEO XIII

Fr Angelini's intervention led the way to an audience with the Pope for Monti on 31 July.

The aristocratic pontiff, who very much appreciated the hospital work done by Monti's religious, was like a loving father to Monti, standing before him.

'I've heard', the Pope said, 'that things are going badly for you. So, let's hear what's happening in the family.'

Bro Luigi told him very simply everything, including the ban on talking to his Friars. He explained that this had caused such a tension that he asked the Supreme Pontiff to relieve him of his responsibility. Leo XIII dismissed the charges one by one, saying that they went against all the rules. Luigi was at peace and was not afraid of the visitor, who could not do anything without the Pope.

'I am the Pope! Don't worry', he said, dismissing him in a fatherly manner.

Monti locked those words away in his heart and the certainty that went with them.

When he returned home he was relieved of the job of superior general and was relegated to the position of superior of the Santo Spirito, where, in fact, he could no longer exercise any real authority.

Monti recounted further episodes to Fr Daniel in a letter which the latter then passed on to the Pope. In fact, only the supreme authority of the Church could resolve once and for all this problem, which had emerged again from the ashes.

Monti put together his own experience with the good counsel of others and presented an objective and sober view of the situation to Bishop Jacobini at the Holy Office, whose opinions were much respected by the Pope. The letter concluded, 'I am sure that you would want to leave no stone unturned until a remedy is found, so that the Institute can triumph, for the glory of God and to the honour of our Immaculate Mother.'

Jacobini thought the arguments were so judicious that he suggested showing them to the relevant authorities, in particular to Cardinal Innocenzo Ferrieri, the highly respected prefect of the Congregation of Bishops and Religious.

Having consulted his spiritual director, Monti showed all the evidence to the Cardinal Prefect, who immediately took an

DISAGREEMENTS WITH TURRICCIA

interest in the case and wanted to take a closer look at things.

Others too supported this approach, including Canon Adeodato Orlandi of Orte, who gave his backing to Monti's arguments. Also the older Concettini, who were well aware of what was going on, sent an appeal 'with tears in their eyes' to the Pope, asking him to liberate them 'from the critical and intolerable state' into which they had fallen 'through the constant imprudence of the Apostolic Visitor.' Fr Angelini also wrote a letter appealing to Cardinal Ferrieri in which he spoke of how 'the whole community loves and respects Bro Luigi, a man of heroic patience and rare prudence who has kept and keeps in good order a religious family. It was through Bro Luigi that many good young men came to the institute from Lombardy. They are my consolation, so good and well-educated are they.'

He added that the removal of Monti would only lead to disorder within and scandal without.

'I have prayed and prayed', he concluded, 'as fervently as I can, that the Most Holy Mary will inspire you and the Holy Father to find a solution as soon as possible.'

At the Sunday council Turriccia noticed a sadness on the faces of the Friars, especially the younger ones, which was in sharp contrast with the permanent expression of joy he had seen when he first arrived. But, instead of softening him, this only had the effect of making him more bitter, to the point that he made more grave accusations against Monti and some of his Friars, including Bro Jerome, who was 'the wisest and most prudent.' It was he who had been elected successor to Monti.

When the visitor had finished speaking, with great respect Bro Luigi asked just one question: 'Your reverence has accused me of being a thief, of stealing six hundred lire from the institute. Can you explain to me how this came about?'

Monti saw it as his duty to defend his good name, as the reputations of others linked to him were also being dragged through the mud.

Monti called one witness after the other and each of them demolished the accusations, forcing the accuser to admit he was wrong.

CARDINAL INNOCENZO FERRIERI INTERVENES

The time of the final decision was drawing near and some of the Friars' spirits were nearing breaking point. In fact, one or two of them had left the turmoil and had opted for a more peaceful existence outside the community. On the morning of the 19 October, Turriccia made yet another attempt to get Fr Angelini's authorisation to expel Monti, or at least have him transferred to Orte. Fr Angelini's reaction was to write immediately to Cardinal Ferrieri explaining all the facts of the situation including the latest developments. The letter is worth reading, as an objective documentation of the facts:

'Most Reverend Grace,

'This morning Mgr Turriccia came to see me and told me of his determination to remove Bro Luigi as superior from the Santo Spirito and send him to Orte where the Concettini have a house attached to the hospital. His intention is to send him there tomorrow. His reasons for doing this are irrelevant and based, as you are aware, on false anxieties concerning Bro Luigi. He asked my opinion and I told him frankly that I did not agree with his request: 1) because it would cause great turmoil in that community who love, venerate and respect Bro Luigi, the person who formed them with his prudence, wisdom and zeal; 2) because all the Milanese, who are the best members of the community and the most numerous, would leave, having been brought to the Santo Spirito by Bro Luigi; the ill-feeling that they all feel towards Mgr Turriccia would explode into outrage.

'Mgr Turriccia admits that these reasons are right, but he still will not accept my advice and change his mind, for he believes that the Milanese and many other Friars as well as Bro

Luigi, to be his enemies. He refers to them as the opposition, whereas they are in fact the best and the vast majority of the religious family.

'Mgr Turriccia approached me with a request to replace Bro Luigi with Bro Gregory, an ignorant man with false ideas on the spiritual way. He is unpopular with everybody and it is he who is advising the Monseigneur and urging him to make changes that will have disastrous consequences.

'I have responded to the voice of the Holy Spirit, who has put a pen in my hand and made me inform you of the imminent ruin which will overcome the institute if urgent action is not taken. Many good souls are helping me to pray to Mary Most Holy that she will come to our aid, and soon.

'The wisdom and rectitude with which the Lord has endowed Your Grace, and the sublime position of prefect and superior of all the religious orders and institutes, open my heart and give me hope that this cause is God's cause, the cause of truth and of justice.'[1]

Fr Angelini was able to explain the contrast between the two men, one of whom had 'formed' the community through his own 'zeal and wisdom', and the other who wanted to exploit it and deform it with his tantrums and prejudices.

The evidence given by the Jesuit father, who was universally respected for his holiness and his teaching, was made even more valid because of its spontaneity and detachment. It was confirmed by other, equally spontaneous evidence from another worthy priest, the chaplain of the Santo Spirito, Fr Salvatore Lai, who really could speak from first hand experience.

Fr Lai said quite simply that Mgr Turriccia's accusations against Monti were 'proven false by the exemplary behaviour of Bro Luigi', whom everyone, with prudence, praised. 'The majority of the professed Friars and the novices are opposed to him [Turriccia], just as they are well disposed towards Bro Luigi whom they regard as their true father and consoler', said Fr Lai.

He added that to save 'such a beautiful work of God and of Mary, the reverend visitor will somehow have to be removed' and the institute put back in the hands of 'Bro Luigi who has already had to revive it on three previous occasions, expelling the spirit of the world and putting the souls back on the road to perfection...'

These interventions had their effect. On 28 October the cardinal called Monti and Turriccia to his house, each without the other's knowledge. The cardinal had asked for an explanation of the dispute between the two men and Turriccia produced a nine-page document written in the early hours of the morning. He read it out to the cardinal, repeating the same accusations as before. Eight days later another meeting was held at which Monti read his account of what had gone on. The meeting ended with the full recognition of Monti's loyalty, administrative wisdom and leadership and with an invitation to Turriccia to resign.

Monti, in a true spirit of humility, turned his thoughts to the Mother of God, who had saved his institute. That night, with all his anxieties removed, he fell asleep with his heart full of gratitude.

In obedience to the cardinal, the following day Monti went to see Fr Angelini to invite him to come to his house. Then he went to tell Bishop Perilli everything that had happened. The latter was delighted with the news and confided to Monti that the next day Cardinal Ferrieri was coming to lunch. The idea came to Monti to arrange things so that Fr Angelini might meet the cardinal and convince him that the time was now ripe for the institute to be given its independence. He managed to convince the spiritual director to go to Bishop Perilli's house, where Fr Angelini had arrived a few minutes before the cardinal. On seeing the good Jesuit, the cardinal said to him: 'While you are here, we could discuss tomorrow's business now.'

In the discussion that followed, it was decided that Fr Angelini would ask for Mgr Turriccia's resignation. Over the next few days Angelini thought about the best way of doing it. In the meantime he was able to inform the cardinal about what had been decided and to assure him that 'calmness, tranquillity and observance' had returned to the Concettini. Angelini also reported that throughout the whole affair Bro Luigi had acted 'with remarkable prudence.'

On 7 November Angelini was able to notify the cardinal that Mgr Turriccia had offered his resignation to the Holy Father a few days previously.

Finally, on the 30 November Turriccia's resignation was accepted and the apostolic visitation came to an end. It also meant the end of 22 years of persecution and the much longed for autonomy of the institute. Bro Luigi saw it as a gift of Our Lady who brought to an end a sequence of trials and torments the gravity of which we cannot conceive. 'Anyone reading the story of the institute in the future', commented Monti, 'will not believe their eyes when they read about all the unpropitious events which ought to have destroyed it.'

With all the power delegated to him as president, six days later Cardinal Ferrieri confirmed Monti as superior general and called on his most trusted Friars to work with him: Bro Jerome Pezzini as procurator general and Bro Daniel Quagliani as novice master.

Notes

1. P. A. Angelini uses the title Fratello (Brother) instead of Fra (Friar). In fact, when the Cappuccini had ceased to govern the Concettini, Monti introduced this title and wrote it into the Constitution. Later on, the Friars started to call Monti 'Father', not just to show their love for him, but also because they recognised in him all the qualities of a father. From now on in this book, these titles will be used.

11

THE FOUNDATION AND THE FOUNDER

THE FOUNDER

In 1876 Don Bosco had called Pius IX the founder of the Salesian Congregation.

In the same year, at an audience given to the Concettini on 15 July, Bro Luigi read an address to the same Pius IX, calling him 'the true founder of the institute.'

During his last illness at the end of 1877, the Pope expressed his paternal interest in the institute, which he saw was now flourishing, to the Commander of the Santo Spirito: 'Oh yes, I love my Concettini... I made them!... Every day I pray specially to the Lord for them at the Holy Mass.'

Monti recalled that daily remembrance in an invocation sent to all the Concettini: 'This prayer, O Holy Father, now that you are blessed in Heaven, you renew in a purer, more efficacious way at the throne of Our Immaculate Lady for the humble society which you promoted for her glory and for the care of the sick. This is the guarantee that our institute, which came to life through you, will flourish through you.'

In his will, dictated at Saronno, Monti affirmed: 'As regards the founders of the institute of the Sons of the Immaculate Conception, recognition should be given to no one except Jesus, Mary Immaculate and St Joseph. These first two guided me in the most marvellous way in the undertaking. The third, St Joseph, provided for the institute in its gravest needs. His Holiness Pope Pius IX has been an eminent benefactor of the Institute.'

This declaration by Monti for the Conceptionists, like that of John Bosco for the Salesians, expressed the deferential, disinterested gratitude of the two founders to an understanding Pope who had offered each of them help at a moment of crisis. But this did not mean that the work of foundation did not belong to the two men. It just demonstrated their humility. St Vincent de Paul was another one who would never have allowed himself to be credited with the foundation of his own institute.

Besides giving the title of founder and father of the institute to the Pope, Monti also gave it to Bishop Fioravanti of Veroli. The latter soon grew to love the Concettini and their work and their spirituality, so much so that he considered himself a 'Concettino Friar'.

Fr Luigi also held Bishop Fioravanti in high esteem. He would joke about his surname, greeting him when he met him with: 'Avanti, Fior!' (Go ahead, flower). Monti made frequent trips to Veroli to see him, and the bishop would return the visit in Rome. They wrote mutually edifying letters to each other for the rest of their lives. Every year Fr Luigi sent him a box of the famous Amaretti di Saronno biscuits. Of course, Fioravanti's title of founder was no more than a courtesy title.

In Rome, the jumble of good, bad and indifferent Friars Hospitaller who worked at the Santo Spirito, received, or recovered, their vocation in the main from Monti's word and example and, under his leadership, it became a real community. It was he who put a stop to the process of deterioration, bringing discipline and conferring the taste for, and the order of, a life of piety. Monti also redefined hospital service, adapting it to meet the needs of the period, first at Orte and Civita, and later at the Santo Spirito. In fact, Monti was putting into practice an ideal he had developed from his youth and which had remained fundamentally unaltered through every kind of trial and difficulty.

For the first time the Friars discovered the ultimate aim of their vocation in an explicit and integral way. They saw that their vocation lay in the sanctity of their work, with the dignity of their care of the sick. It was a genuine asceticism, a prayer composed of deeds and clothed in continuous sacrifice. So noticeable were the effects that Prince Borghese in 1878 asked, on behalf of the new governing body of the Santo Spirito, for all the wards to be served by the Concettini.

Luigi Monti, applying all his talents and with the help of many supernatural graces, was putting together a masterpiece, following the blueprint in his head. It was a simple and living work of art, to which he gave the name the Immaculate Conception. For him, the Institute had to become like the arms of the Immaculate Virgin open to serve Christ in the sick.

It required the genius of a craftsman of exceptional strength, considering the incredible difficulty of the task, and the simple and upright genius of a saint who knew what was needed.

The enormous effort made by Monti in building up the Institute would have defeated most normal people. Monti was the architect and the builder who knew how to transform all the difficulties into a solid, organic construction. Only a holy obstinacy, built on the rock of religious faith, could make something out of that mixed bag of stubbornness, conspiracy, worldly opinions and ignorance. It was like a heap of rubble which to others might seem only fit to be thrown out. But the same kind of exercise has often been carried out, perhaps on a different scale, in the growth of religious orders, beginning with monastic ones.

Those who understood such things recognised Monti's work as a founder. Already in 1878, during the most stormy period, Fr Angelini had written to the Sacred Congregation asserting the fact that the community of the Concettini had been 'formed' by

Bro Luigi. At the same time, the chaplain of the Santo Spirito, Fr Lai, had made the same affirmation in a letter to the same authority. He referred to Bro Luigi as the one whom the majority of the Concettini considered to be the 'true father', and who had restored life to the Institute on three occasions.

1880 had been a year which had been almost completely submerged in difficulties. At the end of that year, in thanksgiving to Mary for the interior peace she had granted, Monti had her statue in the Santo Spirito chapel crowned with a silver crown. He prayed to her as queen and mother and wrote in his diary: 'It can be said that today, after twenty-three years of life, the Institute started to be born. This is due to the excellent vocations, as well as to the fact that we are free of all ties and conflict.'

Without realising it, Monti, with these words, summed up the reasons behind the foundation he had built. The Institute in 1880 had been in existence for twenty-three years, but as an association, not as an order, as an experiment, not as a permanent reality. It had been a collection of individuals whose unity had either never been born or was always about to die. It was, in short, a union lacking any real internal spiritual, administrative or vocational unity. It was held together by material and spiritual goals but it had never shared a common ideal and had never felt like a family. In the better moments, it had been a kind of confraternity or corporation, but apart from the same habit and living quarters, everyone looked after his own affairs. Because of the lack of discipline the members formed into factions, which then broke up again. All this, without Monti's energetic, tenacious, almost obstinate action, would have resulted in the break up of the community. After the collapse of the temporal power of the papacy, not even the fear of the Pontifical police would have kept them together.

The congregation of the Concettini was born of the heart, mind and arms of Luigi Monti. For historical reasons, the birth of the Institute was risky and laborious, but this, rather than making Monti's achievements less meritorious, makes them doubly so.

In 1879 the Institute consisted of:
1) The Mother House in the Santo Spirito, Rome
2) The house of the Immaculate in Piazza Mastai, Rome
3) St Joseph's Hospice at Porta Cavalleggeri, Rome
4) The house at Orte
5) The house at Civita Castellana
6) The Fornai Hospital, Rome

Anyone who has the normal type of foundation in mind, one where the founder draws up a plan which is then carried out, will be rather confused by that of the Concettini. It was, in part, planned by others, using material gathered in the most unusual way, in the strangest of circumstances. It is, perhaps, a confirmation that the Holy Spirit never repeats himself and that he brings to birth his works when and where they are least expected. When he wants to build new areas of the city of God he makes use of fishermen, illiterate women, poor parish priests, craftsmen and 'idiots'.

From his youth, Monti's desire to serve his brothers for the love of God had two aims: teaching and hospital work. With his strong will, clear vision and hard work, these two ideals developed into the education of young orphans and the care of the sick.

Both these aspects of charity recur in the works of the great saints down the centuries. What was original about Monti's work was that he was able to bring a time-honoured ideal up to date, just as Elizabeth Seton, Madeleine di Canossa, Cottolengo, Don Bosco and Cabrini had done in their particular fields. The relationships with Dossi, Pezzini, the Capuchins and others during the hard years, were for Monti a source of supply of experiences to confirm his vocation. But it was already very much alive during his adolescence and youth. At the age of sixteen he felt a strong desire to do good to his peers and had been encouraged in this mission by his parish priest and by so holy a missionary as Fr Taglioretti. He had also been chosen by his superior to study surgery and pharmacy, unlike the other young men who had been asked to teach their own craft.

Dossi guided and encouraged him in one of these missions, and in the other, the education of the young, it was the voice of God speaking directly in Monti's heart. Fr Dossi, Pezzini and Sister Maria Crocifissa Di Rosa directed him towards the sick.

There has been much discussion as to whether and to what extent Monti was the founder of his Institute. Some have their doubts, some consider him only a reformer.

It has been argued that the idea of an order of hospitallers was not a product of Monti's mind, but this is an argument that could be levelled against all, or almost all, founders.

Monti's ideal and initiative passed through various stages, each of which could be identified with a person regarding the hospital work: from Sister Di Rosa, to Manini, Dossi and Pezzini… Each one pointed him in a new direction, in the sense that each one encouraged him in his vocation and provided him with important experiences.

Take Monti away and the experiences of Manini, Dossi and Pezzini dissolve and are reduced to mere historical fragments.

The fact that Monti was the founder is beyond doubt. What is more, we cannot but admire his brilliance, his heroism and the fact that, out of all the difficulties and chaos, he managed to bring his creature into the light. Neither would it be right to talk about co-founders. Those around him were more often trying to demolish or deform what he had built up, rather than help build it. Monti's repeated efforts to reunite the various disparate and disorientated elements is really deserving of merit. They were actions of enlightened charity, of patience and foresight. His attitude was always that of a healer of the wounds of humanity, always in an attitude of service, in order to restore health.

THE NEW CONSTITUTION

With the removal of Turriccia, Monti's institute was saved.

At the end of that year all sixty-five of the Friars made a retreat. In a moving ceremony, they made peace with one another at the feet of a beautiful image of Mary Immaculate. On the vigil of the feast of the Immaculate Conception, they acknowledged her, not only as queen and patron, but also as queen of their institute. This was a pact of fraternity between her sons, a sign of their recognition of her protection, where they ascribed the 'life' of their institute to her after emerging from 'so many long and difficult trials', as it was written in the prayer read by Fr Angelini.

Now Monti wanted to rewrite the constitution. He felt that it did not reflect the new reality of the institute, having been drawn up when they were no more than a kind of Franciscan Third Order, dependent on the spiritual and practical direction of the Capuchins. Such laws and practices no longer corresponded to the needs of the community.

The five-year trial period granted by the church authorities to the old constitution expired on 15 June 1880. So, Monti asked the Sacred Congregation for permission to modify the constitution according to the experience and judgement of the members themselves. Cardinal Ferrieri gave his consent to alter the old constitution as they felt necessary.

Monti got rid of the old rule completely and drew up one more suited to the aims and practices of the Institute.

The draft of the new constitution revealed a mind that had a very clear vision of the whole complex of laws relating to a religious institute. Unlike the old constitution, this draft was not just a succession of chapters, often totally unconnected, many of which contained a variety of different topics. One chapter in the old rule, for example, spoke about the 'duties of the novice master and the bursar.' Monti divided it into four clearly defined sections. The first part, divided into subsections, dealt with the general aims, the form of government, the administration of goods and the admission of novices. The second and third sections covered everything necessary for the perfect formation of the individual regarding his own sanctity and the specific aims of the Institute. Thus these sections dealt with the vows, special virtues, prayer, mortification, silence, work, how to behave towards one's neighbours and towards sick Friars. Finally, the fourth section, entitled "special offices', covered the rights and duties of those with special responsibilities. The section ended with a chapter on the rights and duties of novices.

The new constitution had an organic integrity. Its division into sections, with double the number of chapters, had the great advantage of allowing each Friar the opportunity to consult, easily and with precision, whichever part he might be interested in.

When he had finished the revision Monti wrote: 'This constitution contains no obligations, except for those concerning disregard for, or breaking of the vows, or other defects which contravene the virtues or the laws of God and the Church. Nevertheless, as it has been approved by the Holy See, it provides for the Friars Hospitaller of the Immaculate Conception, the established rule that God requires of them, until they receive their reward from him in Paradise.

'So it is not enough just to know the rule. It must be studied in order to put it faithfully into practice, observing it in every precise detail, in the certain knowledge that by so doing we will become more pleasing to God and loved by Mary the Most Holy Queen and Mother of our Institute.'

For the rewriting of the text, Monti used the Venerable Pavoni's constitution, Fr Angelini's advice and the opinion of other wise people, but most of all he drew on his own experience and meditations. He used rules dictated by life, for life. He wanted the nurse to become a religious, who in carrying out his 'service' to the sick, acted like an angel before the Lord, with a maternal love. In order to be able to do this, the nurse would have to be rooted in a deeply pious life. To establish this cornerstone of the Friars' formation, Monti assigned a supremely important task to the spiritual director. He gave him the job of 'guiding everyone, through a regular and uniform method, towards the highest goals, to which by their very nature religious institutes tend'. Monti wanted him to be 'the promoter of regular observance, a firm guide for individual consciences, the dispenser of supernatural gifts and a channel through which pass the copious graces which God rains down profusely on the community.'

As well as caring for the sick, the Friars Hospitaller could, whenever possible, practise their former trade. They were to do so staying 'close to God', in serenity and recollection, as if in prayer. Here too, Monti was very much in tune with Catholic social teaching, which was at the time in full flow, giving a Christian evaluation of work.

The structure of the 'form of government' was particularly notable. From hard experience, Monti had learned the importance of having a system of government based on the unity of the members with the head, through obedience. Unity is vital for the development of a religious institute and essential for the practice of the principal virtues of the Christian religion. Monti was aware of this and wrote in the new constitution: 'It is therefore necessary for a religious institute to be governed directly by a superior general, who, under the direct jurisdiction of the Supreme Pontiff, directs everything in one single spirit, which brings about one heart and one soul.'

This feeling of oneness which the head passes on to the members through intermediaries, and which they then reflect back to him, from the estuary to the source as it were, calls for the virtue of obedience, understood as the acceptance of the thought of the superior who is seen as representing God. As already mentioned, the Ignatian concept, practised by the word and example of Fr Angelini, offered such a radical model of the rule that it gave a whole new imprint to the new organism.

'This spirit of perfect obedience', wrote Monti, 'will bind the individual member in the same way and for the same ends as all those to whom the superior has entrusted part of his authority. Thus we should be reminded of what St Ignatius instilled in his followers, namely that they should look at the person who has to be obeyed, as representing the one to whom ultimately we must be obedient, Our Lord Jesus Christ. So, whether it is the superior who commands, or one of his representatives, it is in fact God who commands, and that should be the end of it.'

Monti had always said, right from the earliest days: 'Find a religious who is perfect in obedience and you will have found a saint.'

So it is easy to understand why Bro Luigi made obedience the basis of the formation of the Friars Hospitaller. 'The fundamental point to aim at', he said to the novice master, 'is to inspire in them a great respect and love for obedience, in which all the virtues of the religious life are contained.'

In order for individuals to accept this, they needed, along with other qualities, a gentle and sincere nature with a 'firm resolve to abandon themselves to pleasing God, submitting themselves without reserve to the will of the superior regarding where they work and what job they do. Anyone who is stubborn or finds obedience difficult is not suitable for the Institute, where we need religious who are dead to the world and to themselves.' Humility, simplicity and obedience are, for the founder, 'the characteristic virtues of the sons of this Institute of the Most Holy Immaculate Mary.' These characteristics are her virtues, she who by opening herself up to the will of the Father (fiat mihi secundum verbum tuum) and emptying herself, was filled with the Holy Spirit and gave Jesus to the world. Just as she had become the ancilla Domini, the handmaid of the Lord, so her sons had to be servants of God, above all in the poor. Her sons had to become nothing so that they were always ready to do the most humble jobs, as Jesus had come into the world not to be served but to serve.

This is why he taught the novice master to train the novices to suffocate their self love and practise a 'blind obedience... there you will have saints, if you make them truly humble and obedient.' This spirit of abnegation, sacrifice and obedience is nothing to do with discouragement, depression and melancholy, it is completely different. Souls are re-made in God through the mortification of the old man, to participate in the life of God, who is strength, initiative and joy.

One need only look at this normative aspect of Monti's work to have a measure of his greatness and his originality. Through his constitution he founded a new society to which he gave an unmistakable soul, based on the example of the great founders.

EXAMINATION OF THE TEXTS

The constitution was an enlightened summary of psychological, moral and religious wisdom. The author succeeded in blending together the most beautiful ideas from those spiritualities with which he had been in contact, from that of the Sons of Mary, to that of the Capuchins, the Jesuits and the Salesians. It was a blend of the most solid spiritualities from every period of the Church's history, converging in an ideal model for the Friar hospitaller.

On 19 July, Monti presented the text to Fr Angelini, who, in half an hour, read it, appreciated its consistency and goodness and advised him to present it immediately to Cardinal Ferrieri.

The cardinal asked Bishop De Luca, a stickler for the rules, to examine the constitution. He raised serious objections to the section on authority and the duration of the period of office of the head of the institute. He suggested that it should be limited to a specific number of years, as he was afraid it might become purely arbitrary. He also suggested that the spiritual direction should be entrusted, not only to the Jesuits, but also to priests appointed by individual bishops in their own dioceses.

In the midst of the discussions, Bishop De Luca died and his place was taken by Bishop Gizzi, who removed the former's modifications and brought in some of his own. When Monti read the new proposals, he remarked jokingly that they would result in a 'republican government.' At that time in Rome the word 'republic' was synonymous with 'anarchy'.

Fortunately, Ferrieri asked Angelini to carry out the final revision, which he did in agreement with Monti. After consulting his Friars, Monti also proposed changing the religious habit, which was no more than a Capuchin tunic with hood, girdle and cloak. The hood was removed, the girdle replaced by a sash and the skull cap by an outdoor hat.

Besides the care of the sick, Monti also wanted to add the welfare of orphans, but he was not able to include it in the proposed text.

However, the most radical innovation and the one which caused the most difficulty, was that of introducing the priesthood into a lay institute. Over the previous twenty years Bro Luigi had suffered a great deal through the lack of priests specifically at the service of the Institute. In fact it had often been difficult to find a priest to celebrate mass, or perform other sacred functions, as well as provide permanent spiritual assistance from within. On the other hand, he had suffered from interference on the part of clerics brought in from outside to give spiritual direction. He wanted this service, above all, to come from within the family of the Concettini, in the spirit of the Concettini, in a harmony of life.

THE APPROVAL

With the introduction of the priesthood, which meant that some of the Friars began to prepare for Holy Orders, the superior general had not the slightest intention of changing the lay character of the religious family. On the contrary, he wanted to protect it, by giving a priest to each family, as a fixed point for its religious life.

'The idea is to write into the constitution that after fifteen years of religious life a Friar could be ordained to cater for the needs of the family, if he has a good record and has always been well disciplined. This will only be done at the discretion of the superior general, who is empowered to do it. The superior general may also choose not to ordain anyone if, in his judgement it is not the right thing to do. This is to discourage the admission of priests or clerics who join only to perform this task thus bypassing the main aim of caring for the sick.'

This proposal was greeted with silence, opposition even, by both Fr Angelini and Cardinal Ferrieri.

In fact, the presence of priests in a lay community posed new problems, which Angelini and Ferrieri immediately pointed out to Monti.

For Monti, the formation of 'our own priests' meant an assurance that there would be no more outside interference, which even though exercised by pious individuals, was nonetheless, still interference. It was a guarantee that the unique spirituality of the Institute and its religious life could be preserved. But Angelini and Ferrieri drew Monti's attention to the difficulties and dangers. 'Would not a priest', they asked, 'through his very nature and dignity, tend to override the authority of a lay person, even if that person were the superior general?

This was the greatest danger envisaged by Fr Angelini himself, who realised that once the Concettini had their own priests, the institute would no longer have any need of him or his confrères.

But Monti had very clear ideas on the matter and he would never have reduced the authority of the superiors. Even though they were laymen, they must retain their authority. He wanted to take the task of spiritual direction from outside priests and entrust it to Conceptionist priests. At the same time he had no intention of taking this task away from Fr Angelini and the Jesuit fathers, whom he wanted to have, whenever they were available, as spiritual directors for his sons. He was grateful to them for all their advice and help and indebted to them for their many inspirations. For the same reason he had included in the group of patrons to pray to and to celebrate officially, St Ignatius of Loyola, St Aloysius Gonzaga and Stanislaus Kostka.

However, Fr Angelini was not convinced and he went to see Cardinal Ferrieri to tell him that Monti's ideas were Utopian. Ferrieri agreed with Angelini. Thus, with the best of intentions, the spiritual director rejected all Monti's proposals. Monti could not sleep at night. To soften the blow, he decided to explain the reasons for his proposals to Bishop Gizzi, who in his turn explained them to the cardinal. The latter was so convinced that he declared: 'But don't you realise that Bro Luigi is right! Enough of all this. For now we will bury the whole affair and when the time is right it will be implemented.'

The cardinal was a fine diplomat and he had realised that Fr Angelini was smiling at the idea of linking the Institute of the Friars Hospitaller to the Jesuits, and that he did not like the idea of introducing the priesthood, a move that he continued to oppose.

For the moment Monti did not insist, he just wanted the Holy See to approve the constitution. In fact, there was a frequent exchange of opinion between the cardinal and the Holy Father, particularly on these two key points: the appointment of the superior general for life and the fact that the general council had only an advisory capacity. Eventually an interim solution was found. The superior general's period of office would be determined by the Holy See and, in the case of any disagreement between the council and the superior general, the cardinal would intervene.

After the inclusion of other minor alterations suggested by the Congregation's advisers, the new constitution was approved *ad experimentum*, for a five-year period, on 18 November 1881.

The cardinal added his signature on 5 December and Monti made the official announcement on 8 December.

It was the feast day of the Immaculate Mother, whose protection had constantly been sought during the long drawn out negotiations for the approval of the constitution. That morning he went up to the altar and stood in *cornu epistulae*. Fr Angelini, who had been his closest ally during the arduous struggle, was on his right. Monti showed the document to the community and read out the first six articles, declaring that, without a doubt they would now be enacted. Fr Angelini then read the decree of approval and gave a beautiful talk on the subject. After that, two Friars made their triennial profession. At the end, in the bright and decorous surroundings of the church, a moving *Te Deum* rang out and the hearts of all offered thanks to Mary. Inspired by this feeling, two days later Bro Luigi, now known as Fr Luigi, wanted to add to the prayer 'Blessed be the Holy and Immaculate Conception of the Most Holy Virgin Mother of God', the words 'and our Mother'.

THE CHARACTER

If there was disagreement as to whether Monti was the founder or not when he was alive, even after his death, and after the whole of his congregation had exalted him as builder and legislator, there were still those who, in good faith, disputed that title. That struggle which accompanied him through the wards of the Santo Spirito, from time to time also flowered on his tomb.

Monti's personality, as well as the various characters and events surrounding the foundation of the congregation, was part of the problem. He was an imitator of Christ, a sign of contradiction. He wanted to stand firm at a time when everything around him seemed to be in a state of flux.

All his life Luigi Monti felt the effects of his origins as a craftsman who came from a background of poverty. His per-

THE FOUNDATION AND THE FOUNDER

sonality was a mixture of uprightness, honesty and simplicity which was not open to duplicity, half measures and compromise. Turriccia described him to the Sacred Congregation as a clod. To the sophisticated he was a scandal. His personality was not easily tolerated in certain settings where, politeness, feeble smiles and clerical bowing abounded, where one's thoughts were expressed almost in a ceremonial format and any wounds were bound up by the bandage of formality.

Monti simply was not able, apart from when he was joking, to become 'Roman' in the bureaucratic sense that so many of the people he had to deal with had become. The cunning and the hypocritical did not find in him a soft mattress, but a hard wall, against which they broke their necks trying to make a breach. This was his tragedy, the result of his resistance against the ambitions and conspiracies of men who mixed the sacred and the profane in the pursuit of self-interest. Monti could not play their game and so, every year and after every experiment, they realised that there was no hope. Monti was a solid rock, with four direct and certain ideas fixed in his head, like four logs of oak. They tried every way to get rid of him, to expel him. His logical simplicity always reduced the discussion to the most radical basis: them or me, intrigue or sanctity. If he won, it meant an end to all the nepotism, the submissive exploitation, the narrow-minded arrogance and the sumptuous surroundings. If Monti's rule was to be implemented, then a proper religious life would have to be led.

Monti simply could not become used to these ways or even pretend to, not even for the sake of appearance. Whenever there were clashes he just bound himself more closely to Our Lady and St Joseph and to his ideal of a lay institute dedicated to the service of the sick and to the education of the young.

In my experience as an author, and having read many biographies of saints, I have scarcely ever come across so much deception and misunderstanding heaped on to the back of one man, and often conceived by very good people. Monti accepted it all with an enduring patience and strength. He was able to discern the thread of God's plan for him in all of this and unravel it from amongst the thorns. He was like the good farmer, who, when mist, hail and drought have destroyed the fruits of his labours, picks up the hoe and starts again.

In the name of Jesus and Mary, Monti, like an exhausted fisherman, cast his his net in one more time after all the failures, and won.

Although he worked for a long time in Rome and had contact with church officials and all kinds of different people, Luigi never adopted the submissive attitudes and the sycophancy to which he was often either witness or victim. He remained hard and durable like the raw material of his trade. This brought enemies from both outside and from within his own congregation, but it also served to preserve the originality and newness of the Institute.

Thus it fell to him to win one of the first of the modern battles between the mentality of the world and that of the religious spirit, which inevitably came to a head during those first attempts to consecrate lay people in a religious apostolate. It was almost like associating the laity with monasticism in surroundings which until then had always been the domain of the laity.

A pious lady, who had taught one of the Concettini, Bro Guglielmetti, wanted a portrait of Fr Monti. Fr Monti hung his head and could not understand why anyone should want his portrait. On the other hand he did not want to disappoint the good lady, so he sent a portrait of St Aloysius. 'Tell the good lady', he said to Bro Stanislaus who was to deliver the picture, 'that for now she should be happy to pray for me. I am sending her a portrait of St Aloysius, because one of me would cause her to lose her devotion. However, please give her my regards and ask her to pray for me to God and to Mary Immaculate, especially as we are about to make our retreat.'

Such a man was he.

12
THE REBIRTH OF THE INSTITUTE IN A CLIMATE OF SECULARISATION

EXPANSION

Monti's aim, one which he always had kept firmly in mind, was the service of the sick. He wanted to offer a much-needed service to the body and to the spirit. A sick person walks along a narrow ridge with death on one side and life on the other and in the moment of suffering can lose both bodily and spiritual strength.

Monti never allowed himself to be distracted from his task. Having conquered his disgust of his own human weakness, he knew the immense value of such an apostolate, all the more worthy for the fact that it was carried out in a hidden way, in the midst of sickness and misunderstanding. This was why he turned down requests to send groups of Friars to provide other services, such as a seminary in Spoleto, and a farming community in Messina, as well as other jobs in Caiazzo and Mesagne.

Nevertheless he took on board all suggestions and harmonised them with the aims of the Institute and its constitution. Everyone who saw the work of the Concettini admired them and hospitals all over Italy wanted them to come to them. Of course there were still plenty of difficulties, some of them insuperable.

The last part of his life was a time for harvesting the fruits and for expansion. Monti now had full authority and a group of faithful followers, but, rather than slowing things down, he opened up new and greater horizons. At the age of fifty-five and with a rich experience behind him, he began to recruit new members.

On 30 September 1879 he wrote to his trusty friend Fr Giglio Albuzzi: 'We must pray to Mamma and to St Joseph and ask them to send us some good young men to help the Institute to grow. If you think my presence would be helpful in finding good young men I could quite easily take a trip to Lombardy.'

Mgr Mariano Rampolla of Tindaro, President of the Foreign Missions, discussed with Monti the possibility of sending a group of Concettini to Syria. The idea of expanding and going to holy or venerated places like Jerusalem and Constantinople filled Monti's soul with joy. It was another opportunity to give glory to God.

Fr John from the Franciscan church of St Francis at Ripa, near the Concettini's novitiate at Piazza Mastai, Rome, had experienced their piety and their zeal and wanted to transfer the Institute to his own country, to La Paz in Peru.[1]

The idea of putting down roots in that faraway land, with all manner of opportunities and riches, fired the zeal of Fr Luigi who, also because of his early missionary aspirations, wanted to set up a community there. In fact, he was ready to go there himself, with nine Friars, to open the first house in Peru. However, an old missionary and an old friend of Monti's, Fr Taglioretti, dampened his enthusiasm. The Pope himself also poured cold water on the idea in an audience given to the Institute on 11 November 1879. He suggested that the superior general should not venture into America until the Institute had become 'more confirmed'.

It was not easy to confirm a religious institute based in a centre of positive secularism and anticlericalism, which is what the Santo Spirito had become.

Luigi Monti, with his simple faith, understood the meaning of the arguments which were everywhere to be found, on the hustings, in the taverns and in the newspapers. Everywhere the truths of the faith and of the Church, which for him were so limpid and obvious, were being denied or deformed. He realised that an external barrier had been erected, one much more serious than that which he had suffered from the inside.

He had been unable to find a place in Rome for a young sculptor recommended by Fr Giglio. Monti wrote to him in melancholy mood: 'Rome is no longer the Rome of the Popes. Now it is the Rome of misery and iniquity. Imprisoned like this, the Holy Father cannot act as he wishes. Thus there can be nothing but squalor and misery. I, who once knew free Rome, the Rome of the Popes! The difference now is like day and night. Artists of Sacred Worship can find nowhere to stay.'

In the provocative speeches made by uneducated people, he noticed an assumption that the religious era and that of the Popes had now been superseded. There was the ridiculous belief that the light of science had conquered the darkness of the Church of Rome. He saw Leo XIII rise up with prophetic strength against that tidal wave of blasphemous mediocrity and against the politics of the new Italian state. Monti watched with great interest the poor, the workers, with whose aspirations he could easily identify. Monti's ideal was of a community service, where faith was at the service of the needy. This also seemed to him to be the best way of bringing back to the Church a society which had gone away from it, and of resurrecting the person of Christ in creatures who were against religion. The courageous carpenter's ideals of community service fitted in very well with the new social ideals of the equally courageous Pontiff. The faith of a religious community at the service of the needy seemed to Monti to be the kind of apostolate most likely to bring back to the Church a society which had abandoned it and to revive the figure of Christ in people who had set themselves against religion. The spiritual and material needs of the age acted as a stimulus to the powerful leader of the Concettini to win souls through good works.

EVENTS AT THE SANTO SPIRITO

The very same hospital, the Santo Spirito, which had been the cradle of Monti's religious family and which was still its main centre, was turning into a hive of anticlericalism, a meeting point for positivist medical men and illiterate priest-haters.

This situation had caused unforeseen difficulties which tried the prudence of the superior and the patience of the Friars.

After 1870 huge numbers of people from Piedmont, Tuscany and Northern Italy as a whole, poured into Rome and the population of the capital increased, in ten years, from 240,000 to 300,000. The 'outsiders' outnumbered actual Romans by 32,000.

There was a burning political tension between the Government and the Vatican which was turning into a brawl in the daily quarrels between the 'usurpers' or 'boors' and the 'blacks' or 'hare-hunters,' as the two factions were commonly known. The influx of migrants from the north, together with the masses of pilgrims and tourists, brought about a huge increase in prices of food and lodgings. Thousands of people who had made a living from the pilgrimages or who had survived through begging, had nothing to eat.

The situation of religious in the hospitals had become precarious. One of the first acts of the regional government had been to secularise the work done by religious orders. This was followed in 1878 by a subversive action of the ecclesiastical board, under which, in Rome alone, 134 religious houses were suppressed. This was an enormous number in a city with 218 religious houses, considering that, as the capital of Catholicism, it was given special treatment. With all the changes, the free masons had gradually taken control of the Santo Spirito and

THE REBIRTH OF THE INSTITUTE

would have liked to have got rid of the chaplains, the nuns and the Concettini. However, the Pope still retained some influence, for although he no longer had any temporal power, he still represented the highest religious authority and was able to help the religious at the Santo Spirito. The statute which regarded Catholicism as the state religion was also still in place. So the struggle began to employ ever more underhand methods. The chaplains were not expelled, but their ministry was obstructed. The Friars Hospitaller were not dismissed, but their life was made increasingly difficult, so that the appreciation of their work by the public and by important public figures such as Prince Paul Borghese, could be undermined without causing any damage.

The weapon most favoured by many doctors and the majority of the staff, who were either free masons or people who were greatly influenced by them, was to burden the Friars with more and more work, at the same time spreading false rumours accusing them of not carrying out their duties correctly. The number of patients grew, but the number of workers decreased and the free masons used it as an excuse to accuse the Friars of laziness and insubordination. In fact, to the great anxiety of their Father, the Concettini were working themselves to the bone, some of them to the point of complete exhaustion 'martyrs of charity', as St Vincent de Paul used to say.

They carried out their work in the midst of threats and mockery from personnel taken on by the anticlerical faction and put in positions of authority. The Friars were already working in the Lancisi and Baglivi wards, each with a hundred beds, in the new Braccio ward with 197 beds as well as in the clinic and other departments where the pace was frenetic. When necessary they also helped the sisters. At a certain point they were ordered to help out in the San Carlo and Santa Maria wards, under a lay superviser whom Monti bluntly described as being 'just like a copper'. In fact, he was an ex-policeman, rough and ready, and who knew absolutely nothing about hospital work.

But he knew which way the wind was blowing and he was making a career for himself maltreating the Friars and accusing them of being incapable of work and of indiscipline

On 13 June 1882, Monti was still complaining about the situation to Prince Borghese, the hospital's representative, and to Dr Francis Scalzi, an inspector. He told them about the way in which the Friars were being ill-treated, how they were being asked to do more and more work and how their wages were also being reduced. The number of nurses per ward had been reduced from three to two, in order save money. In fact the Friars had to do the work of four people, as they had to do the job of the porters and of the phlebotomists.

'Slaves in prison', Monti remarked with his usual frankness, 'are not oppressed as much as these Concettini Friars, who are serving the poor sick people.'

Borghese, who was becoming convinced that, in that web of intrigue, the position of the Concettini was no longer tenable, took the bull by the horns and issued an ultimatum: 'Either do as you are ordered, or get out!'

'This is tyranny', retorted Monti, 'not the service of the sick.'

That word 'tyranny' came just at the right moment. Borghese, a liberal who was also a conservative of the *Unione Romana,* was proposing conciliatory ideas, against the wishes of the Pope, and was trying to put the devil and the holy water together. He was continually haranguing the liberals about tyranny, that is, the tyranny of others. Hence, following the logic of a certain type of liberalism of the time, he replied abruptly: 'Anyone who doesn't want to stay can get out.'

Poor Borghese, he had started out with humane and Christian ideas, but he realised that right wing moderate-clericalism was growing weaker and left wing anticlericalism was growing stronger. If he had expelled the religious from the Santo Spirito he would have won the favour of Dr Guido Baccelli and other anti-Papists.

THE REBIRTH OF THE INSTITUTE

Fortunately for the Concettini, Fr Monti had a rock-hard character which resisted the anger unleashed on them and on all religious orders.

They had suffered especially after the death of Pope Pius IX, their protector, benefactor and legislator who had collapsed under the bitterness of the disgrace of the dispossession of temporal power and the anti-Papist fury. To add to all this, on the night of 13 July, when the Pope's coffin was being transferred to its resting place at San Lorenzo, a sectarian gang tried to throw it into the Tiber, right by the Santo Spirito.

The uproar during the night reached the Friars' ears and terrified them. Such an attack on a dead body showed them just how much moral degradation had set in.

The following year the number of Concettini who died of exhaustion rose again, and all of them were between twenty and thirty-eight years old: 'God and St Joseph have to free us!' cried their father whose only trust was in the Lord. The difficulties on the wards were exacerbated by poor conditions in the living quarters, where the dormitories were freezing cold in the winter and intolerably hot in the summer. The chapel was tiny and foul-smelling and all the time they were trying to live a religious discipline and wear a religious habit in an atmosphere that was saturated with anti-Catholicism.

To save his sons, Fr Monti would have withdrawn them from the Santo Spirito. But where was he going to find them somewhere to live and a source of income?

A young Prussian, Boniface Junker, who had joined the order in 1881 at the age of twenty-five, was at the point of exhaustion. But he had absorbed the ideal of charity to the point of giving his life. Through his constant union with God he was drawn into ecstatic contemplation. One day, when a patient in a fit of madness was heading for one of the Friars with a knife, he intervened saying: 'Go ahead, kill me, so that I can suffer everything for the love of God!' This was how his superior had taught him. On hearing these words and in front of such charity and such innocence, the patient fell down and threw the knife away. And Junker was not the only one. Only an exceptional spirit of self-sacrifice could explain how he and many other young men could survive under these harsh conditions and in such a hostile environment.

In 1884 a serious cholera epidemic broke out and all the Friars responded to Monti's proposal to offer help. The enthusiasm and courage with which they offered themselves reflected the formation given them by their superior general. Some of their comments indicate their attitude: 'If you are happy that I go and assist the cholera sufferers I am ready, and I give my life for God and the Most Holy Mary.' 'If you, my good father, command me, I am always prepared for whatever you want.' 'I pray to the blessed God and to the Most Holy Virgin for their help and to accept the sacrifice of my life which I offer from this day with all my heart. And you father superior, bless me and do not in the least take my life into consideration.'

When Pope Leo XIII opened St Martha's palace, in the Vatican, to those suffering from cholera and equipped the building as a hospital, Fr Monti offered twelve Friars to look after the sick day and night, ready to give their lives. Later on, when there was an epidemic of smallpox, the same service was offered.

That year at the Santo Spirito, Monti managed to obtain a new place to use as a chapel. The primitive chapel, as already mentioned, was a covered passageway linking the mortuary and the operating theatres. There was always a stench there and, because of the lack of ventilation, in the summer it became a burning pit infested with aggressive insects. Only with great difficulty could the Friars pray or meditate. Fr Monti managed to obtain a larger, better ventilated place and, after a good deal of hard work, he transformed it into a chapel which was opened on 29 July 1884.

St John Bosco.
A portait of this true man of God, a face marked with suffering. He was a prophet of the Church in the nineteenth century, bringing a new vision and new methods of evangelisation to the world of youth.

Pius IX invited him to become involved in the life of the young congregation. He was charged with 'sorting things out'. Don Bosco's idea was to merge the two congregations. There was much admiration for him as a person amongst the Friars, but much opposition to his plan. In the end it was not put into effect because of the action of members of the Roman Curia.

In June 1877, four months after his election as superior general, Luigi Monti had two meetings with Don Bosco in Rome. Monti reiterated the need, felt by all religious, for the independence of their own congregation.

He was grateful for the concession made to him, but he was not fooled by it.

Whatever way you looked at it, his career in the Church militant was a *via crucis*, the intensity of which was only broken by moments of prayer.

THE HOSPITAL AT NEPI

The difference made when Monti became superior of the order and reformed, or re-created it, can be seen in the number of requests for the Concettini to work in hospitals. After the reform, even though there was such vehement anticlericalism, many more local hospitals wanted the Friars to run them. The majority of these requests came from the Lazio region, where the Concettini were best known.

In the spring of 1881 Fr Luigi drew up a contract with Giuseppe Maria Costantini, the Bishop of Nepi, a diocese in Lazio, by which the Concettini would come to work in the hospital there. In agreement with the governing body of the hospital, the contract made provision for three Friars to be employed at the hospital at Nepi on a combined salary of 100 lire per month. This was less than the minimum salary of 50 lire per person.

They started work on 5 May, the feast day of the patron saint of Nepi, Pius V. Monti appointed as prior Bro Gregory Coriddi, who had earlier stirred up a lot of trouble in the community. His appointment was an act of forgiveness and rehabilitation, typical of the generous spirit of the founder.

The little hospital at Nepi flourished under the enthusiastic action of the Concettini. The mayor wanted to expel the Friars from the hospital in order to spite the bishop, with whom he was in conflict, as was the norm in the political atmosphere of the time. But just at that moment, when he was about to rejoice at his victory over the bishop, he was brought into hospital himself suffering from apoplexy. Fr Luigi's nurses saved his life, and from that moment he became their greatest supporter.

For his part, the bishop, happy with the religious and moral success of the work of the Friars, wrote of them: 'Truly these religious have given incessantly such examples of the observance of the laws of the institute of sanctity, of devotion to God, but above all of Christian charity, of selflessness and relief of the sick as well as procuring their salvation, that they are the sweet smell of Christ. They have made their institute not only totally acceptable to us, but also to our people and to the civic authorities themselves. So, he concluded, 'we are convinced that this institute was an inspiration of the merciful God in these miserable times and that the Church will gather sweet fruits from it, especially in cities and in less important places, and, to their advantage, and so because of the sad reduction in the number of priests, may God grant this religious institute prosperity and growth.'

From Nepi the bishop did everything to persuade the Friars to come to Capranica di Sutri where, in fact, after various difficulties, Monti managed to install them on 10 August 1885.

He would also have been very happy to install a group at Ronciglione, another town nestling in the woods, in Bishop Costatini's diocese, but there was a problem. The governing body of the hospital wanted to include in the contract certain clauses which went against the laws of the institute.

In the meantime those Concettini who were settled in the small towns up in the hills were becoming renowned for their service given for love, and not for money, and it generated a great good among the people.

CARING FOR ORPHANS

In carrying out his reform of the institute, Fr Luigi proposed that his sons should start another activity, that is, the care of orphans. Monti, like the other socially inspired apostles of the nineteenth century, such as Don Bosco, Don Cusmano, Don Fusco and many

THE REBIRTH OF THE INSTITUTE

others, recognised the urgent need to gather in the many homeless children off the streets. The problem had been caused, on the one hand by the concentration of workers in the cities, and, on the other hand by the aftermath of the wars.

If these orphans were brought together they could become the cornerstones of a new society and of the Church. If they were left on the streets they could easily become involved with revolutionaries, or with dishonest and unhappy people who hated the Church and its religion just as much as they hated society as a whole. The enormous rebellion against the faith broke out in the streets, from the lowest levels of society, and mingled with this revolution was materialism and class hatred. If, however, these children could be looked after in houses where the law of God was the norm, they would grow up for the Church, consecrating themselves to the service of God, offering the vocations which the Church needed.

Monti's initiative in 1880, was neither understood nor endorsed by everyone, which was another proof of the originality of his actions. His way was to open up new roads and innovations with his own strength and through his own inspirations.

So Monti put aside his idea until the time was right, exercising that virtue which allowed him to hope against hope and to know how to wait for the right moment. One day in 1882, that moment arrived, as several of the Friars gave witness:

'The superior had tried on previous occasions to extend the institute's charity to include abandoned adolescents, the most difficult of all the orphans. Anyway, one day a Carthusian, who did not know who Fr Luigi was, called to see him. He explained why he had come: 'I am from Desio and a few days ago my widowed brother died leaving four children, the oldest of whom is eleven years old. Nobody wants to know about them, which is a great suffering for me, as I, being a monk, cannot look after them. I made a Novena to Our Lady and to Pius IX asking them to look after these poor orphans and when I had finished I heard this inspiration: 'Go to the Santo Spirito, to the superior of the Concettini, and he will look after them and save them.' 'This is my idea as well', replied Monti, 'to work for the well-being of orphans, but at the moment I cannot do it because I haven't got a suitable house for them.'

The monk answered: 'I know nothing. Our Lady and Pius IX told me to come to you and that you would sort it out. So you will have to save my nephews.'

Those words convinced Monti of the genuineness of the monk and, although he had nowhere to put them, he offered to take the eldest child immediately, saying that he would accept the others if his Friars were in agreement. In fact, on 19 April 1882, the first orphan, John Santambrogio, came to live at Piazza Mastai.

In August of the same year, he was joined by another brother, and Fr Luigi took the two of them personally under his wing. He became both father and mother to them. To begin with he kept them out of sight, until gradually the community grew used to the idea. New things were always regarded with suspicion and this was no different. One reason for the Friars' reluctance was the simple fact that it cost a lot to keep the boys, which meant making sacrifices in other directions. But Monti, with his great charity, slowly dissolved the objections and helped the Friars to accept new sacrifices, preparing them to equip another house, with its own staff, to accommodate the orphans in a modern environment. He chose Bro Rocco Battisti for this task and sent him off to study bookbinding so that he could teach the boys a trade. Just like St Vincent de Paul and St John Bosco, he realised the importance of work for the formation of a family as well as for the moral education of the worker himself. Monti saw work as a means of reaching moral perfection, as the great Leo XIII was about to propound in his encyclical of 1891, *Rerum Novarum*.

Then he sent Bro Dionysius Mandelli to do the same, at the college in Staderini. Dionysius went there dressed as a lay person, so that he could study in peace, free from the derision with

THE REBIRTH OF THE INSTITUTE

which those wearing the religious habit were treated in those times. It was quite commonplace in the streets of Rome and of Lazio of that period for priests and monks to be whistled at, or have stones or rotten fruit thrown at them. In fact, when they discovered that Mandelli was a Friar, he could no longer attend the college. Monti himself took him away and sent him to Saronno to start up a bookbindery.

Just three years later, on 8 December 1885, in honour and at the service of the Immaculate Conception, the first orphan was clothed in the habit of the Concettini. He changed his name from John to Evangelist, as a sign of his progression in the religious life. Two years later his brother did the same and in the meantime their two younger brothers had been taken in by Fr Monti.

Orphans of the poor were taken without any payment until they were twenty years old, although benefactors were sought to help defray the expenses, especially in the early years. Those who were better off had to pay the very reasonable rate of 15 lire per month, plus a one-off payment of 50 lire to fit them out.

The orphans either learned a trade or studied and in either case they were given adequate preparation to become good citizens. However, it happened quite often that they decided to dedicate themselves to the apostolate of the Friars Hospitaller, either as religious or as associates, in which case they spent the rest of their lives in the institute. They followed the rule and were treated just like all the others. Of course Monti hoped that most of them would stay in his family, for he felt that they were his children all their lives.

Thus the orphanage was, as he had wished, 'the seminary where the number of religious can grow and be fed.'

Note

1. La Paz, now the capital of Bolivia, was then part of Peru, but later became independent.

13

THE HOUSE AT SARONNO

A VISCOUNT'S RESIDENCE

It was not until 1885 that the Superior General of the Concettini was able to introduce the changes to the habit which had already been decided on in 1880. A couple of years previously he had been able to replace sandals with shoes, which saved the Friars from scalding their feet when carrying hot drinks to the patients.

Now it was time to do away with the habit which was actually that of mendicant friars. So, the white sash of Our Lady replaced the rope of St Francis to draw the blue cassock in at the waist. Having to clothe around seventy Friars was a considerable expense, but they were able to do it because of some savings which they had withdrawn in 1884 and with a gift of 1,000 lire from their cardinal protector.

On the feast of the Annunciation all the priors from Rome came together and were clothed in the new habit at a thanksgiving service. That day, which was a great celebration, the definitive character of the institute could be seen.

The year 1886 was marked by a gift that was to become more and more precious. It was a statue of Our Lady of Lourdes in a silvered metal, presented to Monti by a young cleric, Anthony Anastasius Rossi, who was to become the Archbishop of Udine and Patriarch of Constantinople. Fr Luigi kept it on his bedside table and every evening he knelt before it to say three Hail Marys and the *Sub tuum praesidium* to ask a blessing on his sons in the institute.

That year, out of love for his homeland and because of the rich harvest of vocations he continued to gather there, Monti thought about setting up a centre of the Sons of the Immaculate Conception in Lombardy. So, armed with unceasing prayers to the heavenly Mother and to her Spouse, and with the encouragement of the cardinal protector, he set off for Milan on 19 May. There he met his friend Fr Albuzzi, chaplain at the military hospital. From Milan he went to Saronno where he thought of building the house.

Saronno was near Milan and on fertile land next to the shrine of Our Lady of Miracles. There too another priest friend, Fr Joseph Alberti, who had spent some time as a guest at Piazza Mastai in Rome, carried out an active ministry. Fr Alberti and his colleague Fr Joseph Borella took the project to heart and recommended a house. For Monti, the fact that both priests were called Joseph was a guarantee of their trustworthiness. The house was a rather imposing building which belonged to the Visconti family. It was a sumptuous building of very handsome architecture. There were forty or so rooms, a vineyard, a large courtyard and a small wooded area which could offer guests healthy air and relaxation. They could not have found anywhere which more suited the plans of the founder. 'It is like a cloister', Monti wrote to his Friars and he wanted to take it straight away. But how would they find the money? In his opinion it was worth at least 50,000 lire, and he had scarcely 10,000. It was up to the heavenly patrons to find the difference.

In fact, the owners, two elderly ladies from Milan, wanted precisely 50,000 lire. Monti approached all the priests with whom he was friendly and whom he most respected, from Fr Taglioretti at Rho to Fr Origo at Monza, from Fr Grassi, parish priest at Cascina Amata to Fr Dionysius at Cremnago. He asked them for help, advice and letters of recommendation. He ran from one end of Lombardy to the other and picked up a bad infection in his left leg in the process.

When Monti's counsellor-general in Rome heard about this he became alarmed and suggested they should give up the idea of collecting such a huge sum, as it was more than the institute could handle, even if they were able to obtain an interest-free loan. He suggested making do with rented accommodation. There was clearly quite a gap between the founder's ambitious project and the modest vision of his Friars.

In the meantime, Monti had approached another priest whom he had also met at Piazza Mastai. He was another Joseph, Fr Joseph Rossi, a generous soul who, when he heard that the Concettini were looking for a house, offered them immediately 20,000 lire, which had been made available for 'good works'. Monti could hardly believe it, in fact he was afraid he might not have understood correctly. But it was indeed 20,000 lire, and it was a gift, not a loan. Our Lady and St Joseph had worked the miracle that he had been praying for ceaselessly. Fr Luigi gave the news to Rome right away, and told them to start a triduum of thanksgiving.

Monti explained the miracle to his Friars, pointing out the fact that Providence had made use of four Josephs. 'If we now have a house at Saronno, it is through the great Patriarch. In order to show us that he, and not others, had obtained this great favour from God, the only people he would have help him were those who shared his name. It was a Joseph who put me up when I first came to Saronno; a Joseph who found the house and acted as mediator; a Joseph suggested where I might find help; and finally it was a Joseph who made the whole thing come to fruition.'

His Council in Rome did not share his enthusiasm. They were afraid of accepting the 20,000 lire and of agreeing to take on a loan to make up the difference. They were also afraid that people would accuse them of being spendthrift and materialistic and they recalled certain accusations of liberality made against the superior. The counsellors were governed more by human prudence and an excess of human respect than any higher motives. This incomprehension on the part of the Council was a source of great suffering to Monti, but it also showed that the idea was his, wanted by him and envisaged by him. The others would have remained frozen by fear into immobility.

On 2 June he replied:

'Beloved Brothers in Christ,

'I have received your latest reply and I regret that you have not understood the meaning of my letter. However, it matters little. God is with me, and with his help all is well. Besides, Our Immaculate Mother asked her spouse, our Father, St Joseph, to procure the foundation of a house for us in Lombardy. To that end he gave me four priests named Joseph, all of whom are involved in helping set up this house. Do you want any clearer evidence that it is God who is at work? Not only is the 20,000 lire interest-free, it is gift sent by our Mother through the hands of St Joseph. It was a tremendous joy to receive the 14,000 lire interest-free from the Pope. Should we not now thank Mary and St Joseph? This is why I told you to make a triduum of thanksgiving.'

In the meantime, once again due to the intervention of Fr Borella, Monti had been able to get the price reduced from 50,000 to 45,000 and then to 44,000 lire with permission to pay in instalments.

FIRST FRUITS

When the first Concettini saw the house, they were astounded: 'It's a palace!' wrote Bro Jerome Pezzini from Milan, where he had gone with Monti and Fr Borella to sign the contract. And when Monti returned to Rome, he received words of praise from the Pope himself.

In fact it had been a far-sighted and courageous act, which

gave a new impulse, a new opening almost, to the congregation. In September, five Concettini, including Monti, blessed the house and took possession of it. It was to become much-loved by everyone in the congregation, because it belonged to them, because it offered the possibility of peace and quiet for all, because of its delightful residents and because it was the fruit of the benevolence of great souls.

As well as being a place for the Friars to rest, the house was also used as a surgery for local people who had toothache and other minor ailments.

Right from the beginning Fr Monti also set to work in this section. He threw himself into it and soon they were giving him too much to do. As he wrote in a letter to Bro Jerome: 'I hope Bro Ludovic is coming soon, so that I can let him get on with extracting teeth. Already all the towns around here have heard about us, and every day I am pulling teeth. Thank God, so far everything has gone well... The people have a great respect for us and are happy that we have come to Saronno.'

The clergy too were happy because Monti brought reconciliation between them after the various quarrels and disagreements which resulted from the political events of 1860-70 and from petty rivalry.

The house was modified as the tenants gradually moved out. The vineyard blossomed, thanks to Monti's expert hand, and he cultivated thousands of vines for the production of dessert grapes. The woods had tree-lined pathways, seats and a small circular patio with a statue of the Madonna and Child and a cage containing turtle doves and canaries.

The debt on the house was paid off on 28 May 1887 and the rapid repayment was like the removal of a thorn from Fr Monti, for which he had continuously entreated St Joseph.

One of the first and most precious fruits of the new house at Saronno was the vocation of Charles Pastori, the future Fr Stanislaus, who was to become Monti's successor as rector of the institute. He was clothed in the blue habit in Rome, at the Santo Spirito, before even reaching his fourteenth birthday, but Monti already had an intuition of Pastori's exceptional talents. Writing about him to Bro Ludovic on 27 February 1887, from Rome, he said: 'If you are speaking to Charles Pastori Senior tell him that his nephew is doing well, growing big and strong, and exploding with happiness!!! He bears the name of Stanislaus of the Immaculate worthily.'

He added a comment about the house: 'I hope that you will observe the month of our father St Joseph with the greatest fervour and that you remember frequently to open his treasure chest in May and complete the job started at Saronno!!! I strongly believe that he will not want to look foolish.'

That year Cardinal Innocenzo Ferrieri died in Rome, cared for day and night by the Concettini. As soon as he heard about his illness, Fr Luigi himself arrived, post haste, from Saronno. The cardinal was overjoyed when he awoke one night to find Monti at his bedside. He died peacefully, comforted by the incomparable care of those Friars, who, together with Fr Luigi, accompanied him, praying, all the way to the cemetery.

The life of the community had now become established and Fr Luigi governed it with wisdom and charity.

In July 1888, Monti went to visit his brother Anthony Maria, for the last time, at Monza. Anthony had lived the same ideal of charity as his brother Luigi. With the suppression of the religious orders, he had had to leave the Sons of Mary, with whom he had lived a model life and follow, affectionately and from a distance, his brother's work. He died a holy death, the last but one of a large family. Fr Luigi could have seen it as something very negative, if he had stopped to think about it, like the last remnants of a shipwreck. But he was totally immersed in doing the will of God in the present moment and in serving him in the sick. He was in constant adoration of the Lord's plans, including those for Monti's natural family.

EXPULSION FROM THE SANTO SPIRITO

While the institute flourished in its new centres, things were coming to a head at the Santo Spirito in Rome. Monti realised that this was the finale to which events were leading them. In the logic of the process of secularisation, religious had to be expelled. The masonic lodge insisted on it and the anticlerical press supported it, inventing stories of the Friars' incompetence and insubordination. This method of dismantling pious works and separating them from their origins and often from the funds donated to them by pious Christians down the centuries - and in the case of the Santo Spirito, by Popes - was commonly employed. The various factions did not look after the needs of poor people; on the contrary, they despised them. The feeling of deep gratitude which simple folk felt for benefits received, a feeling which had spread far and wide, frightened the agents of secularisation and they cloaked their actions in hypocrisy.

The main pressure, as already seen, consisted in piling more and more responsibilities and duties on the Friars. And rather than their efforts being rewarded with an increase in pay, they were insulted and affronted, which provoked Monti into saying: 'So, we have to let ourselves be killed to let these Freemasons claim victory?' His working class upbringing urged him to rebel, but his religious asceticism led him to place things into the hands of the real arbiters - God, Mary and Joseph.

Things grew worse by the month until, in May 1885, the Friars were expected to do the work of 43 men when there were only 17 of them. This was the height of exploitation, the fruit of a certain kind of capitalist mentality which had grown out of the political and economic liberalism and which had been empowered by the anticlerical factions. Life had become impossible for the Concettini, whose lodgings were inadequate and also a health hazard. But Monti was always conscious that once they were removed from the Santo Spirito, the Concettini would be deprived of their centre and would have great difficulty in finding anywhere else. So he entrusted everything to the heavenly superiors more than ever.

His struggle to defend the Friars against injustice, or 'persecution' on 'that battlefield' as Pius IX had called it, became exhausting. There was a feeling of complete exploitation when the inspector continued to insult them and the doctors, besides increasing the Friars' workload, hurled abuse at them and rebuked them in full view of everyone, reinforcing the already negative opinion of Prince Borghese. And as if that was not enough, the nuns and the chaplains were also encouraged to add to the list of accusations against the Concettini.

The crisis came to a head when, unable to cope any more with the pressure from the masons on one side and the staunch resistance of the Friars on the other, Borghese resigned. The inspector, Scalzi, also had to go. On the advice of the great clinician Guido Baccelli, he was replaced by a doctor, Achille Ballori, who, though a mediocre doctor, was politically acceptable.

He gave proof of his credentials as soon as he set foot in the Santo Spirito, which had been founded by the Popes and which they had kept flourishing for centuries. He shamelessly decreed the abolition of the recitation of the Angelus and the Rosary and forbade the chaplains to visit the sick, under threat of instant dismissal, unless they had been specifically requested by the patient. He also mounted an epigraph in praise of 'freedom of conscience', which was a real eyesore, in the entrance of the hospital. To begin with, to test the water with the Concettini he smiled at them and praised them, but he then went straight to his cronies and assured them that he could not stand the sight of them.

He filled his lungs with the antipapist and anticlerical passion burning in Rome at the time. On 31 December 1887, without any warning, the government removed Duke Leopold Torlonia from the office of mayor, finding him guilty of sending greetings to the Pope on the occasion of his jubilee.

In 1888 the inspector stung the Concettini in various ways in his attempts to persuade them to leave. Then, on 1 January 1889 he transferred them all to work in the huge San Carlo ward, on the second floor, divided into three sections by a double row of fifty-eight columns. He said that he did not like to see men religious working on the wards with the nuns, and be almost dependent on them. So it was that the Concettini were removed from the most popular wards and relegated to one which was less accessible. Up till then the work had been carried out by thirty-five people, Ballori now said that it should be done by only twenty-seven, twenty-one of whom would be Concettini. By so doing he saved money and placed an extra burden on the religious.

As if this was not enough, a few days later he removed five of the six people who were helping the Concettini so that they now had to do the porters' job as well. The Friars were forced to bring in eight of their confrères to help them, though the latter did not receive any payment for their work.

To understand the zeal that existed against a community which was also a reminder of the much-hated Pius IX, we need to look at the anticlerical atmosphere which pervaded Rome. That year, 1889, saw the fall of the council of the Roman Union, whose aldermen had been forced to resign, allowing the Council finally to approve a plan to erect a monument to Giordano Bruno, something which Crispi, the head of government was keen to do. It was also the year when the deficit in the city council's budget reached a record high and the building crisis was exploited to the full by the free masons. Preparations were being made for the new council elections and amongst the list of candidates were names such as Guido Baccelli, Menotti, Garibaldi, Bacarini, Armellini, Caetani...

In June the monument to Giordano Bruno was officially inaugurated at Campo dei Fiori, accompanied by wild celebrations infused with antipapism and marked only by their exceptional vulgarity.

During the building shortage crisis, the governing body of the Santo Spirito thought up the idea of turning the miserable place used by the Concettini as a dormitory into a surgery. So they proposed that the Friars should move to St Galla, which was to become a geriatric institute linked to the Santo Spirito. St Galla was near Piazza Mastai, and the governors of the Santo Spirito thought that the Concettini could sleep at their novitiate house. In this way the governors would also be able to move them out of the Santo Spirito. To justify the proposal, it was suggested that the old building was going to be demolished to make way for the extension of the Tiber embankment on the hospital side.

Monti realised where this proposal was leading, and it was confirmed by the secretary of the Santo Spirito who openly declared: 'Accept it, otherwise you will starve: the director intends to kick you out anyway.' It was one of those situations in which, abandoned by men, Fr Luigi saw only God. 'At all times', he wrote to the Friars in a circular letter, 'prayer is necessary, but especially in times of tribulation. Sometimes God tests the fidelity of his servants to the limit, but he never abandons them. On the contrary, he himself invites us to run to him in times of affliction with those sweet words: 'Come to me all you who are oppressed and overburdened and I will give you rest.' So let us pray, let us pray fervently, making our need for prayer for our institute felt more than ever. Yes, beloved sons and Friars, we are in the period of tribulation, in the time of trial. But let us humble ourselves and, subjecting ourselves totally to the will of our heavenly Father, let us take everything from his hands, certain that whoever hopes in the Lord will not remain in confusion.'

The circular went on to invite the Friars to celebrate the feast of Our Lady's birthday on 8 September with special fervour. It was a special day because on that day thirty-two years previously 'the first foundations of the new institute' had been launched. And he recalled the many deceased Friars who had 'fallen' in those thirty-two years, in the prime of their manhood, at the service of the sick.

Now they were undergoing a very hard trial, but no one ought to give 'space to any kind of fear, because the work is God's and Mary's.' 'Not even St Joseph', Monti wrote to Fr Joseph Rossi, 'will want to look a fool. On the contrary, it will be a chance for him to show his generosity and fatherly affection.'

Having thus prepared the Friars, he went to see the cardinal protector and told him everything. And, as Monti wrote in a letter to his secretary: 'He [the cardinal] understood immediately the scoundrel's move, and said that it was to be expected, and that if today it is us, tomorrow it will be the turn of the Capuchins and the nuns. I replied to him saying that if they provide us with forty beds for the Friars, with a surgery, medicines, food and sufficient paid staff, like at the Santo Spirito, we can make it. Otherwise we cannot move from where we are, having been born at the Santo Spirito. In such a way we can carry out our duty and no one can complain about us.'

The cardinal protector was in full agreement with Fr Luigi, who added: 'Otherwise we shall say: "we don't want to find ourselves out on the street, so we are not moving from here, unless we are forced out, because reason is useless against brute force." Then we will protest about being moved from the place where we were born. Forced out, yes, but don't let them say that we abandoned our house.'

Clearly, the Cardinal had no illusions. All he needed do was glance at the headlines in *Messagero, Tribuna, Popolo Romano* and other papers such as the satirical *Don Chisciotte* and Crispi's *Riforma* or *Capitale* to know what was going on. Therefore he told Monti that realistically a religious order motivated by charity could no longer live in hospitals where 'the philanthropic hypocrisy under which poor humanity languishes' has taken hold.

He suggested setting up a private nursing home, 'so badly needed in these times', at Rome as at Saronno.

Regarding St Galla, rather than turning to the Holy Father for places to sleep and thereby play into the hands of the masons, the

Cardinal seemed to think it best to let themselves be evicted ('they will kick you out anyway sooner or later' he said). This would also reveal in its true colours the administration to the people.

The Cardinal had hit the nail right on the head. The confrontation took place on 9 September and brought the middle-class MP and the humble carpenter, the opponent of all forms of hypocrisy, face to face with one another.

Monti recounts the meeting, which took place in 'the MP's Herodian room' in his own rough style, in his diary.

'We need to reduce the staff', began the MP, but Monti interrupted him saying, 'Before talking about these things, I am telling you that we do not have a house for the religious community, and you ought to think about how you are going to provide accommodation for us.'

The MP replied: 'It's a waste of time discussing it.'

'Then we'll stay where we are', replied Monti.

'Oh no, by the end of September you will no longer be at the Santo Spirito.'

'So you are kicking us out! What have we done wrong?'

'Nothing, but we need the space.'

'As soon as we have found somewhere to live we will leave.'

'You must be out by October, otherwise I will bring the law in.'

'Do as you please. This is the reward for thirty-two years of sacrifice, with so many Friars victims in the prime of life and grave damage to our administration. This is how are rewarded. Not even thieves are treated like this. Where can I find somewhere to accommodate a family of forty at the drop of a hat?'

Just imagine! Ballori belonged to a conservative political coalition that had a bee in its bonnet about suppressing the revolutionary ideas of the working classes who had already started to go on strike, cocking a snook at the noble and academic titles of their bosses.

Thus he insisted that Monti should vacate the Santo Spirito

by the end of the month, although in fact he made a concession allowing them to sleep there for the whole of October.

At the same time Ballori notified the commander of the Santo Spirito that, because of their insubordination and indolence, the Concettini were deserting the hospital and refusing to move to St Galla. When the news became public knowledge, shouts of joy and showers of insults appeared in the secular press, which praised Ballori for his 'exceptional energy' and raised him to the status of a celebrity.

And this was the recompense for all the sacrifices suffered over thirty-two years, with more than fifty Friars having died in the completion of their duty, martyrs of charity. But these were the requirements of the Lodge!

On the evening of the 30 September the Concettini performed their last duties to the sick, made the beds, swept the wards and then silently handed them over to the new nurses. Then they knelt down, all thirty-seven of them, and recited the *Agimus tibi gratias* with three Hail Marys, as usual, before the altar in the ward. Finally they processed two by two, in silence to the chapel.

There Fr Monti invited them to consider everything that had taken place as by the permission of God and to sing the *Magnificat*.

'I remember the good father', Stanislaus Pastori was to recount later, 'kneeling at the entrance and, weeping, he kissed the ground. "Here Brothers," he said, "I met Pezzini when I came to Rome in 1858."'

They slept where and how they were able and they ate even more frugally than normally.

On 31 October the expulsion was complete.

THE GROWTH OF THE EDUCATIONAL WORK

Even though the house at Saronno had its problems, particularly economic ones, still Monti thought of opening orphanages in other places, starting with Rome. He very much wanted to have a brood of children there, growing like lilies in Mary's honour. The house he had in mind was St Joseph's, near Porta Cavalleggeri, but nothing came of it, in part for economic reasons and in part because no one in Rome really understood the project.

The following year he was offered an old dilapidated convent at Tursi in Basilicata. The local bishop explained to him that the building was crumbling, and would need completely rebuilding. There was also an abandoned church, full of corpses, which was difficult to enter and with which there were various administrative complications. Therefore the bishop asked Monti to send a trustworthy person. Monti wanted to go himself, but first he wrote to the bishop asking him not to welcome him with flowers and hymns, as the bishop had planned, but as an unknown pilgrim. And, as many rumours abounded with all sorts of suggestions for starting the orphanage, Monti added, 'I have no intention of opening the orphanage to make money, but to give a Christian upbringing to poor abandoned young people.'

So, in October he went to inspect the premises, having first informed Fr Giglio, whose idea it was in the first place. It is worth reading this letter, as it reveals something of Monti's inner life, made up as it was of simplicity and realism:

'Next Sunday, at midnight, I am leaving for Tursi with my procurator. The bishop wanted you to come with me, but I think it is impossible. I would have been delighted if it had been possible.

The bishop wanted to know the date of my arrival so that he could organise a crowd to welcome me with olive branches, shouting: 'Long live the Sons of the Immaculate Conception. But I am keeping the day of my arrival secret so as not to receive the *Hosannas* so that there will be no 'crucify him'!!! In fact, he wrote to me recently (even though I had written to him telling him that from the general down to the last Friar, we are laymen). He said that when I arrive in the town I should go to the bishop's residence and that I would have his permission to preach all over the diocese, to hear confessions and to absolve all the special cases. It seems to me like over-exaltation, but let's hope it's all in good faith and that the Lord and Mary turn it to the good. Our cardinal is encouraging me to go and have a look.

'So, full of trust that Our Immaculate Mother wants to pitch her tents there, we are setting off on our journey, otherwise we would return home regretting having spent the money.

'Anyway, pray, united to us, in the hope that prayer will work miracles.'

Fr Monti was welcomed to Tursi with deference by the authorities, and with enthusiasm by the people. However, after a brief visit he realised that it was impossible to build an orphanage in a dilapidated convent, in the middle of nowhere.

The following year, 1892, when Bartolo Longo took in the first Calabrian child at Pompei - the first of the prisoners' children - Monti was struck down with pneumonia. This was the result of his exertions at the service of his neighbour. The illness worried his Friars and Cardinal Parocchi went to visit him. But as soon as he recovered, Monti went back to his work, still eager to expand the institute. He tried to open an orphanage at Viterbo in 1894 and he entered into discussions with the local bishop, through the cardinal protector. The bishop, however, had in mind another task, that of helping at a teacher training college. As the cardinal had presented them as 'obedient, simple, exemplary Friars' who did 'good for the love of God, without a trace of vanity', they did not seem to fit into the bishop's plans.

This happened towards the end of the year.

Later on, between the end of 1895 and the beginning of 1896, Bro Stanislaus Guglielmetti, through Fr Pompeo Rusconi, managed to interest a rich and pious lady from Cantù in the setting up of an orphanage. Cantù was an industrial town on the outskirts of Brianza, where there was an urgent need for such an institute. Mrs Isabella Pogliani, a widow, gave to Monti, through Bro Stanislaus who was at Cantù, a fine house, called

'Casinazza'. It stood on a piece of land surrounded by a wood. Mrs Pogliani also donated an annual grant of 2,500 lire to maintain the Friars and the first orphans. On 5 June, Fr Monti himself went to Cantù to sign the contract. When Monti told the Archbishop of Milan, Cardinal Andrea Ferrari, about the orphanage, the cardinal was very pleased. He had already seen and expressed his appreciation of the orphanage at Saronno and now wanted to visit the one at Cantù. He said: 'I would be delighted if this fine institute could spread throughout my diocese.'

Mrs Pogliani remained a generous patron and a real mother to the institute. Before Casinazza was ready to welcome its new inhabitants, she opened her own home to the Friars who had come with Bro Stanislaus to prepare things.

Fr Luigi returned with his novices to visit the orphanage which was already open on one of those dates which he chose as a reminder of Eternal Glory. It was 21 June 1898, the feast of his own patron saint, and Monti's presence there gave weight to the solemn inauguration of the new institute, which was crowned by the arrival of the authorities and the lay folk and recollected in a solemn religious procession of thanksgiving.

In a moving farewell, Monti kissed the intelligent and untiring Bro Stanislaus, and gave him a blessing, for it was he who had been the prime mover in setting up the new orphanage.

'The Lord', Monti wrote in his report to the cardinal protector, 'has shown us once again, that he is the one who guides, governs and provides for the needs of our institute.'

That year they were also able to open a novitiate at Saronno, which meant that not all the young men had to be in Rome. Monti appointed Bro Stanislaus Pastori as head of the new novitiate and his work in the formation of the Friars immediately gave great encouragement to the founder.

14

THE STRUGGLE FOR PRIESTHOOD IN THE CONGREGATION

FR ANGELINI'S DISSENT

At the general chapter of 1883 Monti communicated his plan to introduce various innovations at the end of the institute's five-year trial period. One of these was the formation of its own priests. A formal request was made to Cardinal Innocenzo Ferrieri on 8 September, once more on the occasion of a Marian feast

'After many years of experience', Monti wrote, 'we have come to the conclusion that the lack of the priesthood in the institute of the Friars Hospitaller, the Concettini, has become such an obstacle to their work and to their spiritual and material development, that without it they will never increase and spread.

'First of all they cannot carry out their work properly, because of the shortage of priests, especially in provincial hospitals where often there is no appointed chaplain and they have no-one they can ask to minister to the patients. They are deprived of the mass, not only on weekdays, but also on Sundays and feast days. It follows that the Blessed Sacrament cannot be reserved in the chapel, and when a sick person requires communion, the Friars have to rush to the nearest parish church, causing curiosity and apprehension amongst the local people.

'But that is still nothing. It often happens that nurses go outside the hospital because of their desire to receive the holy sacraments (encouraged by their brothers) after going a long time without. They go out and still are unable to receive them. But the saddest thing of all is to see patients dying without the sacraments. This happens because the priest in charge is not in and the others, it not being their job, refuse to administer them. Sometime, at night, the Friars have to go out into the town to wake the priest In the meantime the poor soul has died. All this could be avoided by having a Friar/priest in the building, who would always be ready for any event. So, as well as restoring bodily health, he could also restore the spiritual health of the patient and there would be the consolation of seeing him pass away healed in body and soul. In this way the institute would be fulfilling its vocation.

'So the lack of a priest not only hampers the work of the institute, but also hampers its spiritual and economic development. For, in the provincial houses, the Friars have to go out every day to find a mass in different churches, where the times are often irregular. It often happens that, after doing the rounds of the churches they cannot find a mass and have to return home without having heard one. This means they miss it altogether, because their work does not permit them to go out again. The same applies to Holy Communion for which they have no time either for preparation or for thanksgiving. Living like this, rather than acquiring the religious spirit, they lose it.

'Besides all this, a Friar who was a priest would be able to break the bread of the word of God, not just for the sick, but also for his own brothers, which would strengthen them in the practice of religious virtue and keep alive in the families the true spirit of the institute.

'We mentioned that this lack of priests also hampered the economic development of the institute. In fact, if there was a priest/Friar in the provincial houses, as well as the benefits of a mass in the house, there would also be that of the collections, which although small, would help supplement the meagre income which we receive from those poor hospitals. In the house we have in the country outside Rome, where there is no priest, the poor Friars only hear mass on Sundays and feast days, for which they have to come to Rome. If they wanted to have a chaplain there, what small income they receive from the vineyard would not be sufficient to keep him in a dignified fashion.

'Therefore, having examined all these inconveniences, the first general chapter held at the end of May 1883 recognised the extreme necessity of the priesthood in the institute. So that our successors do not have to disturb the Holy See again, the chapter voted unanimously to make it aware of this necessity in order that at the end of the five-year trial period it would allow us to insert an article on the priesthood.'

In previous meetings between Monti and the cardinal protector, the latter had told him that Monti's idea of only promoting to the priesthood those Friars with at least fifteen years experience of religious life in the hospital was a pipedream. But Monti insisted on his idea and explained his reasons: 'We have arrived at this conclusion', he wrote, 'because the work in the hospital is so exhausting that very few manage to last fourteen years and fewer still twenty. The majority succumb to the stress in the first ten years. Those who manage to go beyond fourteen years are usually worn out through illness and unable to work. This is an added burden on the institute, which has to maintain a greater number of Friars with the same level of income. If, however, these Friars were priests, they could be useful to the institute. Through their good example and with the instruction which they would give to their brothers, and economically through their mass stipends, they would help the different Concettini families. In this way we will have the advantage of good resident priests who will give respectability to the institute.

Monti's reasoning was based on the experience gained over the years. In fact, the Sacred Congregation accepted its validity and asked the bishops in whose dioceses the Concettini were

THE STRUGGLE FOR PRIESTHOOD

working to confirm this view. All the bishops' replies were favourable and based on the positive experience of the good service of the Concettini.

Unfortunately, just as the modified constitution was about to be approved, Cardinal Ferrieri died. The Concettini had lost a trusty, loving and intelligent protector.

His successor was Cardinal Lucido Maria Parocchi, the Pope's vicar for the City of Rome and a man who was universally respected.

Fr Angelini, who was against the new proposal, went to see Parocchi to try and block it. He was convinced, and he said so in a written memo, that the introduction of the priesthood would be harmful to the institute, as it went against its original nature as a wholly lay organisation, as desired by Pius IX, 'who founded and established the institute.' The priesthood would be the cause of 'competition, envy, jealousy' and indiscipline, because a priest would not obey a lay superior.

When he saw that the cardinal did not seem to be moved by such reasoning, the Jesuit, who was highly respected all over Rome and well-known to the Vicariate, threw himself at the cardinal's feet and implored him to block the proposal.

The cardinal was surprised by such behaviour which showed perhaps that Angelini was too attached to his point of view and to his responsibility. In fact, Parocchi confessed that he did not share his concerns; on the contrary, he thought it was a good idea.

But Fr Angelini would not give in. He went straight to Fr Luigi Raimondi, the former secretary of Ferrieri and well thought of by the Sacred Congregation for Bishops and Religious, but he had no more success there either. Next he wrote to Cardinal Masotti, the new Prefect of the Sacred Congregation, and to Bishop Trombetta, the secretary. Over the following few days, Monti noted, 'he turned cardinals and Pope upside down.'

Angelini told everyone how the Brothers of Mercy and the Brothers of Christian Schools, who were much more educated than the Concettini, had never introduced the priesthood into their ranks and were thus flourishing, whilst the Fatebenefratelli were suffering because they had done so.

He made it into a question of vital importance for the Concettini and for the Church and, because he was eloquent and sincere and had a good reputation, he sowed perplexity and opposition.

He turned his attention to Cardinal Masotti again, sending him a memo on 5 June 1887, saying:

'Your singular goodness and wisdom give the courage to ask:

1) that the second rule of the Concettini be confirmed, which says 'they should all be laymen', and that this should exclude the petition asking for the introduction of the priesthood, which, for many reasons is repugnant to the aims of the institute;

2) that the superior general should be elected for a six year term and not for life, as laid down in the first constitution;

3) that the general's council should be decisive and not consultative, as laid down in the first constitution. And to prevent them from introducing new proposals, studies should be excluded, which, under the false guise of pharmacy, tend towards the priesthood;

4) that the superior be warned about the way in which he tried to hide from Cardinal Ferrieri, who was extremely supportive of the institute, his secret intention to introduce the priesthood;

5) that the new general and his council, on taking up office, should swear to remain faithful to the constitution and not to alter it.

'May Your Eminence acquire this great merit with the Church, of which you are such an outstanding part, by saving this fine institute, so dear to the Most Holy and Immaculate Mary, from the total ruin into which it would fall if you were to concede the priesthood to it. Support its cause energetically at the Holy See. Have compassion on the extreme suffering of the writer.

Antonio Angelini d. C.D.G.'

He was actually suffering in the extreme. Still not satisfied, he managed to have his arguments presented to the Pope himself, through Fr John Cornoldi, the director of Civiltà Cattolica. Leo XIII, faced with the opposition of such faithful and intelligent servants, decided not to allow the amendments to the first constitution.

As soon as Monti heard of Fr Angelini's opposition, he defended his proposals as best he could. But, above all, he turned to Our Lady and to St Joseph and waited for a 'miracle'.

There would be a miracle, but not yet. The Sacred Congregation was faithful to the will of the Pope and so the introduction of the priesthood was not granted to the Concettini.

Monti's disappointment did not end here, for Fr Angelini continued to bring pressure on the institute. The Sacred Congregation decreed that the vote of the Concettini's general council was not only consultative, but also decisive, and that the superior general would no longer be in post for life, but for six years. This was a major blow to the person of Luigi Monti.

If there was any comfort for Monti in that bitter moment, it came from the cardinal protector, who had not failed to read the significance of this manoeuvre. Monti wrote him a letter thanking him for his support and concluding: 'The institute of the Most Immaculate Mary is the most recent in the Church, and also the most attacked, oppressed and insulted because of the fear that it might rise above other religious orders. Without a shadow of doubt, it can be said that our only support and comfort at this present time come from Jesus, Mary, Joseph and Your Eminence. I am confident that you will protect us now and always, as our most affectionate father in Christ.'

To Monti, it seemed as if he was passing through one of those old crises, when outsiders tried to take the institute into their domain. Fr Angelini too, certainly with the best of intentions, was doing what the 'Capuchins, Don Bosco, Archbishop Turriccia...' had done with equally good intentions. 'But', he wrote to

Fr Giglio in his own simple style, 'Mary Immaculate is more powerful than the Jesuits.'

THE OPPOSITION GROWS

There was a complete contrast between Monti's ideal of autonomy and the proposals for absorption or for interference from outside. Monti's vision was of an institute immersed in arduous activity amidst all kinds of difficulties, in contact with a rapidly evolving humanity. He felt that they should be able to go ahead with their own human talents and under the guidance of the Holy Spirit and the Church. Others, not understanding this new institute, and thinking along traditional lines, felt, most of them in good faith, that it should be supported from outside and be linked to already existing bodies. He was looking to the future; they were looking at the past.

The clash with the Capuchins, because of the resistance of certain elements in that order, had been quite fierce. With Don Bosco it had been much easier because of the dignity with which he had released his grip. The episode with Turriccia had been more insidious, because of his attachment to the prestige of his position. It was especially painful with Angelini, that saintly man, because he, more than anyone else, had loved and served the Concettini's cause. However, on this point, the spiritual director found himself at odds with the founder and with the Friars, who were almost all behind their superior.

Consequently, the Friars found it increasingly difficult to turn to their spiritual director and he gradually began to feel isolated. He was absolutely convinced that the Concettini should remain in the lay state, without any education, so that they could carry out their humble service to the sick. He complained insistently to the Holy See that they were still studying and that the superior general was still in post, even though the six years were up.[1]

Regarding this complaint, which he sent in writing to the

Sacred Congregation on 20 December 1887, Monti had the reassurance of Archbishop, later Cardinal, De Ruggero, who told him: 'Beware of Fr Angelini, who is out get you and who is putting the whole institute at risk. He to wanted nothing less than to go to the Holy Father and tell him that the institute is going wrong because of the Superior.'

It was always Monti, the Superior, who was a sign of contradiction. At this point it is clear that the proof of his consistency as founder lay right there in that serious and continuous opposition, which hit right at the heart of all that he intended and wanted for the institute of the Conceptionists. He realised that 'that good man,' Fr Angelini would not stop until he had achieved his objective. Monti spoke to the cardinal protector, who suggested that he go and see the cardinal prefect.

Before going to see the cardinal prefect, Monti had a dream in which a terrifying dragon perched on the edge of a ravine, fixed him with its ferocious eyes. He was so frightened that he cried out loud: 'Oh my God, help me!' In one leap the beast was on him, and he, even more terrified, pleaded: 'Jesus, help me!' And the Lord promised to help him.

These strange happenings overshadowed the celebration of Christmas that year.

When, on 28 December, he went before the cardinal prefect, he received a reproof for disobeying the orders of the Holy Church.

Monti, prepared by the dream and tempered by the trials, did not resist. In all humility, he tried to explain his behaviour. He was so logical and convincing that the cardinal believed him once again and admitted the rightness of his aspirations to the priesthood. A few days later, using his full authority and having agreed with the provincial of the Jesuits, Cardinal Parocchi organised a reconciliation meeting between the Concettini and their spiritual director on 20 January at the Santo Spirito. The meeting took place in a spirit of humility on both sides and seemed to be leading back towards the kind of helpful and happy relationship that they had had in the past, especially as Monti and Angelini had explained their thoughts to each other, to their mutual benefit.

Fr Angelini was a deeply religious man and so, having begged forgiveness, he put everything into the Sacred Heart of Jesus. Fr Monti was a simple soul who saw Angelini's change of attitude as Mary's intercession. He immediately ordered a triduum of thanksgiving, ending with the singing of the Te Deum on 2 February, the feast of the purification of Mary.

It must be remembered that by now Angelini was an old man who tended to see danger and ruin wherever things were developing too rapidly. The Friars were already used to referring to other spiritual directors, one of whom was the wise and holy Mgr Maximilian Franzini, which made the good old Jesuit suffer. However, he had the satisfaction of seeing the convocation of the general chapter on 22 November 1888, for the election of a new superior. But the chapter, presided over by Cardinal Parocchi himself, voted almost unanimously for Monti. This exacerbated poor Angelini to such an extent that he called for the chapter to be declared null and void. However, the chapter had been conducted in the presence of the cardinal protector, who blocked Angelini's move.

'The Immaculate Mother', remarked Monti, 'had the power to bring down this fourth power whose aim was not to help the institute, but to make it his own... The power of Mary Immaculate has always defended and liberated her sons from little power seekers.'

For Monti it was yet another demonstration of the presence of the Virgin and another chance to sing her praises.

Fr Angelini could contain himself no longer. In his old age he had lost that clarity of judgement which had made him one of the most highly respected priests in Rome. He wrote an anonymous letter (it seems it was the second one) to the Sacred Congregation and one to the Pope himself in which he once more accused the superior general of the Concettini of wanting to introduce the priesthood in contravention of the constitution.

The Sacred Congregation notified Cardinal Parocchi who, saddened to see that 'Fr Angelini had really gone off the rails', blocked this attempt as well, with an explicit statement delivered by hand to the Sacred Congregation by Monti himself. 'Your Eminence can rest assured that the spirit of these good Friars is excellent and most devoted to the Holy See, whose decrees they study to fulfil its desires. In a relatively short time they have won the greatest respect of clergy and people in this metropolis of Christianity.'

With the failure of his attempts to block the new constitution and through the general coldness of the Concettini towards him, Fr Angelini came back to his senses and decided not to minister to them any more. He simply disappeared from the scene.

He stopped opposing them, however, only when he died. In fact, he died a very holy death on 12 October 1892. We know that, even between saints, there have have been, and there will be differences of opinion on particular issues and we should not be surprised by such disagreements. Monti never ceased to be grateful to his spiritual director for the many graces received, and during Angelini's illness and after his death he prayed and asked others to pray fervently for him.

FRESH ATTEMPTS

Monti returned on 18 March 1893 to present the changes to the constitution, including the priesthood.

When he presented the new text to the Sacred Congregation, it was accompanied by testimonial letters from bishops who, having had first-hand experience of the goodness of the institute, spontaneously gave their support for it to have its own priests. For example, Mgr Angelo Mantegazza, vicar-general of the Archdiocese of Milan, expressed his own satisfaction with the house at Saronno. He also commented 'that, given the number of members of the pious institute and the scarcity of priests, who are too busy looking after the souls of this large town, some members of the institute should be ordained priests, like the Fatebenefratelli. In such a way', he added, 'much better provision could be made both for the congregation and the sick.. There would no longer be any need to go to neighbouring towns to find confession, the local clergy being busy with the care of souls.'

A similar testimony was given by the bishop of Civita Castellana and Orte: 'I vote', he said, 'that the Holy See, in giving final approval to the rule of this institute, for the good of the suffering, permits them to have at least some priests of their own. This would be for the greater benefit of the sick in hospital and would make up for the increasing deficiency of priests in the diocese. They would be able to bring spiritual comfort to the dying, who accept it much more willingly at such a time from a religious who has offered them tender and unstinting bodily charity. Through personal experience I can vouch for the institute and for the even greater good which I am convinced they are capable of achieving.'

Comforted by these and other testimonials, Monti spent the whole of 1893 rewriting the text of the constitution and for the whole of 1894 he waited to gain the support of the various cardinals concerned, from Parocchi to Graniello, as well as other officials more directly involved in the process.

He worked furiously, with his indomitable will, often sacrificing his own physical health. In June, for example, he received the text back with a request to make a few corrections. As it could not be sent back again unless it was completely rewritten, he spent a whole night rewriting it by candlelight. This further damaged his already failing eyesight, to the point that there was a risk of blindness and he had to spend the next three months in darkness.

Top: The shrine of Our Lady of Santo Monte at Varello.
Below: The shrine of St Mary at Oropa.

In Fr Monti's spirituality, frequent pilgrimages to shrines played an important part. For him, they were places for receiving special graces and for strengthening one's faith.
In his youth he went on pilgrimages to Santo Monte at Varese, to the shrine at Rho and to Our Lady of the Woods at Imbersago (Milan).
In Rome he had a special devotion to Our Lady of St Augustine, to whom he confided with great human warmth all the problems of the birth pangs in the eternal city.
He asked Our Lady of Varese for the recovery of his physical strength.
He entrusted to the Brown Madonna of Oropa the final months of his life and the future of the congregation.
Here, two months before his death, he had a foretaste of heaven.

Gradually, Monti's conviction and the transparency of his faith seemed to have overcome doubts and opposition, and during a visit to St Joseph's vineyard, in October 1894, the cardinal-vicar told him: 'By Easter, whether the constitution is approved or not, we will bring two Friars in their third year of theology to Rome, and within a month, two weeks even, I will ordain them.'

However, even though Monti had convinced many eminent people, the difficulties continued. Fr Arcangelo Lolli, the consultant, let the whole of 1895 pass without taking the revised constitution to the Sacred Congregation to be examined. On 17 September of that year, on his return from Lombardy, Monti confronted him. Lolli's excuse was that the strongest resistance was coming from Cardinal Verga.

Monti told him openly that the opposition was coming from opponents of the institute, who maintained that they were afraid that having its own priests would be its ruin. He, on the other hand, as a member and as superior general and after thirty years experience, felt that the institute without the priesthood was like a body without a soul. To counter the fears expressed by the opponents, Monti said that he had inserted special provisions in the constitution to prevent the entry of men who were already priests and who had been ordained outside the Conceptionist atmosphere and spirit. He explained how future priests would be chosen from those who had been exemplary nurses, at least twelve years in religious life and having made their final profession. They would have to follow a proper course of study and would not be ordained before their thirtieth birthday.

He had also devised all sorts of precautions to block any possibility of the priesthood becoming part of a career structure to be exploited by ambitious men who might cause dissent and internal conflict with the lay Friars.

'Fr Luigi', noted Spreafico, 'could have brought his own example as proof of the lack of ambition of the members of the institute. Not only did he, many years ago, refuse to rise to Holy Orders, when the bishops were almost forcing him to do so, but even when he became convinced of the necessity of the priesthood for the institute, it had never entered his head that he himself should study theology. In fact he had directed some of his confréres to take up such studies, which they did very successfully.'

In recounting this meeting, Monti revealed that he had made it clear to those Friars who were looking after the sick, that they also needed to look after their spiritual welfare 'thereby avoiding the danger of seeing them die without the sacraments.' This is something that he had seen happen 'because there was no resident chaplain in the hospital.' 'And this would not have happened', Monti went on, 'if one of us had been a priest, who, besides being a spiritual director to the religious family, could also be chaplain to the sick in our care.'

'I also pointed out to him how some ancient religious orders, in order to adapt themselves to current needs, open up rules which have been closed for centuries, changing their original objectives, and sometimes even going against the spirit of their founder, and it is permitted. Whereas for our institute things are being made very difficult, despite the fact that our rule is still open precisely in order to be able to add to it those things judged necessary for its completion, and to remove those which are harmful to its discipline. And so, having added the priesthood to our rule, we have simply added something that was lacking. Those who felt that this addition was not in line with its nature, have taken it as a reason to target the institute in all kinds of ways.

'It does not matter', concluded Monti 'the people who, at present, are studying ways of obstructing the institute and who are maliciously trying to delay the approval of its rule, sooner or later will, to their cost, feel the uncomfortable effects.'

Fr Lolli seemed to be convinced by Monti's reasoning and

by his clear-cut answers to the various objections. As he was leaving Monti was able to say to Lolli: 'Father, many of those who were an obstacle are no longer alive. I hope that now you will keep your word. Do not have any doubt: God and Mary Most Holy will reward you.' In reality, when, finally, in 1896, Fr Lolli, as consultant, decided to present the new text to the Holy See, he added his vote against the priesthood, adding a rather unfavourable comment on the Concettini's obedience.

Regarding the priesthood, Fr Lolli quite simply and literally repeated the words he had written in the 1887 vote:

'1) The priesthood goes against the reasons behind the foundation of this institute which was to assist the lay workers in the care of the sick in the hospitals. This can be found in the first edition of the constitution approved for a five-year period by this Sacred Congregation, under article No 2 of the first chapter: 'All will be laymen.'

2) The priesthood in a lay institute is a source of competition, jealousy and envy amongst religious, *experentia teste*.

3) The subjection of a priest to a lay person is a contradiction both *de jure* and *de facto*.

4) Study, which is absolutely essential for priests, cannot be reconciled with the constant care and assistance which the Concettini, if they wish to remain faithful to the spirit of their own institute, have to give to the poor sick even in their most basic material needs.'

During 1896, while the 'dossier' was held in abeyance, underneath a pile of other similar 'dossiers' in the filing cabinets of an office in Rome, Monti had to convince himself even more, if he was not already convinced, of the sanctity of the initiative for the priesthood of the Concettini. In fact it happened at Saronno that for three consecutive weeks there was no priest available, not even to renew the consecrated species. When the cardinal protector heard about this, he was surprised and saddened and suggested going to talk to the local bishop, Andrea

Ferrari of Milan. So Monti hurried over to Milan from Saronno where the bishop, after yet again expressing his appreciation of the institute's work and his wish that it should spread throughout the diocese, decided to suggest to Rome that three or four Friars should be ordained priest for each of their houses. He said that he himself would call on them in an emergency, to help from outside the institute. So saying he embraced Monti.

Monti's trusty old friend Fr Luigi Raimondi, always ready to give a hand to a work of God, made a useful suggestion. He suggested sending a petition to the Pope, endorsed by the cardinals who supported Monti. The petition was sent off on 12 August 1896 and at the Congress of the Sacred Congregation, on 1 September, it was unanimously approved.

When Cardinal Verga, Prefect of the Holy See, was about to present the document to the Pope, an aggressive letter written by a Concettino arrived.[2] It stated that the priesthood, which the ambitious superior wanted to introduce, had been the real reason for the expulsion of the Concettini from the Santo Spirito, and that he personally, because of this deviation from the lay nature of the institute, had left the order.

The cardinal, if not totally against the change, had serious reservations about it. He presented his vote against it, along with the petition, and on 7 September the Pope rejected the proposal.

Fr Monti was at Saronno when he received the bad news. One can imagine the reaction in his soul, but he described it himself in a letter to the superior in Rome, Bro Stanislaus Guglielmetti on 11 September.

'I am replying to your letter', he wrote, 'in which I read of the terrible decision regarding the priesthood. Your previous letter arrived on the morning of the 8th at nine o'clock, the feast of our Immaculate Child Mary. When I heard that Cardinal Verga, a disciple of our deceased Jesuit father Angelini, was going before the Holy Father, I felt that my heart had been pierced, which made me sad and melancholy. But I went straight to the chapel and, in front of the Blessed Sacrament and Mary, I offered up whatever happened, offering myself to Jesus to drink the bitter chalice to the last drop. This morning at Holy Communion I was still sad, but my heart was ready to receive whatever the news was, and when I read the letter, or rather when I was opening it, my hands were shaking, my eyes were dazzled and I read it with great difficulty. After I had read it I went back to the chapel in front of our Mother Mary and the Blessed Sacrament. I made an offering of what God had disposed and prayed to them for my opponents asking for their good and that their souls would be saved, for they had done no more and no less than God had permitted. This would make the institute even more resplendent and, in spite of the diabolic scheming, it would eventually triumph in even greater splendour... Peace, tranquillity and prayer...'

And this reaction, of strength and humility, shows the level of sanctity to which his soul, in the midst of such hard trials, had risen.

FACING UP TO FAILURE

He told the Friars to accept the Holy Father's decision as the will of God and to forget about books and study completely, and they put their full submission in writing.

Cardinal Verga wanted to go further. He thought about removing the superior general from his position, for Monti had given him plenty to do and was never content. For this task he employed the Holy Father's auditor, so that the resignation could be obtained with the Pope's approval. But first of all the auditor wanted to speak to Fr Luigi Raimondi who, amazed at what was happening, exclaimed: "What on earth are they doing? Don't they know that this superior general is the founder of the institute? He drew up the rule and he had the right to change and modify it as he wishes.'

The auditor was convinced by this and a few days later Cardinal Verga was promoted to another post, thereby leaving that of Prefect of the Sacred Congregation for Bishops and Religious. Verga was succeeded by Cardinal Serafino Vannutelli, another friend of Fr Angelini, and thus another opponent of Monti's aspirations. However, he had the intelligence and the virtue to accept Monti's arguments which were put forward by Fr Luigi Raimondi. He conceded, to the great relief of the priest, a clause which said that the priesthood of the Concettini would depend on individual bishops.

Monti, was delighted by the concession, although he was justifiably worried by the clause which meant that in some way his priests would be drawn away from the institute, or at least they might be tempted to do this. He communicated his concern, through Raimondi and Mgr Gizzi, a friend of the cardinal prefect, in December 1897.

But the via crucis which had lasted seventeen years and which only someone with Monti's extraordinary courage could endure, was not yet over. After so many trials, he was in almost constant pain. In February he had what he jokingly called 'a lovely influenza', but one which frightened his sons.

After much hesitation and rethinking, the commission convened on 25 April 1898 to give final approval to the text of the constitution, which Monti had revised through illnesses and trials of every kind. Once again Fr Lolli spoke out against the priesthood of the Concettini, calling them deceitful and disobedient, while the Jesuit, Fr Bucceroni, repeated all Angelini's old arguments and judgements. In the end instead of the text being approved, it was decided that the Friars Hospitaller should be invited to submit to the 'above-mentioned decision of the Supreme Pontiff and to the rebuke given by the Sacred Congregation, and to re-present the correct constitution, as a matter of duty, to the definitive examination of the same Sacred Congregation.'

It might have seemed like the last straw, but for some time Monti had placed every hope in God alone. Having heard the decision from his secretary, Jerome Pezzini in Rome, he replied to him on 3 May 1898:
'Dearest Bro Jerome,
'You rightly tell me to be ready for anything. The sad news that you gave me yesterday was like a thunderbolt in a clear sky. But to tell you the truth it did not hurt me too much. What else can you expect from men? - nothing, other than tribulations and thorns. I firmly believe that it will eventually come about and that the Lord will find a way. He who made water flow from rocks can also look after our affairs. And just as he has not abandoned us in the past, I am sure he will not do so in the future. The institute is, without doubt, his work, and so it is he who will look after it and make it triumphant, bringing down all those who relentlessly and for no known reason want to interfere in our affairs. We have palpable proof of his help and his providence. That is all.'

Fr Luigi looked up to heaven, trusting only in God and in Mary Immaculate, whilst men were nailing him ever more firmly to the cross. At the congress of the Sacred Congregation held on 6 May 1898, the concepts put forward by the commission were found to be right and just and were unanimously approved. The outcome was conveyed to Monti in a letter written by the cardinal prefect himself:

'In truth, it is a great wonder that, despite the requests refused, even in the august name of the Holy Father, for the plan to transform the institute over which you preside, with the idea of promoting some of its members to the priesthood, you have continued to pursue the idea and have the audacity to introduce new articles to your constitution. These are in open opposition to the rebuke you have already received. Thus this Sacred Congregation believes that it is its duty to issue you with a serious warning not to make similar attempts in the future and to maintain the institute in the conditions which are essential to its nature. May God let you prosper according to his pleasure.

'Serafino Card. Vannutelli Prefect'

'It is clear that the devil has unleashed himself against the Concettini', said Bro Jerome Pezzini, commenting to Monti on the Cardinal's letter. 'But it gives me greater hope', he added sharply 'because the more acute the problem becomes, the nearer it is to a solution.' Monti replied thus:

'Dearest Bro Jerome,

I am deeply saddened by the deliberations taken by the Sacred Congregation over our constitution. Let us be patient. Let us adore the plans of the Lord. If he wants it like this, then he knows why. Humanly speaking, it can only be attributed to human wickedness and, it would seem, we do not deserve such treatment. But given all of this what can we do? Nothing else but pray.'

Once again, his religious formation helped him contain himself, but beneath it was the grief of a man of God misunderstood and opposed in a plan which was obviously at the service of the Church. All this opposition, he felt, was the result of misunderstanding, of distortion, through which a direct attempt to increase the ministerial services and the spiritual resources of hospitallers, patients and orphans appeared to be audacity and rebellion. This simply could not be. For Monti it was by the permission of the Lord that the devil conducted his battle against the family of the Immaculate Conception. But he was convinced that the good cause, which was for the glory of God and of Mary, would triumph.

He repeated these concepts on various occasions to the Friars Hospitaller, to Raimondi and to all those close to him.

He confided something to Raimondi with that simplicity which characterised his faith: 'I am right to have firm hope, because Jesus and Mary are persons of honour.' He recalled an apparition of Jesus and Mary that he had had some years before where they had assured him of this 'triumph'. He could have been thrown into the sea like Jonah, but the glory of God and the good of the institute for which he was toiling, could not be overthrown.

His trust in God was rare indeed when the cardinal prefect sent him the declarations which clearly excluded Monti's ideas. 'Everything is fine', the cardinal said, 'but the priesthood is absolutely impossible.' Monti was strong, like an Alpine rock, against the storm. Certainly, physically he was a wreck and he was now confined to a chair. Nevertheless, in October 1898 he had to journey to Rome to face up to the troubles which were waiting for him there. It was a journey that was almost too much for his poor health.

He went back to Lombardy in February 1899 and, almost without any physical strength left, he spent the days and most of the nights, praying rather than working. In May of that year he wrote again to his trusty Raimondi:

'Before the month of Our Lady comes to an end I will send you a calamus with which you will mark the era of the priesthood and the rule, or rather the triumph of the institute of the Immaculate, now so much targeted. That I will already have departed from this miserable world matters little, as long as the day of the renewal of the institute can be seen joyfully on the horizon.'

Notes

1 The same Cardinal Masotti, Prefect of the Sacred Congregation for Bishops and Religious, made them postpone the chapter.
2 Joseph Hamentien, a shady character, had already left the institute when he sent in the false report. He asked Fr Monti to forgive him for what he had done.

15
THE MAN AND THE INSTITUTE

THE INSTITUTE

Having reached seventy and after all that he had done and suffered, Luigi Monti was rather like an ancient oak, which soaked up the sun and was battered by the winds.

His sons were alarmed at how bent and how physically weak he was becoming and they feared for the institute, the leadership of which needed a firm hand.

But Monti was one of those characters who remain unbowed with the years. He went ahead, perhaps with his mind, when his legs could no longer carry him, as if he was just at the beginning.

His congregation and its many works were firmly planted. There were seventy or so Friars, many of whom had revealed administrative and organisational talents as well as moral and religious virtues. The venerable old man, when he caressed the untidy hair of the orphans, knew that they would always be well cared for, even after his death.

The chief characteristics of the institute were already well established through the drama of the various ups and downs. It was a community of nurses devoted, through gospel charity, to the care of the sick, with an eye also on the health of the soul. They were providers of overall health.

To this end the Friars received an increasingly specific formation, both in the care of the sick and in their apostolate. They were dedicated to both the corporal and the spiritual works of mercy. Some of the nurses even studied 'basic surgery,' so that in every hospital at least one of them was able to perform simple surgery, as was the custom at that time.

In Monti's mind there was a plan to send some of the Friars to study pharmacy, which they were already practising to some extent, and also to study medicine itself. Then with the desire to introduce the priesthood it is clear that the specific task of his community was to provide personnel for every type of hospital care. He wanted to create a self-sufficient institute, but his plans ran into every conceivable difficulty. In the end however, his plans would be fulfiled. Of that the founder was certain.

The institute was vivified, as by the blood of Christ, by the essential virtue of Christianity, something which had become more vital than ever in an era where the supernatural had been eliminated and where charity had been replaced by philanthropy. It was a real satanic seduction whereby man became more easily separated from God in his daily life. Thus it also became easier to establish those forms of materialism which lead to a deadly totalitarianism.

Monti said that what blood is for the human body, love is for the religious organism. And he repeated along with the Fathers of the Church and with the mystics: without love everything is nothing. The substance of Luigi Monti's teaching and action lay here. He did not know much theory; he knew only enough to be able to live according to the second commandment of God: charity. And charity generates unity.

'But how can it be' he asked, 'that we are here to love, to do good to others and there is not union, love amongst us? We are sons of Mary Immaculate, in her institute. Shouldn't peace, charity reign there?'

Recalling these words of his father and master, Bro Clement Longhi noted: 'if there was a lack of charity he was blazing.'

MAN OF CHARACTER

It was not true that Monti wasted the community's money. All his life he had been a conscientious and severe administrator who preferred to impose sacrifices on his own Friars rather than go into debt. Nevertheless, he took some courageous decisions, urged on by charity and trusting in Providence, but with an enlightened shrewdness.

'I don't mistrust God's providence', he said, 'but I don't want to tempt it either... Let's cut our coat according to our cloth.'

All his life he was tormented by the fear of going into debt and by the necessity of doing so. His letters talk of loans and expenditure, savings and payments... they remind one a little of the letters of St Teresa, whose ecstasies were punctuated by worries about bills, legacies and bank balances.

To some people Monti could have seemed quite a hard man. More precisely he was a simple man, not used to subtle expressions and sweet talk. When he knew he was right, because it was a question of God and human souls, he said so and made his words count, perhaps with a certain roughness.

On the other hand, the kind of people he often had to deal with constrained him to defend himself forcefully, both against the 'old Concettini' who were scheming and rebellious, and against the hospital administrators. After the collapse of the temporal power of the papacy, the popes, following the Masonic and secular trends of the time, tried to limit or deform the religious character of the Concettini by intervening in their organisation. In Monti they found someone who gave them a run for their money. Tenacious and logical, it was he who taught them the use of and respect for freedom and the observance of contracts.

He spoke in charity, but at the same time in truth. This was his divine strength, and his human weakness, in many difficult situations. As Bro Clement Gamberini said to him in the Orte period, if 'he was targeted and held to hostage by everyone, it was due to his overwhelming sincerity...' He called a spade a spade...

In fact he told Bro Clement that he would never change his approach, that he was happy to suffer for the truth, and that he prayed constantly to keep away from intrigue, duplicity and from so-called 'politics.'

His quarrels with the directors of the hospitals of Santo Spirito, Capranica di Sutri, Civita Castellana and Fornai were always provoked by his resistance to secular intrigue and, or, attempts at abuse. He always remembered his duties as a member of the Church militant, something which was almost instinctive in him.

Without his energy, innumerable abuses would have been perpetrated which would have damaged the institute and its members. His was a real work of construction for which some were not ready and to which others were opponents. And it all took place in a period in which popular faith was being worn down in the heat of the political furore. 'Good grace with all', he said, 'but to each his own.'

His was an arduous life, the life of a pioneer.

While he was collecting and ordering the documents for the institute's archives, Bro Stanislaus Pastori wrote to him: 'I am continuing with the archives. I am making a register of everything between 1857 and 1896 with all the papers and letters which are in our archive. I am writing in the register a summary of every document, a task which takes a lot of time, as I have to read each one before summarising it. I have included everything, even the less important letters which the P. V. has kept. And here I cannot but exclaim, "How come the institute and the P. V. have managed to conduct so many battles." My God, my God, what a set up! It is unbelievable. I have come across many writings, especially for the years '78 to '81, which made my hair stand on end and my eyes burn. I felt my blood boil when I read those hurtful, inflammatory, deceitful, ironic papers, and I said to myself, "How on earth did that poor man keep going?"'

However, that tough, peasant hide with its steely outer layer was the outer surface which protected a precious substance - love. He had become a religious, and that particular kind of religious, at the service of the sick, the most thankless of tasks, for love. His hardness helped him on more than one occasion to preserve the rights of love which had been violated in a world dominated by selfishness, intrigue, hypocrisy and exploitation. But in reality he was always a brother and a father, humble and in complete donation to his institute. At times he was full of fun, making gentle ironic quips, and he loved Our Lady precisely because he loved those gifts of meekness, humility, goodness and joy which were contained in her. This is something that one must never forget if one wants to understand him: that in the secret depths of his soul a special love for Mary was always burning, like a lighted lamp. And it was from this that his every thought was formed.

He had to deal with lay people at every level and from every sector of society. There were good Catholics and underhand members of sects, especially after 1870, when the presence of religious nurses was opposed so that, in the name of progress, science and freedom, the middle-class 'reformers' could lay their hands on the Church's property, on the deposits of charity. In fact, the great majority of the revolts against the Popes down the centuries, under various flags, were for this one reason.

Inasmuch as his personality allowed him, Monti was deferential and prudent, and as far as he was able, he tried, *pro bono pacis,* to maintain respect in a relationship, making concessions whenever possible. But more often, especially in Lazio, faced with hypocritical attempts to put the Friars in impossible positions, he was guilty of being too honest, too definite and decisive. For him it was either black or white: keep to the contract or I will withdraw the Friars.

He was never afraid. If God was with him, who could be against God?

VIRTUES

His humility lay in his simplicity. He was someone who 'longed' to be converted, as if he was always full of sins and ungrateful to the Lord. Even in his old age, he could be seen frequently going down on his knees in the refectory to ask forgiveness and to kiss the feet of the older Friars. It required an heroic humility to put up with the insults and accusations from superiors who did not know him and from corrupt subordinates, and he never defended himself, except when it concerned the interests of the institute. And it was because of his humility that he never wanted, as many other founders had legitimately done, to claim his rights and title to the foundation he had brought to life.

It was the exercise of charity itself, as with the great Vincent de Paul, which led Monti to that humility whereby authority appeared only as service. He expressed this relationship in words that typify his simplicity: 'In church and in the refectory we are all equal.' There can be various functions, but in front of God, as when faced with the necessities of the physical life, we are all the same, we are all hungry. The spirit hungers for God, the stomach hungers for bread. It was a concept which was strong enough to strangle the shoot of pride.

Although, for the sake of the discipline of his religious family, he had had to ask for life-long overall authority for himself, he never confused his own person with his responsibility. He insisted every morning when he rose on putting his room in order and cleaning it. His sons had to be sharp and cunning to beat him to it, rushing in to his room whenever he was away from it. 'He was like the others', was Bro Alexander Cesana's summing up of Monti.

He wanted perfect equality also in what he ate and in every situation, as for example when he was ill. He never allowed any special treatment.

If there was an exception, it was that he would look for the worst food, the most tiring task, the greater mortifications. He would do penances that he would not let the Friars do, as they were already so tormented by their heavy workload.

He had eye problems and suffered various other illnesses such as hernias, ulcers and a fistula, but for as long as possible he would keep quiet about them. He considered physical suffering to be a dutiful contribution to divine justice, which did not dispense him from practising the rule of the common life. He recognised the value of suffering and never wasted it by complaining. Humility was the virtue which typified him and was inseparable from him.

He had realistic awareness of his own limitations. He knew he was not cultured, not endowed with the priesthood, that he had to face continuous hostility... while he was working hard for the glory of God, but without ever thinking anything of himself. In fact, with his common sense and his religious awareness he was admirably equipped, on more than one occasion, to take some of his Friars down a peg or two.

Since he was so humble, his opponents could heap scorn and lies on him. He was bowed by this burden as he had been under the piles of timber when he was a carpenter, and he transformed all that rotten material into the raw material of good.

Whether in the general foundation of his institute, or in forming the consciences of his fellow-workers, he was always inspired by the virtue of charity. The spirit with which he infused the institute was that of 'beautiful charity'. Monti's sanctity consisted essentially in the love of God, Mary, the saints in heaven and all the Friars on earth, starting with the worst.

So his was a simple, almost working class, holiness of the type needed by a society which was emancipating the workers.

He did not think of himself, he thought of others, and he never stopped suffering for his children, both nurses and orphans. He enquired about them, did things for them and wrote to them.

He replied to every letter and if he did not receive a letter he would want to know why. He often did this jokingly, as for example when he chastised Bro Anastasius Monti for not sending him any news of himself: 'Perhaps you are dead? Why did not you let me know, so at least I could have prayed for you? Why is it that the Montis have to be different?' Or, as he wrote to his beloved Stanislaus Pastori, who was doing military service: 'If I were to receive a letter from you every day, it would be a great comfort to me. In fact, I am keeping them all for your beatification... the ball's in your court.' On one occasion he replied to Bro Isidore 'on the same letter', that is, on the same piece of paper: 'In order to send you a strong Friar as cook we will have to ask the brickworks to make one..., because we don't have any here...

'You tell me that you are in poor health because you have to wear a truss. If it is true, a third of the Friars would have to remain seated with a servant at their side. In fact, everyone worked hard, like all those who are healthy and strong.'

As a matter of fact, he too wore a truss because of his hernia.

Even in his old age, with failing eyesight and when the pen weighed like an iron bar in his hand, he tried to reply to everyone.

He wrote to Pastori, who jealously kept all Monti's letters, in 1893 and 1895: 'Don't show my letters to others, or I shall lose my credibility as superior general, for I am sure they will say: "A general writes like this?" Joking apart, you must forgive the scrawl and the crooked lines in this letter.' On another occasion he writes: 'This has been written by a poor cross-eyed, half-blind man. Nevertheless, I have to thank the great and good God for having kept what remains of my sight. In fact I am writing this without spectacles.'

He wrote above all to those who were suffering, going through trials or in military service.

'I can assure you', he wrote on 10 February 1886 to Bro Stanislaus Guglielmetti, serving in the Forty-Fourth Infantry Regiment, 'that all these Friars love you with a great love and that never a day passes without thinking of you... I keep your picture at the feet of my statue of Mary under the little veil that you made for her. Every evening, at nine o'clock, before going to bed I say three Hail Marys and the *Sub tuum praesidium*, and then I bless you with my little statue of our Mother and all our families in the different houses. I will leave your picture at Our Lady's feet until you return...

'Oh, how often I have said to myself (and also to others): how happy I would be if I could fly over and embrace my son Stanislaus once again! But I will have to put this desire in the hearts of Jesus and Mary Our Immaculate Mother. Yes my son, let's resign ourselves in everything, because everything that God does for us is for our greater good. So let's live in the peace of the Lord.'

'Your last letter consoled me a lot', he wrote, 'to hear of your courage, that you are ready even to die rather than offend God and that you have great confidence in Our Immaculate Mother... *Mater Immaculata, virgo potens, ora pro nobis! Sub tuum praesidium...* let these be your frequent ejaculations, and do not be afraid.' 'Yes, my dear son', he wrote on another occasion, 'I assure you that day and night you are in the depth of my heart. And every night before going to sleep I give you a blessing with Our Immaculate Mother.'

The letters were written in a very simple style and included various quotations. They were not, however, completely free from slight mistakes in spelling and grammar. They reveal the ingenuousness of this man of such strong faith. They talk of modest, practical things, but they confirm the co-existence, the continuous co-operation almost, of Our Lady and St Joseph.

When he was not writing, he was talking, and not just one to one. There are many convincing testimonies to both the content and the effectiveness of his private and public talks. 'In the chapel', affirms Bro Eugene Arlati, 'very often he gave us exhortations. They were well prepared little talks, meaty, apt for correction and persuasion. His way of speaking was at the same time moving and convincing. We listened happily to them. He was able to unite arguments on the love of God to those of justice. He emphasised offence to God, showing his strong dislike of this, as for example in the case of malicious gossip.'

'When he found out', says Arlati, 'that there had been a lack of compliance, or especially malicious gossip against superiors, he would come to the Santo Spirito and call to his room all the Friars who were not on duty. He would sit behind a shabby little table with the Friars around him.

'He would give an exhortation, taking examples from Holy Scripture. I remember when, talking against gossip, he recounted very vividly how Aaron and Miriam gossiped with the people against Moses. I was moved to tears. He always referred to facts from Holy Scripture or from the lives of the saints in order to change the Friars and persuade them to do good. He had an ease with words and always managed to give good advice and he knew how to convince us.'

Also Fr Faustino Monti affirms that Fr Luigi 'had facts and sayings from Holy Scripture at his fingertips, and he quoted them whenever necessary, drawing examples from it to encourage this or that virtue.'

Bro Clement Longhi says: 'Fr Luigi came often to visit us at the Santo Spirito from Piazza Mastai. How generous he was in giving us comfort, both privately and in public! How much light he gave us in those meetings in the chapel and in the refectory! Like an expert pilot he knew how to keep his ship safe with his reasoning. At the slightest hint of friction on the ward or at home he would immediately intervene and his words would heal all the wounds.' 'His talks always gave encouragement', confirms Bro Celestino Turchi.

Fr Luigi wanted the Friars to be dutifully instructed in Christian doctrine. He taught them himself every Sunday without fail at the Santo Spirito. He was not content, as eye-witnesses verify, just to explain theology point by point, but he quizzed them on what they had done the previous Sunday, and they had to know the answers off by heart.

'After the lesson', explains Bro Virgil Santambrogio, 'he would take the opportunity of giving some further religious instruction, perhaps illustrating a particular virtue which he knew was not practised much, or those points of the constitution which were not fully observed.' He taught especially the observance of the constitution, the practices of piety and brotherly love of the sick. He also emphasised the nobility of their work of caring for the sick, quoting as examples St Camillus and St John of God and encouraging them to see the person of Our Lord Jesus Christ himself in the sick.' 'During the conferences', Bro Michael Martinelli testifies, 'he always recommended the observance of our holy vows. He often spoke on the importance of the vow of obedience and particularly on the vow and virtue of poverty.'

Monti quite often mentions these conferences in his own diary, which shows how important he felt they were for the good of the institute. Sometimes during these meetings he would expand on the disastrous political currents which were damaging the Church and the religious institutes. In 1891 he wrote: 'During the conferences in the chapel, the superior makes the Friars aware of current events and of the tyranny of the sectarian government which is intent on destroying the Catholic religion and on bleeding the people white. Poverty and misery were constantly on the increase. The superior encourages the Friars to be good religious and to observe their rule, maintaining the true spirit of the institute and still prepared to feel some of the discomfort of poverty. The Lord's Providence will never be lacking and the Immaculate Mother will never fail to come to the aid of her sons. So, the superior advises them to stand firm, for, no matter what punishments the Lord God allows his children to suffer, the Sons of the Immaculate Conception, if they live well, will suffer less than the others.'

It is no secret that the thing that worried him most was the watering down of the true religious spirit. He felt it was that which had been the prime cause of all the problems that had beset the institute in the past. Even the slightest shadow of this was enough to disturb his peace, and to get rid of it he would use uncompromising words: 'How we must fear the judgement of God', he wrote, 'for not responding to our vocation. In fact, I must say that, in general, there is no religious spirit at all and therefore we need to reform our spirit completely, otherwise we run the risk of destroying the institute. So let us offer our warmest prayers to Our Immaculate Infant Mother Mary on this holy day of her birth. May she obtain for us, from God, her divine son, all those graces that we desire for the sanctification of our souls, including a renewal of our spirit, as many saints found necessary when founding their orders.'

He added private conversations to the general conferences. He would call some into his room or welcome the novices and the Friars who wanted to speak to him, or with whom he wanted to speak, and they would confide thoughts and feelings to guide everyone towards the same objective.

In Monti, poverty was inseparable from humility and charity. Poverty was something he had lived all his life, not so much because of either his natural or his supernatural family, as through his conviction that, without it, the other virtues could not be cultivated. Fr Spreafico comments on this aspect: 'Often he saw holy poverty as a chance to make ever new mortifications. From the beginning of his time as superior general up until 1895, the servant of God always received 10 lire every month and sometimes a bit more for any extra necessities, especially for the post or the bus.

'With a precision that by itself would be enough to reveal his love of poverty, he wrote down everything he spent, even if it was only a tiny amount, in a book which he still keeps today. At the end of the month he showed his accounts to the bursar.' But in the final years, Fr Luigi, although superior general, was deprived even of that small sum, due to the excessive rigour of the procurator, and had to ask every time for the small amounts of money he needed. An eye-witness, Fr Angelo Proli, quoted some examples of this: 'On more than one occasion I happened to be with him when he wanted to take a tram. He said to me: "I feel tired" and I said "Let's take a tram." He replied, "But how can I, I haven't even got one centesimo?" "Then ask the bursar." "I ask him and he gives me 50 or 60 centesimi at a time. Can I waste all my time asking him?" "Tell him that, after all you are the general. Do you keep quiet for the sake of peace?" Fr Luigi replied: "With silence, peace is not broken and we keep in good harmony."' And Proli concludes adding, 'He arrived home tired, dripping with sweat but with a smile on his face and never a complaint.'

We know, however, that even when he had money with him, he often chose to return on foot from the Santo Spirito, the general house, because, as he himself said to whoever was accompanying him, that small saving would allow him to buy an extra loaf for his orphans. Fr Faustino Monti tells us that on many occasions when Luigi was tired and going round the town he would refuse to take a carriage, even if invited to do so. 'I will have a good rest at home', he would say as he continued on foot. It was clear that it was above all the spirit of mortification that motivated him to do these things and which found in that heroic practice of poverty a discreet and certain ally.

Convinced of the fundamental value of poverty, he practised it in person and at home, in a Franciscan manner. His clothes were clean but poor and shabby. It depended on the attentiveness and the cunning of his sons to persuade him, on rare occasions, to change his garments. He would sometimes give his own shirt to one of the Friars who needed one.

He was not a scholar, but he loved to read and instruct himself in religious things. In his old age he studied a little Latin. With regard to the philosophical trends of the time, he simply kept his confrères to the Church's line and to do this he took advice from reputable clergymen. Thus he was advised not to follow the Rosminian method as it was questionable and not recommended. He had been told the same thing by his Jesuit spiritual director. He made sure that no books or journals condemned by the Church found their way into any of his houses. He was a simple, but faithful observer of rules given by the Pope and the hierarchy in every area.He was therefore a great defender of the Papacy and wanted his sons to be the same as long as the Roman question was being debated. This was also out of a deep sense of gratitude to Pius IX, who had permitted the setting up of the institute and had affirmed it.

Writing on 25 August 1880 to Fr Giglio Albuzzi, Monti confessed: 'Rome is no longer the Rome of the Popes.. now it is the Rome of misery and iniquity. I who know Rome, free Rome, or rather the Rome of the Popes, can see there is a vast difference, like going from day to night. The artists of sacred art have nowhere to go. The punishment of God! As long as the head of the Church is imprisoned, there will be nothing except misery and quarrels, or rather iniquity. Freedom turns people into slaves and makes them horrible.'

'Free Rome', 'freedom makes people slaves…' In his own innocent way, Monti was indicating the difference between freedom in the Christian sense and freedom in the liberal sense. For him the latter was licence, or abuse of freedom, which generates true slavery of the spirit.

THE FORMATOR

He was also the formator, the master of his institute, and his success was based on the fact that he was able to blend together a group of largely uneducated young men from different backgrounds around a precise ideal. But, one may ask, did he have the teaching skills to avoid clashes with his students? No, he did not, in fact he provoked clashes, or at least he did nothing to avoid them, because even to the Friars he said what he thought and he said it in very stark way, to the point of being rude.

An example of this can be seen from the letter he wrote to Bro Benedict M. Antonietti, the prior at Civita Castellana, in August 1897. Monti was already having problems with his eyesight and was confined to a darkened room. The community at Civita Castellana was tormented from the outside by a doctor, and from the inside by a wayward Friar, Gabriel. He wrote: 'Tell Bro Gabriel straight, if he intends to do good, good; but if he wants to carry on with his sulks and tantrums, tell him that this time he is sadly mistaken. I am sick and tired of catering for miserable pig faces. I let him take his vows because he promised me all kinds of things, but I can soon release him from them and put him out of the door. Tell him to make up his mind either to do good, or to clear off.'

But this straightforwardness also helped give a certain character to the institute.

All the same, his elementary teaching method on the one hand attracted those simple souls who gave themselves to God, while on the other hand it was a discriminating factor for those who were cunning, underhand or introvert. He made himself everything for everyone, with an effort, in certain cases, which leaves one speechless.

In every case he was someone who placed great value on the 'rule' with regard to the conduct of the Friars and for the institute as a whole.

Everything he did was aimed at the observance of the rule, on which he depended for the formation of the true religious. So he impressed it on them and explained it to them through circulars, talks, letters and, above all, through his example. For Monti, the practice of the rule equalled sanctification. It was the guide with which one went, with certainty, to paradise.

'The greatest and most pleasing honour we can give to Mary', he wrote on 28 April 1899, 'is to reproduce in ourselves the virtues which she possessed to the highest degree. So let humility be the basis of the structure of our sanctification, obedience the direction of our efforts and precise observation of our constitution the rule of our life.'

Like the founders of all well-established and sound religious families, he gave a special emphasis to obedience, seeing in it the royal road to sanctity. He valued it because the great saints had done so, but he understood its importance in the light of the disorder and the ensuing structural weakness caused by disobedience experienced over many years. Obedience, together with acquiescence, united everyone with the superior and with each other. But obedience was itself charity, an act of love and it had to flower from charity, which unites.

'Mary Immaculate', he said, 'sees fit to keep us always in the spirit of our institute. In other words, she keeps beautiful charity always burning in us, she forms us into one heart. It is an indispensable virtue for the souls of religious, but especially for us who profess the charity of Christ towards the sick and to orphaned children.'

'When there was a lack of charity he would be blazing', affirmed Bro Clement Longhi, one of his most beloved sons. 'How sad he was when he heard that tenderness did not reign amongst his sons! What is needed is a spirit of compliance', he would say. Mutual tolerance and forgiveness of imperfections became everything for everyone, to win all of them for Jesus Christ.' Because he saw the perfection of religious community life in 'one heart and one soul' and as he had on various occasions observed the effects of disunity, the work of the devil, he never stopped praying to God that fraternal charity was never lacking, either between superiors and those under them, or amongst the Friars.

Like St Vincent, he realised the supernatural value of living together as confrères in charity, knowing that if they were united in the name of Jesus, then the Lord would be in their midst Thus he always found it difficult to be away from the community for very long.

The Concettino Friar had to be a copy of Mary, and thus he needed to base his life on the virtues of humility, compliance and love, in purity. 'The house of the Immaculate Conception will always flourish where humility, charity and holy purity reign', he wrote in his diary on 12 December 1884.

He was among the first to bring about a reawakening of the Marian dimension of the Christian life, in which Mary, the Mother without stain, is presented as teacher and model, as queen and patron to obey and to imitate. Anyone who watched the behaviour of the Friars should have been able to see Our Lady reflected in them.

An essential point of the discipline, for Monti, was always going out in twos.

'The Friars should always live in harmony with one another and away from the things of the world', he wrote in 1893, 'and especially they should never go out of the house alone. Today particularly, there are plenty of snares around, and the world, even the very air we breathe, is so polluted. Those religious families which have ignored this essential aspect of discipline, are now regretting it, so much damage has been caused. We don't want to be like those who are in religious life but whose heart is attached to the world, putting their soul at grave risk, to the detriment of their community and giving grave scandal to the weak. Ah! Let such mishaps not weigh down the institute of Mary Most Immaculate.'

So, neither superiors nor inferiors were to go out alone, except in cases of 'extreme necessity.' His reasons for this rule are also explained in something he wrote in November 1890: 'The times we live in are very sad. The world is becoming worse every day. Happy are we who have the good fortune to be in the safe harbour of religion, away from all those dangers which drag so many souls into the infernal chasm. But what use will the security of this place be if we expose ourselves to these dangers? Then we will have to fulfil that saying of the Holy Spirit: '*Qui amat periculum, peribit in illud.*' So let's encourage everyone to keep away from these deadly dangers, placing their trust only in God, seeking peace only in him, and refuting everything that could displease Jesus and Our Immaculate Mother. So, for us, the spirit of freedom, excessive wandering, or over-indulgence in pastimes, should be proscribed. So, we too must avoid the exchange of visits between Friars of different houses, even though it may be done for the best of motives and to boost morale. Because, in fact, rather than strengthen the spirit, it weakens it, in such a way that one gives in to, and falls at, the tiniest hint of temptation.'

He followed the novices personally one by one, on the principle of making sure of their vocation so that then he could establish their formation, which he saw as a continuous preparation for sanctity. He wanted them to be in good health, both in the spirit, as they had to become copies of Mary, and in the body, as they had to work for the poor. The ideal which he presented to the boys was such that it encouraged a large number of vocations. In fact, he did not have enough space to accommodate them and, sadly, had to send them away. When he could take them in, he was happy. He accepted them even though they were poor or wretched. He looked only at their interior condition.

The feeling with which he followed these novices from both near and far away, can be seen from his letters. The following is a quotation from one which he sent in reply to greetings he had received on the occasion of his feast day, in June 1897.

'There are many things I would like to say to all my dear novices, but over the last few days my eyes are tired and the pen is heavier than an iron rod! So, you will all forgive me if I cannot express all my thanks and gratitude for the affectionate and exquisite greetings you sent me on the occasion of my feast day, and for the prayers to the angelic St Aloysius, to God and to Our Immaculate Mother, for the prosperity of the institute.

'My dear sons, I left you, anxious and in tears, without being able to express my fatherly affection, having to separate myself from you, who are so dear to my heart. However, because of your filial affection, I was not afraid that you would not keep me in your hearts and in your prayers to God, to Our Immaculate Mother, and of everything which you assure me in your dearest letters to me. I too remember you every day, and, every evening, before going to bed, I bless you.

'I beg you always to be faithful to your prayers, and we will be sure of holy perseverance, and thus of our eternal reward in heaven.

'I leave you in the heart of Jesus and under the sacred cloak of Mary Our Immaculate Mother, blessing you.'

His was a human-divine family, composed of his confrères on earth and of Jesus and the saints in heaven: a living together with God in the grace of charity.

It was a family modelled on that of Nazareth, where Mary the 'Immaculate Mother' and Joseph, 'the provider' ruled.

'I believe that the Very Reverend Father', he wrote to the general of the Capuchins at the beginning of 1872, 'will be happy to see the institute prosper, first for the glory of God, second for good of poor languishing humanity and third for the poor Friars.'

So first comes the glory of God, then, as a projection of that, service to humanity. Monti keeps to the fundamental values of religion and bases his social mission on supernatural foundations. It is charity in action: love of God, and love of men and women, out of love for God.

Thus he wants Friars 'capable of carrying out their duties skillfully, but, more than that, with a religious spirit, because even if just one thing is done badly, it immediately lets down all religion, in the eyes of the local people.'

FATHERHOOD

The religious education of the Friars, in charity and in purity, was therefore severe. So that they could become totally consecrated to God, detached from the world, imitators of Mary, he did not want them to waste their time with parties, academic pursuits or plays, even when these were held in holy places. Their recreation had to be amongst themselves, in the practice of mutual love.

He was not happy for them to take part in crowded, noisy religious celebrations, which he felt were held only to pass the time.

'You may think these measures too severe', he said. But they were all part of his system of severity and simplicity. 'We are religious and this is enough for us.'

Those young men came mostly from working-class backgrounds and they brought them certain habits which were difficult to reconcile with the religious life. Monti, with patience and prudence, modelled, or better, remodelled them on the ideal type of hospitaller Friar. He favoured gentleness rather than a rebuke, raising them like sons of Mary Immaculate, making use of experience and common sense, without hurry and without anger. His patience with the unruly and with the half-hearted knew no limits, and, before putting them back on the streets, he would beseech all the saints in heaven and try everything legally permissible on earth for such Friars. He was a father and he forgave them and sympathised with them.

He cared for the unruly, the lazy and the half-hearted with unremitting attention, trying to win them over through love, and usually he succeeded. Only after the most powerful resistance, which turned into scandal, or ran the risk of becoming a scandal, did he resort to punishment and to expulsion.

'More than paternal, his correction was maternal', affirmed Fr Faustino Monti, 'he did not fail to let them know the gravity of their actions when this was appropriate, but never in such a way that he exasperated them. He was always gentleness and charity.'

'When some error had been committed', said Faustino, 'and he found out about it, he would look serious but not severe, his normal lovable smile disappeared, and he then felt duty bound to go to the culprit as soon as the superior was free. Once, I remember, to the question " Why, father, do you look so serious?" he replied, "You yourself know that." The questioner would then offer his suggestion and Monti would explain the real reason and correct him. He preferred it if we told him why he looked serious.'

Because the corrections were the fruit of love, from someone who wanted the good of the other, the culprit usually ended up by blessing the person who had helped him.

His formation was available for everyone, when necessary, even for superiors on whom he placed grave responsibilities with corresponding difficulties. 'It is impossible', he once wrote to Bro Anastasius Monti, 'for a superior to do something, even a very good thing, without someone criticising it. If you were in my shoes you would despair.'

It was true and this was why he could sympathise with and understand them. He knew how to make himself one with each person, and, in sustaining them and reproving them, he varied his approach according to the person. Here is one example: 'For some time', he wrote to one of them, 'I have wanted to write you a few lines to help you live better the sufferings in your position as prior, as superior of the family entrusted to you. The weight carried by a superior has always been heavy, but it is even heavier in times when faith is lacking. Nevertheless we must not lose heart, as happens when we lack God's spirit, which animates the person who wants to become a saint and give glory to God on earth and in heaven for all eternity. Now is the right moment to ask this grace on this day, the feast day of the birth of the Child Mary, Our Most Immaculate Mother. Yes, let's pray to our most affectionate Mother both for the prosperity of our poor institute, which is incessantly the target of Satan's anger, and for all our needs, so that our souls do not perish with the great grace of our religious vocation.'

If, alongside the virtues and sacrifices, he discovered defects and opposition, the good father would raise his voice and, if necessary, the lash. He wrote to one Friar who wanted to leave Capranica: 'Dear Brother, the Brother secretary has told me what you wanted him to communicate to me: either I get out of this house or you will.

'My reply to you is that if you wish to remain where obedience at this moment holds you, then stay there. If you do not wish to stay there any more, then please leave the institute and go and find elsewhere that peace and freedom that you do not find amongst us.'

How did he handle unruly individuals who were never willing to make sacrifices and who were a weight and a nuisance to the rest of the community? Monti's suggestion was always to be prudent and to have charity. 'He's as sweet as sugar', he wrote of one of them, 'and he must be protected with all the precautions suggested by brotherly love.' When he replied to these Friars he never failed to impress on them the fact that sacrifice is the rule of life for a religious. 'Many times you have promised me all kinds of beautiful things, above all obedience', he wrote in a letter to one of them, 'but now, once again you are upsetting me and I am very sad. You too know that in this world there are always tribulations, but the merit lies in knowing how to put up with them for the love of God, as a penance for our sins. If we accept them in this way we will find some consolation, first on our death bed, then in the next life.'

He taught them to 'suffer cheerfully', as he wrote in a letter to Pastori during his military service.

FORMATION OF THE YOUNG

Even military service, which was so remote from religious life, he knew could be transformed into a tribute to God. He realised that, in the secularised world, a soul could give witness to Christ in carrying out the most profane duties. It was almost like squeezing the sacred out of the profane, like raising a ladder from the human to the divine.

On 13 May 1893 he wrote: 'Not all evils come to do us harm, but some do us good. With God's grace we can find ourselves in the fire without being burnt, as long as we don't go there of our own volition... The military uniform does not stop us from acting as a religious. Underneath the military uniform there can be the religious habit, or religious works... How much good you can bring back from the army! Firstly, you give good example to your companions. Even though they may appear to despise you, they have to confess in their hearts that good is good, and that they have strayed from the path. Secondly, there are many of the devil's tricks that you did not know. Now you know them, and this will help you keep away from Satan's grasp when he comes to seduce you. You will be able to avoid many evils and, therefore, win many souls for God. So from the school of evil you learn how to stop the devil himself from ruining souls and taking them from God. You see, my son, how much good you could do on your return from the army to religious life! I have good and holy aspirations for you and I hope in the Lord that they will come true.'

He follows his soldier sons, and especially Stanislaus Pastori, with moving tenderness, more like a mother than a father. He wants to immunise them from the barracks and from the world.

'Take courage my son', he writes from Rome on 3 January, 1894, 'remember that you have with you the treasure of virginity. There is a proverb which says 'Whoever is clothed in gold is watched by thieves'. So, modesty in the eyes, modesty in the ears, modesty in the hands, and beware of familiarity with people, especially with women, however good and holy they may be...'

And after many other pieces of advice, he sends 'a kiss and a thousand blessings', and adds: 'I don't know if you will be able to read this...'

He was particularly kind and affectionate to any Friar who was suffering physical illness or spiritual trials. He would even have sold the house and the most sacred objects to help them. He knew, as did few others, the sufferings of the sick, and as soon as he was told

Portrait in oil of Luigi Monti painted in 1896.

Monti's second successor, Fr Stanislaus Pastori, was accepted by Monti as an aspirant to the religious life at the age of fourteen. He became his most beloved disciple and a trusted archivist.

Monti, in true fatherly spirit, wrote to Bro Stanislaus many letters while Stanislaus was doing military service and, at the same time, studying philosophy.

Pastori commissioned this portrait to show his gratitude. In it Monti has an omnipresent look which communicates strength of soul and the austerity of his life.

that a Friar had taken to his bed, Monti would run to him, or send someone immediately without any thought as to the effort or the cost involved. He would pray for them and ask others to pray.

'I remember one occasion', recounts Bro Eugene Arlati, 'when one of the novices, Bro Isidore Moreschini, had to have ten hot iron discs applied to his back, alongside the spinal column. Fr Luigi wanted to be present at the operation. While the surgeon was applying the burning irons to the flesh, Luigi clasped the sick Friar to his breast and encouraged him with loving words, reminding him of the example of Jesus Christ and helping him to suffer for the love of God.' When they were convalescing, he wanted the Friars close to him, or else he sent them to a house in the country where the air was clean, the diet healthy and the surroundings peaceful.

Fr Spreafico defined paternity as Monti's special characteristic with regard to the Friars. He recalls various episodes of tenderness and magnanimity when Monti was giving orders which sometimes were unpleasant.

Monti knew that to command is to serve, an act of charity and, apart from when dealing with particularly hard or stubborn cases, he never made his authority felt. Bro Eugene Arlati recognised the grace with which Monti prepared their spirits when he required a special act of obedience. He always put his command in the context of the plans of divine love.

He was a man of mercy and because of his many experiences he was able to understand and sympathise with them all. Although the religious were completely dedicated to God, he never forgot their humanity and he took it into account, identifying himself with the sacrifices imposed.

The younger men were attracted by his comprehensive love, which was open and simple, and they confided in him, finding in him a breadth of understanding and a readiness to listen. They felt him to be a father, who lived for them, prayed for them and who wanted them to be healthy and holy. The letters which they wrote to him, thanking him and asking his advice, were spontaneous and expressed the unity which linked them to that understanding father, their veneration and trust in him. The orphans too felt him to be a father to them.

The clashes with certain 'old Concettini' are understandable in the light of the programme of sanctification he had planned for their formation. In fact one appreciates even more the success he had with the new recruits, formed by him to be obedient, penitent and prayerful. In the history of the institute many of the Concettini formed by Monti are remembered as blameless, holy creatures, men like Bro Stanislaus Sauda, and Bro Boniface Pavletic, whom he had put in charge of the novices. Bro Boniface (called after Bro Boniface Junker) died a saintly death and was a little like the patron saint of the novitiate, St Stanislaus.

Already in 1883, Fr Luigi had gathered together a series of 'edifying biographies of the Friars Hospitaller,' written by Fr Angelini and published in the periodical *Il Corrispondente del Clero*.

He gave Bro Seraphim Banfi the job of collecting material for a biography of Bro Boniface Pavletic.[1]

Monti was very fond of the blue cassock with the white sash and the skull cap, Mary's clothing, but he knew that it was not the habit that made the monk. He knew that consecration was a spiritual phenomenon and that every state could have and did have, its own perfection.

He believed in and promoted the apostolate by example. Even in a barracks chilled by the winds of anticlericalism, if someone gives a good example, then eventually he will leave a ferment of goodness in the souls there. He wrote to Pastori the soldier: 'The military uniform does not stop you from being a religious in action. So, underneath the military uniform there can be a religious habit, or rather religious works.'

The form of relaxation Monti liked most was to make a pilgrimage to a religious shrine. He would normally take the novices with him, to fill them with zeal.

One of his favourite places was the Madonna of the Woods at Montina on the Brianza, in Lombardy. While in Rome he preferred the Three Fountains by Porto San Paolo, and the catacombs of St Callistus. On one occasion when he was walking to the Three Fountains with a group of novices, he quipped: 'I am becoming young again.'

During the journey through the countryside under a beautiful clear blue sky, he started singing hymns to Mary, the favourite one being '*Ti lodo, o Maria*' (I praise you O Mary) and after prayers in the church, he took his novices outside for refreshments and recreation, ending with edifying stories.

He was a jealous and spirited custodian of the purity of his sons. 'Remember', he wrote, as he had reminded the soldier Pastori, and had repeated to every one of his sons who was far away, 'that you possess the treasure of virginity.'

The most convincing lesson on this was given by his own long life, which was sealed by virginal purity and which made him seem like an angel.

SEEING JESUS IN THE SICK

In him, faith took on the expression almost of the incarnation, in other words of a direct service of neighbour, as representing Christ, which was a particular characteristic of the social sanctity of the last few centuries. It was a service through which Christ, in the person of the helpers, comes back into contact with those who are suffering. And the sick, out of thankfulness for that service, return to the Church from which they were, to a greater or lesser degree, separated.

For Monti too, the sick were 'Christ's poor' and the nurses had to be, not helpers, but servants. This was a reflection of the vision of St Vincent de Paul, who wanted his followers to be 'servants of the poor'.

'No mother', Monti said, 'who sincerely loves her children will give them the same level of maternal care as the Friar hospitaller should give to Christ's sick. The Friar is totally and firmly convinced that he is serving in them the sick members of Christ. He will give them all the care that the divine Mother would have given her divine Son in the same circumstances. As an angel of consolation, sent by God and his Immaculate Mother, he will stay unceasingly by the bed of their suffering. He will comfort them, relieve their sufferings with love, and help them in all their bodily needs, by day and by night, and in every time and place.'

To serve the sick was to serve Jesus. As Monti had written to Bro Stanislaus Sauda in 1872: 'Mary Immaculate, our most loving Mother, is waiting for you to serve her divine Son in the person of the sick.'

In this way he was drawing upon the inspiration and the rule of the fundamental mystery of the Redemption.

His profession and that of his Friars was nursing, but they were nurses who gave a moral and religious value to sickness and to nursing care. He knew that one reached the soul through the body. He inculcated in the Friars the concept of the moral identity of the sick person with Christ. Monti was offering them a very high apostolic ideal: 'In the sick person try to see Jesus Christ, because if you don't do it for a supernatural goal, you won't be able to persevere.'

His own experience had confirmed this. For years, he and his Friars at the Santo Spirito had given themselves beyond their own strength, in the cold, in the heat, in hunger and in contempt, and at times, even in the ingratitude of the patients themselves. And they had persevered, tenacious, invincible because they never forgot the transcendent nature of their work. This is why they loved to remember their many confrères who had become saints at the bedside of the sick, having discovered eternal values in the dressing of wounds.

'A nursing religious has this huge field before him', he said: 'How many souls to win for Christ, to introduce into blessed eternity!'

He based the prayer life of the institute on devotion to the Sacred Heart, to the Immaculate Conception and to St Joseph, with the aim of conforming its life to that of Jesus Christ. Wednesdays continued to be specially dedicated to St Joseph and Saturdays to Mary.

When he took over the direction of the institute, he not only rebuilt it juridically and administratively from the foundations, but he also wanted to carry out a radical reform of its devotional life, its doctrine and its discipline. Such an undertaking took a great toll on his health and he was sometimes forced to make hard decisions. But he received much joy afterwards when he saw a plant rich in flowers and fruits grow out of a wild bush. Through him, the Friars Hospitaller became givers of health, in the life of the spirit as well as the body, because they gave witness to the Gospel in their daily lives.

'For these good citizens', he had written to Bro Prior Gregory Coriddi at Nepi on 25 August 1881, 'you will be a help in their needs, but more than that you will be an example of virtue to them through a true and good religious demeanour.'

In May of the same year, Monti had written: 'What I recommend most is a good example to the good citizens; and you will be this when you work only for the love of God.'

Note

1 The biography was written by Silvio Vismara OSB. -*Fr Bonifacio Palvetic dei Religiosi Concettini*. Milan Tip. S. Giuseppe 1922.

16

THE MAN OF GOD

MAN OF PRAYER

Monti's vocation can only be understood in the light of his prayer and devotional life. His soul hungered for the divine, which he sought powerfully and with humility in prayer and in the sacraments, in the reading of holy books and in listening to holy priests.

In an examination of conscience made during a retreat at Brescia in 1852, he declared, with the utter simplicity of a down-to-earth working man, that he had understood that the whole point of existence was to journey from God, the origin, to God, the end. He longed to become a saint, if possible living without even the tiniest sin, and offering every breath and every work for the greater glory of God.

'I come from God; to God I must return. God has put me on this earth just to serve him, to win eternal glory in paradise. How have I served him up till now? How am I serving him now? How have I responded to him so far? How many times have I promised God to serve him as the saints have served him? In other words, have I done it with great diligence, without giving him even the tiniest displeasure, not committing the slightest deliberate fault? Am I ready to die rather than commit one? Have I been faithful? Good God, forgive me.'

These reflections on his own end and on his generous correspondence to divine grace speak for themselves. They show the level of perfection that Luigi had already reached. Just like the saints, he had reached a level of perfection that touched heroism.

Even more significant in this respect is the practical examination of conscience which follows this reflection. It is, in its simplicity, a precious document, for it allows us to penetrate the most intimate part of his soul and to gain a deep understanding of what he meant by serving God.

These are the questions he put to himself:
'How is your humility?
How is it going with regard to charity?
How are you finding purity?
What about obedience?
How are you living poverty?
How much do you conform to the will of God?
How do you fulfil the practices of piety?
How is the examination of conscience going, particularly in the small details?
Are you going forward or backward with regard to perfection?
What about silence?
How many times do you make a spiritual communion each day?
Is your every breath and action for the greater glory of God?
How many ejaculatory prayers do you say each day?

He lived in the world as if in the Father's house, determined to do His will and convinced that every event was part of God's plan.

He lived with his feet firmly on the ground, but with his heart and mind always linked to heaven. The beauty of creation, the miseries of human beings, joys and tribulations, everything revealed the lines of an eternal plan. More than ever, faith and joy were flowing out of his soul. His wisdom lay in always being on the path of the will of God. 'Here I am Lord, do with me what you will. Life and death are equally sweet to me when it is your desire.' He wrote this to Bro Stanislaus Guglielmetti on 10 November 1885.

So his whole existence, like his institute, was always inseparably linked to God. Luigi Monti always acted and thought under the Lord's loving gaze and his heart was in constant conversation with him. It could be said that he was a humble collaborator with God Most High and of the Immaculate Mother. He considered himself an executor of orders, placed there to carry out a special plan of the Lord. He prayed continuously, both vocal and mental prayers, even though, because of his work with the sick, he often could not say all the official prayers. In church he was instructive, and in his exhortations, both written and oral, he almost always recommended prayer. It was with prayer that he drew upon the graces for his active life. Pray, and pray well, was his ideal. It was his daily resource and his reserve to call upon in critical moments. When everyone seemed to be lined up together against his family, he would announce a *triduum* and start to pray. Once he had established his link with the eternal, he had no more fear and he became strong with God's strength.

In one of his last circulars, of 18 November 1898, he said: 'Prayer, my beloved sons and Brothers, prayer is a priceless treasure, an infinite fount of grace. In fact if we look back briefly at our past life, at the difficulties overcome, the graces received, the great favours obtained, we owe it all to prayer. Through prayer we come to perfect self-knowledge; enlightened by prayer we follow the path which leads us safely to our ultimate end; and finally it is through prayer that we constrain God himself, as it were, to rain his favours down on us.

'And this is why, on the occasion of the approach of the feast of the Immaculate Conception, a special feast for our institute, we consider it our bounden duty to address you and to encourage you in prayer. The novena and the retreat which precede this feastday will serve to widen your awareness of the importance and excellence of prayer.' He then goes on to remind them that the Immaculate Conception has shown them in many different ways and with special graces, the protection she has always given to the institute.

He added, 'This should animate us and comfort us, certain, as we are, that with prayer we can obtain from our Immaculate Mother all the graces necessary for our institute.'

A man of action, he cultivated his devotional life in simple contemplation; contemplation which had blossomed with love. 'His work', recalls Fr Elia Airoldi, 'prevented him from staying long in church, but his visits were very frequent. I would not be exaggerating if I said I had seen Fr Luigi go into the church to make a brief visit, at least twelve times a day, besides his normal devotions.'

This tells us where he found the strength to face up to the never-ending battles. On days when a particular battle was raging, he would, if possible, stay longer in church, as he needed more light and more energy. And the Lord would flood his graces down on Luigi.

Every evening he would spend a long time praying in his room, on his knees, or pacing up and down, sometimes in the dark. He alternated prayer with an examination of conscience and with meditation. It was with this daily interior exercise that he built up his strength together with his great virtue. Words and actions were, over many years, distilled one by one from this union with God.

His last invocation before going to sleep was the *Miserere*, whose verses he recited with monastic solemnity. In them his humility found the valve for drawing the omnipotence of God into his own human misery.

Whether working or walking, if he could he would pray. His favourite prayers were the Litany of the Blessed Virgin Mary, the *Magnificat, the Ave Maris Stella, the Memorare* to the Virgin and to St Joseph and the *Sub tuum praesidium* to Mary, in which he asked above all: '*a periculis cunctis libera nos semper.*' Daily life was like a stretch of road covered in deceit and he felt the need for some superhuman assistance.

Normally, walking was for him a prayer; almost like ploughing a furrow through space with a beam of prayer. The same went for work and for sleep. He would doze off while praying and every time he woke up again he would carry on with the prayer, as with his normal breathing. 'He prayed all the time.' This was the testimony of those who were close to him.

He prayed for the Pope, his superiors, the whole Church and the whole of humanity, but he remembered especially his benefactors and his enemies.

When he spoke to his Friars 'there could be no doubt that it was God who was speaking', noted Bro Ludovic Sala. Ludovic's behaviour was sometimes rather too free with regard to Monti, which makes his judgement all the more valid.

Monti was someone who kept his feet firmly on the ground. He took note of the difficulties and the disagreements and went ahead, tenaciously, but prudently, making use of the human instruments at his disposal. His head was not in the clouds nor was his heart ruled by sentiment. But the way ahead for him was illuminated by a faith that kept him constantly in union with God. He let himself be led by the Immaculate Virgin, in whose name and for whose glory he had done everything. It was she who had given direction to his life and helped him undertake a task which was superior to his own strength. And through his love for Mary, her spouse St Joseph also helped him. In fact, the absolute faith that he had in St Joseph was reminiscent of that of St Teresa of Avila. For her it seemed impossible that if Jesus had obeyed his foster father on earth, he would not continue to do so in heaven.

St Joseph was the saint whom Fr Luigi most wanted to be like and from whom he took his inspiration. St Joseph reminded Luigi of the people, his own home town and his original trade, but most important of all, he reminded him how he should love Jesus and Mary.

'It is a tangible fact', he said, 'that the institute is a work of God and of Mary who have left the job of caring for our needs to the great Patriarch St Joseph.'

This trust was his strength. When he heard the news that they intended to evict the Friars Hospitaller from the Santo Spirito hospital after thirty-two years of hard work, he wrote to Bro Jerome on 26 August 1889: 'Do not be afraid, because God can draw good out of evil. As they say, if men close a door then God opens an even bigger one. And anyway, as sons of the queen we have nothing to fear!!! And do you think St Joseph wants to look foolish?

'Never! On the contrary, he will redouble his efforts, much to the annoyance of the enemy, and he will make the work of his Immaculate Spouse triumph. So keep calm and we will pray to the two most important people in heaven.' His trust in the patrons of his family, Mary and Joseph, was indeed simple and straightforward.

On 18 March that year, in the midst of the latest furore, he had entrusted the institute entirely to the protection of St Joseph.

When, a few days later Mgr Negretto expressed his wonder at the protection offered by the Pope to a community so threatened, Fr Luigi said to him: 'It is a prodigy, a prodigy of Mary Immaculate.'

He always saw a connection between events at the institute and the liturgical feasts of its patrons. He wanted to make the Friars' hard road towards sanctity into a sustained effort at insertion into the supernatural life of Mary and Joseph: a humble collaboration on earth with the highest saints of heaven. He wanted his Friars to be 'True sons of Mary Immaculate and true followers of St Joseph.' In fact, this desire, expressed in March 1900, was, in a way, his spiritual will.

The high points of his prayer life were marked by sacred names: the Eucharist, the Heart of Jesus, the Passion of Christ, the Immaculate Virgin, and saints Joseph, Aloysius Gonzaga, Philip Neri, Jerome Emiliani, Camillus de Lellis, John of God. The latter two were particular favourites because they were heroic hospitallers. He loved St Philip because he had loved God in joy and St Aloysius because it was his baptismal name.

With patron saints like these, his prayer life was as spontaneous as a mountain spring. He was convinced that the attacks on his institute were instigated by the devil, because it was a work of Our Lady. Every speech he made, every letter he wrote and all his reasoning started and finished with Mary and Joseph. His efforts to save his own institute were tenacious and prudent (a prudence tempered with the cunning of a country peasant) and supported by friends, protectors and benefactors on earth. But in the end he entrusted everything to his heavenly patrons, in whose service he was certain he worked, as a humble collaborator.

But there was nothing surly in his way of religious life, and it most certainly was not monotonous or boring. This was why he did not like devotions that went on too long. In fact he cut them short if they were going on and on. His way of praying was light-hearted and loveable, a projection of love, not of fear. The same thing applied to the work on the wards, even on the smallpox wards. He wanted everything to be carried out in a 'light-hearted spirit'.

As a man from peasant stock, he wanted feast days to be celebrated as such, with great joy. Of course, he saw a clear distinction between joy and chaos or enjoyment for its own sake. When he celebrated a feast he linked his heart in joy to the angels and saints gathered around Mary and Jesus.

SON OF THE IMMACULATE

In Monti's prayer life and in his trust in the Immaculate Conception there is a certain boyish, peasant naïvety. Her name recurs continuously in his speech, in his writings and in his thoughts. He began, continued and ended as a Son of Mary Immaculate.

Our Lady was the Mother, the Teacher, the Queen, the model of life. She was everywhere in the institute. Its members had to have her with them always to be like her, through the practice of modesty, humility, purity and sacrifice.

The Concettini's year was filled with feasts in her honour, with *tridui*, novenas, prayers and all kinds of celebrations. For them, every year was a Marian year. The most loved, most intimate feasts were those during the month of May, but the most important of all was that of 8 December, the Immaculate Conception. The Friars prepared for this feast with an eight day spiritual retreat beforehand, during which they renewed their own spirit.

In the last two years, Monti also mentions 'Our Child Mother Mary.' This could be due to the influence of the order of sisters of that name, or it could be because of a statue donated by the widow of the famous Roman archaeologist, John Baptist De Rossi. It was a beautiful life-size statue of the Child Mary. Monti had a great love for that statue, which he valued more than if he had been given 'a million lire,' and which would be nothing 'compared to the Infant, who inspires devotion and almost seems to be alive.'

Then immediately afterwards he added, what was for him a glorious and inseparable epithet to the word Child, 'the Immaculate Child,' he called her.

From his boyhood, Monti had wanted to be a son of Mary and he consecrated this filial relationship in the very title of the institute. His devotion to her grew every day of his life and he introduced many special ejaculatory prayers to her in the devotional life of the institute.

One of these, which he had composed and which he particularly loved was: '*Mater Immaculata, ora pro nobis.*' It was constantly on his lips and in his heart. To another, 'Blessed be the Holy and Immaculate Conception of the Most Blessed Virgin Mary, Mother of God', he added 'and our mother', thereby putting a seal on that filial relationship he felt so deeply. He was the son of Mary's motherhood and he wanted his institute to be the same. Like a true son, often when he invoked her and spoke to her, he would go beyond the series of venerable titles given to Mary and call her simply 'Mamma'.'

'I cannot take any more! Immaculate Mother, help me!' he would say in a moment of tribulation, '*In Te Domine et Domina, speravi: non confundar in aeternum.*'

He pleaded with her, using the sweetest, most heart-breaking expressions 'sweetest, dear, most affectionate'.'

The pattern of his daily worship and of his religious talks was interwoven with hymns, ejaculatory prayers and invocations to Our Lady. He never ceased calling to her, imploring her, praising her. He was in love with her. She was his poetry and his strength in his darkest hour. Mary seemed to him to be like a flower of light and peace, who re-created him. His sanctity was permeated with love for the Virgin; his day a hymn to the Immaculate.

He was also a passionate distributor of the booklet *Tributo*, which was considered a kind of anthem of the Concettini. In the preface to the 'Spiritual Manual' he wrote: 'Above all, I would like you to recite the prayers and praise to the Immaculate Mother of God in the daily *Tributo* with all the affection of sons. I would like you to remember that the true follower of Mary, he who honours her with purity of mind and heart, can be sure of his eternal health. This is something that we have seen in the death of so many of our Friars from the birth of the institute to the present time. Asked if they felt tempted by the devil at the moment of death, they answered that they had never felt so much peace and tranquillity in the spirit. They said it was like a foretaste of heaven. It was like this for men such as Bros Stanislaus Sauda, Angelico Epifanio, Boniface Junker, Boniface Pavletic and many others, whose holy deaths most of you have witnessed. Oh that their example could encourage us to recite this holy *Tributo* with ever greater devotion, as is prescribed in our holy rule.'

In 1898 a printing press was set up for the training of those orphans wishing to take up that trade. On the occasion of the inauguration of the press he said to the assistant: 'Look here, Elia - the first thing these characters should print is the *Tributo della Madonna*.' And he explained why, because as it was for Our Lady, they should use the most spotless characters.

In fact, the first job to come off the press in the print shop was the *Tributo della Madonna*.

One could say that he honoured Our Lady twenty-four hours a day, in the sense that she was never out of his heart or off his lips. He would repeat: 'If you are seeking consolation, run to Mary, invoke Mary, pay respect to Mary, pray to Mary.'

Both his oral and his written exhortations were packed with anxious love. The clothing of the Friars, or their profession, the institute's most cherished ceremonies, were always held on Mary's feast days so that she could be honoured.

He had planned his institute and brought it to fruition out of love for Mary, in honour of Mary. 'Our Lady thought up my institute' he would say. In a nutshell, you could say that his life was like an outpouring of love for the Mother without a stain. This work was a moving and visible expression of the popular devotion to Our Lady. It was also an expression of the deep feelings of ordinary folk for the official recognition of the Immaculate Conception with which the Pope, and through him, the Church, wanted to honour Mary in her highest grace.

Already in 1880, Monti had had the idea of realising an old dream, that of building a church dedicated to the Immaculate Conception, with a house for novices and orphans. With this in mind he had started a savings book with an entry of 12 lire, money he had saved from walking round Rome rather than going by tram or by carriage.

This minuscule amount did not worry him at all. It was Providence, through Mary's hands, that had to find the rest.

17

THE PEACEFUL PASSAGE

AN OLD MAN AMONGST YOUNG

Fr Spreafico describes Monti in his later years:
   'Physically, the servant of God had the distinctive features of the healthy and vigorous peasant folk of Brianza. Everything was in proportion to his size. On his rectangular face were drawn the clear-cut and rather wide mouth and full lips, marked by two lines at the ends. His nose was slightly prominent and he had thick eyebrows with little brown eyes whose eyelids showed clearly the marks of suffering. He had a broad forehead, which had become lined only in recent years, and his hair, though greying at the temples, for the most part retained its original dark colour. He had the calm look in his eyes of someone who has been through many trials and has known suffering. He always walked at the same pace, slow but light, a little bent in later years and his general appearance revealed the interior composure of his spirit. Only the deep red colour of his face betrayed his spirited, fervent temperament; a spirit so profoundly dominated by virtue that one never saw him lose his composure, not even for a moment. In 1894, his beloved son Stanislaus Pastori sent a portrait in oil of the founder to Monti himself. Monti commented, in good Milanese, on the pallor of his face: 'I did not think I was so pure white.' Purity was a feature of his soul, a

feature that he had kept under the firm and decisive domination of his will power, in complete response to divine grace.'

That same year he had taken part in the jubilee celebrations of the priesthood of Leo XIII. Not only did he offer the Pope a gift and join in the prayers and the religious solemnity, but he also opened his house to pilgrims, who had come in great numbers to join in the celebrations. This meant a great sacrifice for him for many months, putting up the pilgrims, helping and serving them. It also meant many sacrifices for the institute and enormous disruption for his religious. All this effort also took its toll on his health.

But Monti used every illness and every trial as a means of freeing himself from human attachments.

Like all true Christians, he saw old age as growing closer to God. Rather than fussing over his aches and pains, he concentrated on preparing himself for the final moment, so that he would not be caught unawares.

He had written to 'Dear Stanislaus Guglielmetti' in 1892, mentioning the rheumatic pains he was suffering after having been soaked in sweat after helping with the harvest at Saronno. 'I have finally realised now that I am good for nothing. So, all that remains for me to do is to retreat to a cave, in solitude, in a forest somewhere.'

In fact, Monti did eventually retreat into solitude whenever he could. He would go into his tiny room and pray for a good death, for himself and for all his sons, and for all those who had left or been expelled from the institute. One evening in 1882, in the chapel at Saronno, he had heard a voice speaking to his heart. It said: 'Pray for Bro Francis who is about to die and who is in danger of damnation; pray, pray.' Fr Monti said out loud immediately: 'Let us pray for a soul about to die who is in danger of damnation.' The Friars looked at him in amazement and raised their eyebrows to one another as if to say: 'The superior general has gone mad.'

A few days later a letter arrived from the parish priest, saying that the former Bro Francis had died having received the sacraments. The fact was that no one had heard anything about him since the day he left the institute.

In 1896, everyone at Piazza Mastai was struck down by a kind of epidemic, turning the house into a hospital. Monti commented: 'The Lord has come to visit us and he does good to us. Our necks are stiff and he humiliates us, which is fine.'

For the last four years of his life, though always vigilant about every aspect of the life of the institute, Monti dedicated himself in a special way to the orphans. He found amongst them something of the child-like spirit that most attracted him.

The orphanage at Saronno, with its work-training schools, was so successful that huge numbers of boys applied to be accepted. And Fr Luigi accepted more than the financial resources could cope with.

It broke his heart to say no, whenever he was asked to take in an adolescent.

More often than not, charity overcame reason, and he would accept the boy. 'I am just made like that; I cannot say no... ' He would jump through hoops to find a way of squeezing another bed into the dormitory, to welcome another postulant, for to refuse anyone seemed like 'letting a soul redeemed by the blood of Christ go into the devil's mouth.'

This generosity brought with it quite a few headaches.

Just as with the great founders of religious orders, Monti's greatest concern was to reconcile charity with economics. Fortunately, generous benefactors came to his aid. One of these was an old priest, Fr Luigi Lodini, who, at the age of 70 had retired to his home town of Legnano. He had found out about the work of the Concettini through one of Monti's old friends, Fr Luigi Albuzzi. Later, when Lodini was ill, he had experienced personally their charity and their professional expertise. The result was that he gave to Monti all his savings, some 13,000 lire, quite a tidy sum in 1897. Monti saw it as a special intervention by Our Lady at a critical moment in the development of the house at Saronno.

He used the money to set up a new book-bindery and printing press.

He gave his best efforts to the young men. For them he was teacher and bursar, master and companion, educator and father. They saw him as a strong and tender father, whose mere presence could move them to tears.

When summer came, Monti would leave the oppressive atmosphere of Rome and go up to Saronno. Here he felt rejuvenated surrounded by this swarm of adolescents, so pure and so grateful. His arrival was a celebration, as his successor, Fr Stanislaus Pastori recounts.

'You should have seen those delightful and lively lads preparing themselves from early in the morning to receive their benefactor, their father, in a worthy manner. When the time of his arrival drew near they were all there ready, lined up by the door that leads in to the vast garden. As soon as he appeared they all crowded round him, asking his blessing, kissing his hand and showing their affection in so many different ways, suggested to their tender hearts by their innocence and their gratitude. And he, the good father, surrounded, or rather, assailed by his dear sons, had a caress, a smile, a toy, for each one.

'After letting them express their enthusiasm in this way, he would then let them calm down and accompany him to the house singing 'I praise you, O Mary', a hymn they knew Fr Luigi was very fond of.

In fact, sung by those innocent souls, by those silver voices, it was sure to remind him of the angels in heaven.'

He found that hymn very moving. He loved to hear them singing. It reminded him of the meetings held at the various shrines when he was young. He liked to hear them singing the hymns of his youth, at the same shrines that he visited with the

'Brothers' from Bovisio, and especially Montina.

When he wrote to these boys, sending them his regards and telling them to be good, he reminded them that they should become saints. And they would reply to him from Saronno promising him the sanctity he wanted so much.

At Christmas 1896 he wrote them a letter from Rome:

'My dear orphan sons,

'The letter that you all wrote to me with your Christmas greetings was a great comfort to me. I can see that you are behaving like true sons of your father superior. This act of filial affection gives me great hopes for you. You should always be respectful and obedient, not only to me, but to all your superiors and brothers and especially to your dear prefect, who does so much for you. I was certainly pleased to hear from the prefect that you are all well-behaved and good.

'I hope that, on Christmas Day, you will all give your hearts to Baby Jesus and that you will ask him to bless the institute and to send some providence so that the many other poor orphans who write to me from all over the place can be received. I would like to do good for them as I have for you, and as we continue to do. In fact, my heart would like to do the same for all the orphans in the world. But if you don't pray to divine providence to send me the means, what can I do? On that day, pray too for your father, who is in great need... especially to come and see you all soon and to find you all good and holy.'

He added a note for the prefect: 'Read the enclosed letter to the orphans and tell them they have a loving father who always remembers them.'

In another letter written to Bro Luigi Monti[1], the prior at Saronno, announcing his visit there in March, he adds a note for his orphans: 'Ask Bro Angelico to tell our dear orphan sons that I will be coming to see them soon. If they are well-behaved and obedient I will let them come to the station to meet me with a brass band! However, if anyone behaves disgracefully, he will be sent away as soon as I arrive.'

His arrival was planned for April, and announcing it in a letter to 'Dear Luigi', he writes: 'Tell Bro Angelico that I would love him to come to the station with the orphans.'

He arrived at Saronno on 13 April.

Besides spending time with the orphans and the sick, he also busied himself with the vineyard, the nurseries, the bower, the wine butts, the wheat, oil, rice and so on.

Among his letters there is a request to Bro Jerome to send two bottles of Gallipoli wine 'for Fr Procurator to sample, who maintains that grapes trodden by the feet make better wine than do those crushed by machine.'

On 19 March 1898, the feast of St Joseph, the structure of the Institute was defined. 'As the rule makes provision for five provinces in Italy, we will start by establishing two, in Rome and Lombardy, with two provincials resident in Rome (until another, 'a healthier and more suitable one, can be found outside Rome) and Saronno. There will also be a novitiate in each province.'

He himself informed the Cardinal protector about the opening of a new house at Cantù on the feast of St Aloysius in 1898. In this new house the Lord had wanted to show that it was he, the Lord himself, 'who guides, governs and provides for the needs of his institute…'

In the letter Monti recalls the visit he made to the Cardinal of Milan 'to ask him for the grace of a priest', necessary to open the house at Cantù. The cardinal had replied that he did not deploy priests, not even for the parishes. Monti had returned home disheartened. But there was a letter waiting for him with news of a most worthy priest, Fr Peter Capo, who was asking to be received amongst the Concettini, as a Concettino. It was something Capo had been hoping for for many years, but he had been blocked by his spiritual director, Fr Angelini. With the permission of the Cardinal protector, the priest was welcomed into the institute and brought to Cantù. Monti described him as 'a model for all Concettini priests, and', he said, 'much to the shame of the proud opposition, I have a firm hope that the priesthood will be allowed to us whether I am, like Jonah, thrown into the sea, or dead in my grave.'

THE FINAL ILLNESS

Fr Monti went towards death with the same assured, rhythmic step with which he had trodden the streets of this world for more than seventy years. He had pains in his eyes and various other ailments that were largely the result of the grave trials both in body and in spirit that he had suffered.

On 15 February 1897 he wrote of himself: 'The Lord was kind enough to visit the poor superior, and it served him right. He has now been suffering for more than a month and has had three or four rheumatic fevers. Now he is well, and he will soon take up his bad habits and miserable ways again.'

The remission did not last long. In fact, because of his state of health, he could not go to Lombardy in April. It was not until June that he was fit to make the journey. But then even at Saronno in the summer he was racked by a persistent cough. He felt a bit better when he went on a trip to the shrine at Oropa, where he went with a guest of his from Rome, the parish priest of Santa Maria in Trastevere. Then the pains in the eyes returned and he was forced to spend twenty days in his room in total darkness.

He suffered badly from changes in climate, especially in hot, humid conditions. Nevertheless, he managed to drag himself back to Rome again, and from Rome to Capranica, to meet Bro Eugene Arlati. When the Friars there saw him, they took fright, seeing him suffer so badly and so close to death.

In the spring he seemed to recover. April appeared once again to have a positive effect on his health. He felt strong enough to contemplate the journey to Lombardy, his homeland to which he was so faithful. He regarded it as free countryside, where the contact with the young novices and the orphans seemed to give him a new feeling of youthfulness. He wrote, 'Tell the novices that when I arrive, we will go together to look for magpies' nests.' He also added a note for the orphans: 'Tell the Friar prefect to let the orphans know. Tell them to start to polish their shoes and to keep them shining, because when I return they will be invited to welcome me at Saronno station. They can carry me home on their shoulders, taking it in turns. I use the word 'shoulder', because they might need to bring a coffin with them. However, they should study hard and be good, otherwise none of this will be allowed.'

In late spring, Fr Luigi left Rome, his second homeland, and in many ways his first, knowing that he would probably never see it again.

He arrived at Saronno to be welcomed in an atmosphere of great celebration by his confrères, the young men and his friends. He was already not only well-known, but venerated far and wide. He was completely exhausted. He hoped to be able to recover a little, through contact with nature, but he could no longer walk on his own. He went round the garden paths in a wheelchair pushed by one of the orphans, with whom he would chat in such a simple way, just right for an adolescent.

That year he happened to clothe Andrew Celestini in the religious habit. Andrew had come to the house with two brothers; all three of them showed symptoms of tuberculosis, the disease that had struck down their parents, and one which, in those days was both terrifying and incurable.

At eighteen, Andrew knew that his days were numbered and he asked Fr Luigi if he could die a Concettino. Monti granted him his request, admitting him on 21 June 1900, his own saint's day, and he saw him die a peaceful death just a month later.

However, Monti never put pressure on the young men to enter the religious life. He respected their freedom, tried to find out what they really wanted to do and pointed them in the right direction. He uncovered their interests and talents and developed them, thereby forming both excellent religious and excellent workers.

He wrote the following to the vicar general at Saronno: 'On more than one occasion I have expressed my ideas on the workshops. After supper the prefect should give some instruction to his orphans and the master to his novices. After recreation you should read something instructive to the professed Friars and you should let everyone know about it. You should also make it clear that the workshop instructors should have nothing to do with the orphans, and even less with the novices, except when in the workshop. When they are in the workshop, their authority extends only and exclusively to work and discipline. Otherwise the devil creates confusion and disorder. I think you have grasped the idea and that you will apply it to the family.'

In the hope of relieving his physical suffering, his sons decided to take him to the shrine at Oropa. There he would be under Mary's sweet smile and would breathe purer air in a more recollected atmosphere. On previous occasions he had regained both physical and spiritual strength from that sacred and secluded environment.

He went up to the sacred mount once more and through his tears he contemplated the Brown Madonna. Over the centuries many famous people and many humble souls had looked up at her, as a heavenly Sovereign, in faith. Silvio Pellico, Don Bosco and Fr Joseph Cottolengo had been there, as had Quintino Sella, who had been moved to tears. His friends from his youth and Fr Dossi had been there too, as well as many other people dear to Monti. They would come up there for a couple of weeks and breathe in that pure mountain air, that peaceful atmosphere of paradise. With the loving help of one of his religious, he began to feel better. He returned to Saronno much stronger and took part in the celebrations for the feast of the Assumption, when several new recruits to his institute were professed. He felt a tremendous joy within and communicated it to his followers. He had lunch with them all and seemed full of fun. When it came to the dessert course he ate a delicious bunch of grapes with great gusto.

On 1 September he went with the novices and the orphans on a trip to Bovisio. It was like going back to his roots. He did not go up to Montina with them, but waited for them instead in the parish priest's house. He took them to see the baptistery saying: 'This is the place where we were baptised', as if he were uniting his entire family to himself. There was a note of nostalgia, or tiredness, in his voice.

His strength was failing fast. His body was becoming increasingly bent and he was now almost nailed to the wheelchair. His face had become pale and his stomach could hardly take anything. He realised that he had reached the evening of his life. He had no self pity, as usual, and never complained. The only concern in his heart was the good of the institute. He felt that it was still not solid enough and that it was in the hands of men who were still not sufficiently formed. Some of the Friars were still hostile. At Saronno itself there was one such: Bro Anastasius Monti. Luigi Monti did not trust him, he was, according to Fr Luigi, one of those people who simply refused to recognise the authority of the superior general, and who was waiting for his demise so that he could change the direction of the congregation. As Fr Luigi had predicted, by praying, most of them saw the error of their ways. Bro Anastasius kept this bee in his bonnet for a good ten years, and after the founder's death he left the congregation.

If Anastasius Monti never went to visit Fr Luigi in his room, another Monti, Faustino, did. Back after military service, he brought great joy to Fr Luigi. 'Our Lady has granted you the grace to assist me at my death', he said.

He was now certain that he was going to die. 'We won't be seeing each other for much longer', he said to the Friars who came into the little room where he remained until his death. He spent most of the time in bed now. Occasionally he would get out of bed for a few hours, with the help of a Friar. He would sit by the window and every now and again, with a great effort, he would poke his head out to bless the orphans. He was still concerned and remained concerned right to the end, with the affairs of the institute, and most of the time he meditated, prayed or chatted with the Friar who was looking after him. He told everyone not to worry about him. He said he was like 'an old machine', that he had to undergo some suffering and that they should concern themselves with the institute. He knew that there were still some rusty wheels squeaking in the machine which was driving the institute. He never ceased praying to Our Lady, 'Our Mother,' so that everything would be properly completed.

From about half-way through September he never left his bed again. He suffered serenely, though his suffering increased due to various complications, and he appeared to develop a grave form of dropsy. The doctors doubted whether, at his age and in his condition, surgery to remove water from the abdomen was advisable.

DEATH

On 23 September Fr Luigi asked for the Viaticum, and all the Friars and the orphans accompanied the priest in procession, to take the Lord to him. They all gathered around his bed, together with Bro Jerome Pezzini, the secretary-general, and Bro Elias Airoldi. It was a like a farewell ceremony for the father and patriarch who, full of virtues and good works, was returning to the heavenly Father, through Mary.

In a moving scene with everyone at his bedside, Fr Luigi managed to whisper: 'I ask forgiveness from all of you if I have ever given you bad example or failed in my duty to you in any way.'

On the afternoon of 24 September, with Monti's consent, the doctors operated on him. The operation brought him some relief and he took advantage of it to dictate his will: 'It is my last will to submit the institute to His Eminence the Most Reverend Cardinal Lucido Maria Parocchi, protector of the same institute, and to Fr Luigi Raimondi, archivist of the Congregation for Bishops and Regulars. I also pass the government of the same institute to my secretary, Bro Jerome Pezzini, whose integrity and talents I know very well. I wholeheartedly wish him to be my successor and also in this way many possible complications can be avoided.

'For the rest, I entrust the institute to the Cardinal Protector and to Fr Luigi Raimondi, they who have helped and defended it for many years.

'No one other than Jesus, Mary Immaculate and St Joseph should be recognised as founders of the institute of the Sons of the Immaculate Conception. The illustrious benefactor of the institute was His Holiness Pope Pius IX.

'I recommend to all the Friars that, besides persevering in their vocation, they should study to become faithful observers of our holy constitution.

'I ask forgiveness of all those whom I have offended in any way and I forgive everyone.

'I want my funeral to be as it would be for the least of the Friars.

'I beg all the Friars to remember the soul of this poor wretch, so that God will see fit to welcome it into heaven.'

The Holy Father, who was following the progress of Monti's illness with great sadness, sent his blessing through the cardinal protector. He would have preferred Fr Luigi to transfer to Rome, where he would have received more suitable treatment, but those closest to him knew that such a journey was unthinkable. In fact, Monti was in great peace, joy even, and was already thinking of the final journey. He expressed this wish to the person treating him, the good Dr Nigris, who was trying to hold out hope of a cure: 'I know very well how this illness ends. My hope is to go to Paradise.'

Then the Apostle's overwhelming desire '*Cupio dissolvi...*' came to the fore.

On 26 September he received Extreme Unction. He received it with full knowledge and deep devotion, so much so, that all the Friars and orphans at his bedside could not hold back the tears. After administering the sacrament, Fr Joseph Borella, prayed to the Father, asking him to bless the community around him. Fr Luigi looked each one in the eye and entrusted them to Pezzini, whispering with difficulty: 'I entrust these Friars and orphans to you. Have charity; be merciful to them; remember that they are souls sent by God to fulfil his plans.'

His secret, his burning love, he lived right to the end.

With a supreme effort he lifted himself up as much as he could and, taking the small statue of Our Lady in his hands, he blessed them, making the sign of the cross with it. Then he closed his eyes and lay flat, exhausted by the effort. When he opened his eyes again he saw that they had all left the room. He sighed and said to the Friar attending to him: 'The Lord has given me Moses' prize: to see the promised land without being able to enter it. But, as soon as he died, they entered. The same goes for me: I am dying without the fortune of having a Friar-priest at my side, but you will soon have one.' And he recollected himself in holy thoughts.

Some time later, when he opened his eyes again, he saw that the Friar attending to him was weeping. He smiled and said to him: 'Why are you weeping? It is a waste of time. I weep for another reason: when you reach the end of your life, you wish you had done much more than you actually did', and he closed his eyes once more.

The illness worsened. In his suffering the only words he could be heard to say were ejaculatory prayers, calling on the Lord and on Mary Immaculate. Every so often, with a great effort he would kiss the crucifix.

To the Friars who were assisting him and who were eager to carry out his every desire, he offered looks of gratitude and of warning. They understood what he was telling them. He was making a final appeal for harmony, charity and mercy. He was, in effect, giving them his will.

On the evening of 27 September he became delirious.

The following morning the doctors discovered a blockage in the liver. In a lucid moment, Pezzini read him a letter from the cardinal protector which seemed to console him.

The delirium stabilised and then stopped altogether and on the evening of 30 September he was able to give another blessing to the Friars.

The next morning he entered into agony and at midday he began gasping for breath. At about six in the evening, while Fr Borella was saying the prayers for the dying, he died. It was a peaceful death, like a migrant soul arriving back home.

On his death bed his body seemed to regain the look of peace and strength it had when he was alive.

At Saronno, Milan and Rome, wherever his works were known, there was an immense feeling of loss.

Fr Albertario's Milan-based newspaper, *L'Osservatore cattolico*, captured the general feeling on the death of Luigi Monti. The day after his death it reported: 'God has welcomed his faithful servant into his peace. He now has the reward for charity, lived with an admirable goodness, the goodness of the saints, which is completely unpretentious. May the beloved deceased remember his sons, the orphans and all of us who have admired his exemplary virtue.'

The funeral was humble, as he had requested, but it was also solemn because of the presence of so many religious and civic dignitaries. Many ordinary people also came to pray at his tomb, people who came to acknowledge, at his death, the gifts he had given during his life. In the midst of the political and social upheaval and in the wake of *Rerum Novarum*, the profile of a Church weighed down with problems, but with priests and religious dedicated to relieving the sufferings of humble folk, was emerging even amongst the anticlericals and the atheists. Monti, the humble working man, had managed, with the minimum of resources and struggling heroically against superhuman forces, to found a truly magnanimous work at the service of the poor.

Forty years after his death, in 1940, to great popular acclaim, Monti's tomb was transferred from the cemetery at Saronno to the church by the orphanage. In the parish church the Latin Patriarch of Constantinople, who knew Monti, recalled the glorious deeds and the merits of the great servant of the poor, who had become great through the love of God and with the help of the Immaculate Mother.

Note

1. Luigi Monti's nephew.